ABOUT THE AUTHORS

GARDINER C. MEANS, a distinguished economist for over forty years, has served as Economic Adviser on finance to the U.S. Secretary of Agriculture, Director of the Industrial Section of the National Resources Committee, Chief Fiscal Analyst of the U.S. Bureau of the Budget, and Associate Director of Research on the Committee for Economic Development. He is the author of *The Corporate Revolution in America, Pricing Power and the Public Interest, The Structure of the American Economy,* and *Industrial Prices and Their Relative Inflexibility,* and co-author of *The Modern Corporation and Private Property* (with Adolf A. Berle, Jr.), *The Holding Company* (with James C. Bonbright), and *The Modern Economy in Action* (with Caroline F. Wave).

JOHN M. BLAIR, currently Professor of Economics, College of Business, University of South Florida, was formerly Chief Economist of the U.S. Senate Anti-Trust Subcommittee under Senators Kefauver and Hart (1957-70) and, before that, Assistant Chief Economist of the U.S. Federal Trade Commission (1946-57). Professor Blair, who directed hearings on economic concentration and administered prices, is the author of *Economic Concentration: Structure, Behavior, and Public Policy,* his most recent book, as well as of numerous articles in professional periodicals and journals.

P. SARGANT FLORENCE, is Professor Emeritus of Commerce and formerly Dean of the Faculty of Commerce and Social Science of the University of Birmingham, England, and Vice President of the Royal Economic Society. He has been a consultant to the governments of Great Britain and Jordan and to the U.S. National Resources Planning Board (1940-41), and was Visiting Professor at the University of Cairo, Johns Hopkins University, and the University of Rhode Island. His books include *The Economics of Fatigue and Unrest, The Logic of Industrial Organisation, The Logic of British and American Industry, The Economics and Sociology of Industry,* and *Ownership, Control and Success of Large Companies.* He currently serves on the editorial board of the *Journal of Industrial Economics* and has testified before the U.S. Senate Subcommittee on Anti-Trust and Monopoly.

JOEL B. DIRLAM, is currently Professor of Economics at the University of Rhode Island and has been appointed, at various times, Visiting Professor at the University of Paris and the University of Aix-Marseille, France. He was formerly a financial analyst for the Securities and Exchange Commission, an economist with the Brookings Institution, and consultant to the International Bank, the U.S. Department of Justice, the National Economic Research Associates, and the government of Jordan (sponsored by the Ford Foundation). Currently an Advisory Editor of the *Antitrust Bulletin,* Professor Dirlam is co-author of *Fair Competition* (with Alfred Kahn), *Pricing in Big Business* (with A. D. H. Kaplan and R. F. Lanzilotti), and *An Introduction to the Yugoslav Economy* (with J. Plummer). He testifies periodically on economic affairs before numerous Congressional committees.

HELMUT ARNDT, Professor of Economics and Director of the Institut für Volks- und Weltwirtschaft at the Free University of Berlin, is the founder of the "Institute for Problems of Economic Concentration" and former President and currently a board member of the German Economic Association. A consultant to several governmental institutions, he is editor of *Schriften zur Konzentrationsforschung* and author of numerous books on concentration and economic power, including *Schöpferischer Wettbewerb und klassenlose Gesellschaft* (Creative Competition and Classless Society), *Mikroökonomische Theorie* (Microeconomic Theory), *Recht, Macht, und Wirtschaft* (Law, Power, and Economy), *Markt und Macht* (Market and Power), and *Wirtschaftliche Macht* (On Economic Power).

H. W. de JONG, is currently Professor of Economics at the Netherlands Institute of Business in Nyenrode, a member of the Royal Commission on Competition and the Advisory Commission on Merger Policy, as well as a consultant to the E.E.C. Commission on concentration in the Netherlands. He is the author of several works on competition, notably *Dynamische Concentratietheorie,* and *Ondernemings Concentratie* (Enterprise Concentration).

NORTON T. DODGE, is currently Professor of Economics at the University of Maryland and serves as consultant to the Department of Health, Education, and Welfare. He is editor of a specialized series on Soviet economics and author of *Women in the Soviet Economy* and (with Robert Tsuchigane) of *Economic Discrimination Against Women in the United States.*

ALFRED E. KAHN is currently Chairman of the New York State Public Service Commission, Professor of Economics at Cornell University, and was formerly Dean of the College of Arts and Sciences at Cornell University. He has served as economist for the Antitrust division of the U.S. Department of Justice, the War Production Board (1941-43), and as senior staff member for the Council of Economic Advisors to the President (1955-57), and has also served as consultant to the Federal Trade Commission, the U.S. Department of Agriculture, the Economic Advisory Council, the Ford Foundation, National Economic Research Associates, the National Commission on Food Marketing, American Telephone and Telegraph Corporation, and the government of Algeria. He is the author of *Great Britain in the World Economy* and *The Economics of Regulation*, and co-author of *Fair Competition: The Law and Economics of Antitrust Policy* (with Joel B. Dirlam) and *Integration and Competiton in the Petroleum Industry* (with Melvin G. DeChazeau).

HOWARD N. ROSS, who has contributed an appendix to this volume and has taught at both Yale and Columbia Universities, is currently Associate Professor of Economics at Baruch College, the City University of New York.

THE ROOTS OF INFLATION

THE ROOTS OF INFLATION; the international crisis, by Gardiner C. Means and others. Burt Franklin, 1975. 315p il tab 75-4552. 15.00. ISBN 0-89102-036-5. C.I.P.

CHOICE SEPT. '75
Economics

A collection of essays by eight economists concerned with the presumably odd phenomenon of the late 1960s and the 1970s of rising prices and concurrent substantial employment. The general theme of the writings is that the current inflation is not entirely attributable to traditional "demand push" but more importantly to "nondemand" causes within the basic institutional structures and policies in many countries, both capitalist and socialist. Their emphasis is on fuel, energy and labor costs, the "administered pricing" system of large corporations in concentrated industries, and the behavior of governments, businesses, and trade unions. Both Means and Blair link "market power" and inflation. Kahn's article presents a more balanced discussion of the inadequacies of traditional microeconomic theory in explaining chronic inflation. Both the analysis and policies expressed by the writers have engendered much controversy. The volume serves as a useful platform and will lead to further debate. The collection is suitable for undergraduate consumption and is germane to studies of inflation, industrial concentration, and comparative economic systems.

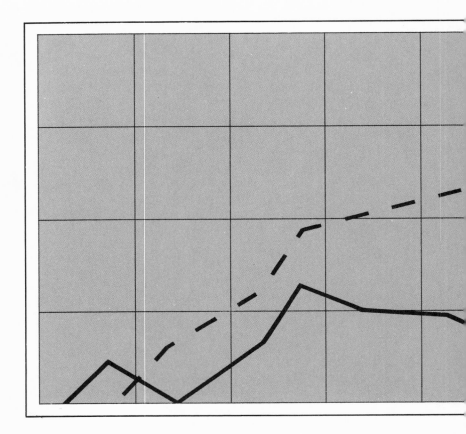

THE
ROOTS
OF
INFLATION
THE INTERNATIONAL CRISIS

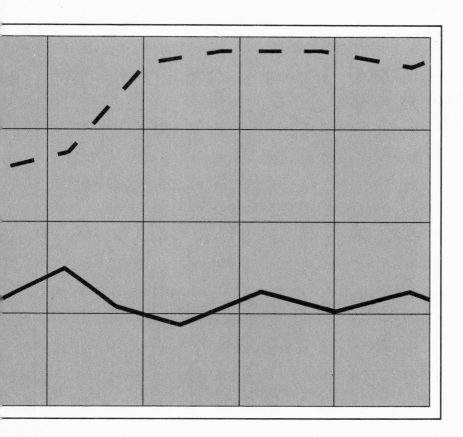

Gardiner C. Means
John M. Blair
P. Sargant Florence
Joel B. Dirlam
Helmut Arndt
H.W. de Jong
Norton T. Dodge
Alfred E. Kahn

BℲ Burt Franklin & Co., Inc.

THE ROOTS OF INFLATION
The International Crisis

© 1975 Burt Franklin & Co., Inc.
235 East 44th St.
New York, New York
10017

Library of Congress Cataloging in Publication Data
Main entry under title:

The roots of inflation: The international crisis.
Includes bibliographical references and index.
1. Inflation (Finance)—Addresses, essays, lectures.
2. Economic Policy—Addresses, essays, lectures.
3. Unemployed—Addresses, essays, lectures.   I. Means,
Gardiner Coit, 1896—
HG229.R66   332.4'1   75-4552
ISBN 0-89102-036-5

INTRODUCTION

From the latter part of the eighteenth century through the first third of the twentieth century, the central issue of economic inquiry was how to make the best, or "optimal," use of scarce resources—labor, capital, and land. From the early 1930's through the middle of this century, the central issue was how to prevent depressions in the short run and how to maximize economic growth in the long run. In each of these eras, economists developed general theories—the microeconomics and macroeconomics, respectively, of today. During the 1950's, there began to emerge a third central issue which cannot be explained by either microeconomic or macroeconomic theory—rising prices occurring in the face of substantial unused capacity and, even more dramatically, actual declines in production and employment.

This new phenomenon was brought home forcibly in 1974 when, for the first time in its peacetime history, the United States experienced "double-digit" inflation, while, at the same time, unemployment climbed to over 7%.

As its title is meant to convey, this book is *not* concerned with what is referred to as "demand inflation"—too many dollars chasing too few goods. Rather, its concern is with deeply-rooted causes which cannot be corrected by simplistic macroeconomic policies designed to reduce overall demand.

Some of these sources of inflation are subsumed under the term "cost-push," of which the most well-known is an increase in unit labor costs. The term also embraces the worldwide increases in the costs of fuel and energy resulting from the recent sharp increases in the price of oil. But there are other "nondemand" causes not usually associated with the concept of "cost-push." Among them are actions by governments that provide a powerful impetus to the inflationary

v

process. Another important source of inflation that is neither "demand-pull" nor "cost-push," as the terms are customarily used, is the type of pricing system employed by large firms in concentrated industries. To a greater or lesser extent, all of these underlying sources have been at work in each of the major industrialized economies, though their importance has varied from country to country and from time to time.

Throughout the world, the failure to distinguish between the "demand" and "nondemand" causes has led governments to adopt policies that not only fail to arrest the inflation arising from the latter but tend to induce or aggravate recession—resulting in needless unemployment and substantial underutilization of resources:

> This comes about as government officials, assuming a competitive industry structure (or at least one that responds more or less the same general way to expansions and contractions in demand) attempt to check an upward movement in prices by reducing the general level of demand through the application of restrictive macroeconomic policies. To this end either fiscal or monetary policy, or both, may be employed. Under the former, taxes may be increased and government expenditures curtailed; under the latter, the growth in the money supply may be reduced and interest rates increased. While disagreeing strongly (and at time acrimoniously) over the efficacy of the two approaches, the proponents of both have shared the common assumption that, given a reduction in demand, prices will respond by declining or at least not rising. True, there will be frictions and lags (of unspecified duration) which may delay the impact of the restrictive policies. But nowhere in the fiscalists' or monetarists' models (which in their more elaborate forms embrace hundreds of variables) is there any variable representing an acceleration of the rate of price increase for a substantial segment of the economy accompanying a reduction in demand.[1]

Not only can the sources of nondemand inflation bring on a recession by serving as the cause of mistaken public policy; they can also aggravate a downswing by depressing sales in industries whose demand is sensitive to price changes, as can be illustrated by the behavior of the automobile industry in 1974. Automobile manufacturers raised new car prices, according to *Forbes* magazine,[2] an average of $1000 per car, to which the buying public reacted strongly by abstaining from purchasing automobiles in record numbers, causing a reduction in industry sales of about 25% in two months in the fall of 1974. Automobile plants were closed, massive layoffs ordered, and unemployment soared, not only in the automobile industry itself, but in all of the other industries dependent upon it as well. When automobile dealers, unable to move their mounting inventories, urged the car-makers to lower prices, the manufacturers initially claimed that price reductions were impossible owing to the increase in their unit costs resulting from the decline in sales.

To make matters even more complicated, the form of behavior illustrated here by the automobile industry was not characteristic of all sectors of the American economy. To contain the inflationary spiral of 1973-74, the government relied on the traditional macroeconomic policy of reducing demand principally by limiting the supply of money and raising interest rates. As a result, products in the competitive areas of the economy, such as cattle, whose prices continued to be responsive to changes in supply and demand, experienced sharp price declines which, incidentally, were only partially reflected at the retail level.

Thus, as a recession proceeds, price declines in the competitive fields will tend to offset price increases in the concentrated industries, thereby shifting attention away from inflation to unemployment as *the* major economic problem of the moment. But measures to end the recession by increasing overall demand will cause the competitive prices to turn upward, thereby shifting attention back to inflation.

During the earlier recession of 1969-1970, the anamolous behavior of rising prices in the face of falling production had become sufficiently extensive in the United States to be reflected in the overall price series. Since most competitive prices continued to display their customary and expected tendency to decline with falling demand, this meant that rises in oligopolistic prices were of sufficient weight to more than offset the decreases in competitive prices. As can be seen in the following table, both the overall wholesale and retail price series during the previous postwar recessions had almost invariably declined.[3] But between November 1969 and November 1970, the wholesale price series, excluding farm and food products, rose 3.6%, and the consumer price index mounted 5.6% in the face of declining industrial production and mounting unemployment.[4] This divergent behavior reappeared during the recessions beginning in November 1973. And by December 1974—the latest month for which such figures were available for inclusion in this volume—both industrial production and real GNP had fallen (7.2% and 5.0%, respectively), while the unemployment rate had reached a level of 7.2%. At the same time, the increases in both the wholesale and consumer price series (27.0% and 13.2%, respectively) were without parallel in the history of economic downturns.

Table I

COMPARISONS OF CHANGES IN ECONOMIC ACTIVITY AND PRICES; SIX POSTWAR RECESSIONS

	11/73 to 12/74*	11/69 to 11/70	5/60 to 2/61	7/57 to 4/58	7/53 to 8/54	11/48 to 10/49
Economic Activity						
Industrial Production	−7.2%	−6.8%	−6.1%	−12.6%	−8.2%	−8.5%
Real GNP	−5.0	−1.1	−1.6	−3.9	−3.4	−1.9
Unemployment Rate	2.4	2.6	2.3	3.8	3.6	4.5
Peak in Unemployment	7.1	6.0	7.1	7.5	6.1	7.9
Prices						
Wholesale Prices**	27.0	3.6	−1.3	−0.5	−0.5	−5.5
Consumer Prices	13.2	5.6	0.0	−1.0	−1.0	−4.2

*4 Quarter GNP   **Excluding farm and food

By 1974, this paradoxical behavior finally made its appearance in the major European countries. In Great Britain, France, and West Germany, production peaked in the last quarter of 1973. During the six-month interval between November 1973 and May 1974, each experienced a decline in output of from 4% to 6%, accompanied by an increase in wholesale prices, ranging from 5% in West Germany to 28% in France.[5]

The American contributors to this volume realized several years ago that the United States was experiencing a new and potentially dangerous form of price behavior for which there existed no satisfactory explanation and which appeared to be centered in industries whose structure did not resemble the model of competitive theory. Out of this background emerged the idea of bringing together, for an informal discussion, economists who for many years had intensively studied the industrial organization of the Western world's major economies. The result was the Cremona conference of August 1971, so named because it was held at Cremona farm in southern Maryland, the home of one of the participants, Professor Norton Dodge.

The conference was highly unstructured: no papers were given, no minutes recorded, and no positions taken. For each of the participants, the conference proved, instead, to be a learning experience. Inasmuch as the European nations had experienced no postwar downswings at all comparable to the American recessions, the economists from abroad had an opportunity to become familiar with a new form of economic behavior—"perverse price flexibility." For the American participants, the conference provided an opportunity to learn about the sources of nondemand inflation in the European economies, the importance of which varied from country to country—trade unionism in Great Britain, government policy in France, and the reestablishment, through industry mergers, of market control in the Common Market. It also became apparent that the Soviet Union and the other countries of Eastern Europe have not by any means been free of inflation. Some of the causes are unique to socialist economies, but others bear a striking resemblance to factors present in capitalist countries.

As the conference drew to a close, a consensus emerged among the participants that each should put his thoughts down in writing. In actual practice this proved to be more difficult than had been anticipated. The principal problem experienced by all was the difficulty of obtaining data, since when it comes to providing data essential to the study of industry structure and behavior, governments differ only in the inadequacy of their performance. Because what is provided differs so much among the various countries, each of the contributors has been free to develop his own organizational structure, emphasizing those factors which, in his judgement, are of greatest importance to his particular country.

But while their form of exposition may differ, the authors are in general agreement concerning both the nature of the central issue and the public policy questions which it raises. In all industrialized nations, public policy makers are now confronted with the necessity of, first, distinguishing between the different causes of inflation and, then, of applying the particular and differing types of public policy appropriate to each. Where inflation *is* the result of an excess of demand over supply, restrictive fiscal and monetary policies are, of course, the appropriate remedy. But where inflation is not the product of demand-pull, restrictive macroeconomic policies will not only fail to arrest inflation: by inducing or aggravating an economic downturn, they will be counter-productive. It is in developing public policies appropriate to nondemand inflation that the greatest difficulties are encountered, since the sources of such inflation are deeply embedded in the underlying structures and policies of industry, labor, and government itself. The real value of this volume should be in expanding our knowledge of those institutions whose importance as sources of inflation requires new thinking, new approaches, and the development of new public policies to ensure a sustained expansion in economic activity — free from the crippling economic and social burdens of continuing inflation.

John M. Blair
University of South Florida
January 1975

CONTENTS

I

SIMULTANEOUS INFLATION AND UNEMPLOYMENT

A CHALLENGE TO THEORY AND POLICY

Gardiner C. Means

Inflation is an age-old problem. So is underemployment, though it seems to have become more acute in the twentieth century. But simultaneous inflation and excessive unemployment is something relatively new.

According to traditional theory, simultaneous inflation and underemployment are not possible. Inflation can occur if an excess in aggregate demand develops. Deflation can occur if a deficiency of aggregate demand develops, and experience indicates that deflation can result in excessive unemployment. But the received theory provides no possible explanation of a general rise of prices in the presence of excessive unemployment.

Yet in recent history, many examples can be found of inflation which has occurred in the presence of heavy unemployment of both men and machines. In the United States, both wholesale and consumer prices have nearly doubled in the last twenty years, but in only two of those years, 1967 and 1968, has there been an excess in overall demand, and these two years accounted for less than 4% of the total price rise. For most of the period, there was a deficiency in demand, while unemployment averaged 5% of the civilian labor force. Clearly, experience is in conflict with traditional theory, and new theory is required.

This chapter is concerned with the new inflation as it has arisen in the United States and the issues of theory and policy it raises. To

1

understand this new phenomenon, it is necessary to distinguish between five types of inflation, three to be found in the classical literature and two nonclassical types.

CLASSICAL TYPES OF INFLATION

The classical theorists have recognized and taken into account three types of inflation: (1) demand inflation arising from an excessive increase in aggregate demand; (2) price increases due to crop failures or a comparable shrinkage in supply; and (3) a rise in the domestic prices of both imports and exports due to monetary devaluation or foreign inflation. None of these could explain simultaneous inflation and excessive unemployment. But it is necessary to understand each in order to distinguish them from the nonclassical types of inflation.

Classical Demand Inflation

Most important in the classical literature is the familiar inflation which arises from excessive demand. In popular terms, it comes from too much money chasing too few goods. Technically, it occurs when there is already full employment and aggregate demand expands beyond the output which can be supplied at full employment. Then prices and wage rates rise more or less together.

This is the type of inflation discussed in the traditional textbooks under the head of inflation. It is properly called "demand inflation." It occurred in the United States both during World War I and following World War II. If this classical demand inflation were the only type of inflation, traditional theory would be correct in holding that simultaneous inflation and excessive unemployment are incompatible.

Supply Shortages

The second source of price rises accounted for by classical theory, supply shortages such as crop failures, does not alter this classical conclusion. Bad harvests could raise not only farm prices but, to a lesser degree, other prices as well since living costs are reflected in the price of labor. The same could be expected from a temporary cutoff of crude oil supplies. In both cases, the price rise would not only be temporary but, according to classical theory, the market

would continue to absorb all that could be produced consistently with the classical condition that marginal cost and marginal revenue are equated by price. Unemployment would not be involved in this type of inflation.

Foreign Trade

The third type of classical inflation, that originating in foreign trade, would likewise not involve unemployment. Inflation abroad would raise the prices of a home country's imports directly, while the prices of domestic exports would, in turn, rise as foreign countries bought more from the home country since domestic prices would be lower in terms of "their" (foreign) currency. This rise in the prices of goods in foreign trade could result in a rise in other prices as well, partly as imports entered as raw materials in the production and costs of domestic goods, and partly as they affected living costs and the price of labor. Essentially the same result could be expected for a country which devalued its currency. But in neither case would the postulates of classical theory allow the result of the price rise to be the creation of unemployment. The two would be incompatible.

The Basis of Traditional Theory

The classical incompatibility between inflation and unemployment rests on the postulate of price and wage flexibility, with prices moving in the same direction as demand. Traditional theory assumed that prices and wages were highly flexible, constantly adjusting to equate supply and demand. The haggling and bargaining in the marketplace was expected to clear the market just as, in the wheat market or a stock exchange, the bids and offers are matched and the price adjusts. All who are willing to sell at the current market price sell all they want to, and all who are willing to buy at the current market price buy all they want to, thus clearing the market. Whether markets were formally organized or not, prices were expected to respond quickly to changes in aggregate demand, falling with a decrease in demand and rising with an increase. Even monopoly prices were expected to be flexible as the monopolist constantly adjusted his price to equate "marginal cost" and "marginal revenue." Any inflexibility was treated as a "friction" and not taken into account in the theoretical models on which traditional theory based

its policy conclusions. Prices which behaved in this classical fashion
can properly be called "classical market prices" or more simply
"market prices." If the great bulk of market transactions took place
at such flexible market prices, general inflation and general unemployment would be incompatible.

NONCLASSICAL PRICE BEHAVIOR

When actual transactions in the modern world are examined, it is
found that prices (other than those of farm products and some raw
materials) are seldom highly flexible and that supply and demand in
the traditional sense are seldom equated by price. For most goods,
the price has been set, usually by the seller, and kept constant for a
period of time and a series of transactions. At the price set, more is
likely to be offered than is currently demanded, and the seller would
usually be delighted to sell more at the same price. Sometimes
demand exceeds supply, and some form of rationing occurs other
than through a change in price. Only by chance are supply and
demand equated and the market just cleared by the price which has
been set. Such a price has been called an "administered price" — and
is the type of price at which the great bulk of commodity and service
transactions take place in a modern industrial society.

Market vs. Administered Prices

The contrast between "market" and "administered" prices is clear
in the field of retailing. Haggling and bargaining is still the standard
procedure for arriving at prices in oriental bazaars. But prices in a
modern chain store are set by the store management and kept
constant for a series of transactions. Sometimes a given item will be
offered at the same price for weeks or months at a time. In a well
stocked store, supply is usually in excess of demand, with stock
immediately available to fill whatever demand arises at the fixed
price. Occasionally demand exceeds supply, and a customer is told,
"Sorry, we are all out of that item. Come back next week." Even the
oriental bazaars have been turning to price administration. A Turkish
shop selling at administered prices is likely to post a sign "Prices à la
Franca."

Most industrial prices are administered prices, not classical market
prices. The bulk of such prices are set by the administrative action of

the seller. In the steel industry, prices are not only set for periods of time, but for such long periods that a price change often becomes front page news. Many prices are set in open-ended contracts negotiated between buyers and sellers for a year or more at a time, with the actual purchase transactions not occurring until the buyer decides how much to buy from time to time at the agreed-upon price. This procedure has also become traditional for wage rates, with the "price" set either by the employer or by an open-ended contract negotiated between management and labor. The actual amount of labor employed is then usually determined by the requirements of the employer.

The Relative Inflexibility of Industrial Prices

Studies of actual behavior of industrial prices show great inflexibility of prices. A study concerned with the Great Depression of the 1930's shows that for a fifth of the weight in the wholesale price index of the U. S. Bureau of Labor Statistics, the average frequency of price change reported by individual sellers was once every two years. For another fifth, individual sellers reported on the average only one change about every eight months.[1] A recent study by the National Bureau of Economic Research indicates that for a sample of twenty-seven important industrial products, the price paid by an individual buyer reporting in each month over a four-year period changed on average less frequently than once every seven months.[2]

The only concrete examples of this infrequence of price change given in the National Bureau study are contained in a chart for bulk ammonia which is reproduced below. The series in the chart were chosen in the Bureau study "to display the varieties of price data reported: unchanging prices, irregularly changing prices, broken price series, and frequently changing prices," and ammonia is referred to as ". . . our illustrative commodity . . ." The chart gives the wholesale price paid by each of four substantial bulk buyers of ammonia who reported the prices actually paid in successive months in the period 1957 to 1966.

Examination of Chart I shows a high degree of inflexibility. Buyer C reported that it paid *exactly* the same price each month for eight years. Buyer A, though it did not buy in every month, paid only four different prices in a ten-year period. Buyer D reported only five price changes in ten years. And Buyer B reported fifteen changes in nine years, but many of these were temporary seasonal changes. If one leaves out the seasonal changes, the four series show eleven changes in a combined life of thirty-six years, or an average change of once every three-and-a-quarter years.

Chart I-I

AMMONIA: SELECTED INDIVIDUAL PRICE SERIES

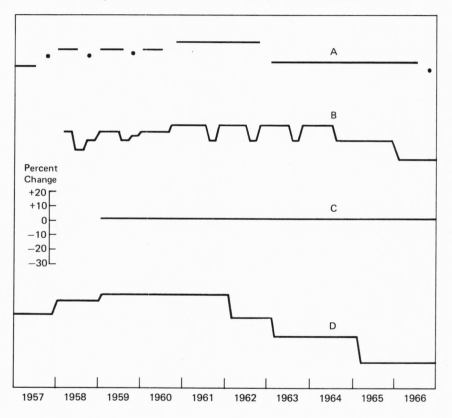

The chart also shows that when the prices did change, the change came in quantum jumps. The three changes reported by buyer A averaged 8%. For buyer D, the average change was 9%. For buyer B, even including the seasonal changes, the average change was 6%.

These National Bureau data collected from buyers reinforce the evidence collected by the Bureau of Labor Statistics from sellers that for many industrial products, prices are administered and held constant for very considerable periods of time; and that when changes are made, they take quantum jumps.

Clearly the behavior of administered prices does not fit the expectation of traditional theory. It is not credible that for a seller of a given product, marginal cost and marginal revenue are constant for a matter of months at a time and then, suddenly, change so that a price 8% higher or lower is the price which just clears the market by equating marginal cost and marginal revenue. It would be even less creditable that marginal revenue and marginal cost both changed over a prolonged period in such a fashion that the price at which they were equal was constant and then, suddenly, was 8% higher or lower. Such price behavior implies not only significant market power in the determination of prices but also the use of pricing discretion in ways not expected from traditional theory. And most important here, it gives rise to two types of inflation, one which occurs when there is less than full employment, and the other, which can occur whether or not there is full employment—neither of which is consistent with the received theory.

THE REFLATION OF PRICES

The first of these nonclassical types of inflation grows out of the quite different reactions of market prices and administered prices to business fluctuations.

In a recession, the general drop in demand produces a fall in market prices, although production tends to remain level, as classical theory would lead one to expect. At the other extreme, administered prices tend to drop little, while the fall in demand for such products works itself out in reduced sales, production, and employment. Other administered prices behave in an intermediate fashion, particularly those in which flexible, market-priced commodities constitute an important raw material. In such intermediate cases, both prices and production tend to drop to an intermediate degree. Thus, excessive unemployment develops along with reduced production in those sectors with relatively inflexible administered prices, while the classical reduction in market-determined prices comes mostly from competition. The net result is not only excessive unemployment, but also a severe unbalance in price relationships.

In a recovery from depression, the rise in demand operates

primarily to lift employment where prices are inflexible, to lift flexible-market prices without much change in supply, and to lift both prices and production to an intermediate degree for the intermediate items. Because the rise in prices is a natural and necessary part of the process of recovery, it is "a good thing" and deserves a separate name. Here it will be called *reflation.*

A spectacular case of deflation and reflation occurred in the United States during the Great Depression of the 1930's. Chart II shows the behavior of five price indexes during the depression for products at wholesale which differ in the frequency of price change and therefore tend to reflect differences in the extent to which market power and administrative discretion are exercised over price. The chart shows the movement of the five indexes from the relatively full-employment years 1926 to 1929 as well as the depression and recovery years from 1929 to early 1942 when full employment was again achieved and the price-wage structure was frozen under wartime controls.

As can be seen from Chart II, the market-dominated index E, made up of such items as wheat, cotton, beef cattle, hides, lead, zinc, lumber, and scrap steel, fell over 60% and recovered an equal amount so that at the time of the price freeze in 1942, it was back to approximately the level of 1929.

Index A, the most administration-dominated, comprising such items as agricultural implements, iron ore, hand tools, plate glass, and sewing machines, fell less than 10% and recovered by about nearly the same amount.

The intermediate indexes behaved in an intermediate fashion.

As a result, the five indexes which had diverged during the recession came somewhat together in the partial recovery of early 1937, diverged again in the 1937-38 recession, and came together again by early 1942 when prices were frozen under the war powers. As can be seen, the five indexes bore nearly the same relation to each other at full employment in 1942 as at full employment in 1929.

During this period, the fall in production and employment and the recovery of both occurred primarily in the industries whose prices had dropped least in recession and recovered least during reflation. This can be seen in Table I, which gives the drop in the prices and production for each of ten major industries from 1929 to 1932 and their recovery to 1937.

Chart I-II

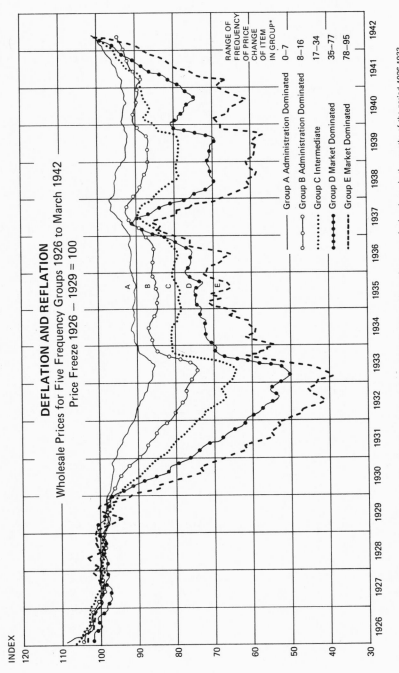

DEFLATION AND REFLATION

Wholesale Prices for Five Frequency Groups 1926 to March 1942

Price Freeze 1926 – 1929 = 100

RANGE OF
FREQUENCY
OF PRICE
CHANGE
OF ITEM
IN GROUP*

——— Group A Administration Dominated   0–7

—o— Group B Administration Dominated   8–16

·········· Group C Intermediate   17–34

—•—•— Group D Market Dominated   35–77

– – – – Group E Market Dominated   78–95

*Price indexes are for 731 items included in the B.L.S. wholesale price index grouped according to frequency of price change in the months of the period 1926-1933.

Table I-I

PRICE AND PRODUCTION BEHAVIOR IN
RECESSION AND PARTIAL RECOVERY

	Decline 1929-1932 in Percent of 1929		Rise 1932-37 in Percent of 1929	
	Prices	Production	Prices	Production
Motor Vehicles	12	74	2	64
Agricultural Implements	14	84	9	84
Iron and Steel	16	76	20	67
Cement	16	55	20	24
Automobile Tires	25	42	27	24
Leather & Leather Products	33	18	29	27
Petroleum Products	36	17	21	37
Textile Products	39	28	24	24
Food Products	39	10	24	−1
Agricultural Commodities	54	1	36	8

Source: *The Structure of the American Economy*, National Resources Committee, Washington, D.C., 1939, p. 386.

Thus, the rise in aggregate demand during recovery lifted the sensitive market prices and increased employment where prices were least sensitive, thereby restoring the pre-depression price balance and full employment.

This same differential behavior of prices occurred in the recession and recovery of 1957-58 and in that of 1960-61 according to the new price data collected by the National Bureau of Economic Research from buyers of products.[3] There was this significant difference, however: in the National Bureau sample, a substantial number of administered prices, not only did not go down in recession, but actually went *up*, while a substantial number went *down* during recovery.

This nonclassical type of inflation would not be possible if all prices, including wages, behaved in a manner that satisfied the classical postulates of price flexibility, market clearing, and the equating of marginal cost and marginal revenue.

The reflation of prices in a recovery from a preceding recession should be regarded as a natural part of the recovery process and, in this way, is wholly different from an inflation due to a general excess in demand. Both come from an increase in aggregate demand. But only the recovery rise in prices is constructive since it is an integral part of the recovery process and tends to restore price balance. Because it is a "good thing," it presents no major problem of policy, except that of recognizing its appropriateness and not trying to prevent it. However, in the period of recovery before full employment is reached, it does involve a rise of prices in the presence of excessive unemployment.

ADMINISTRATIVE INFLATION

The second type of nonclassical inflation also arises from the exercise of "market power," but can occur whether employment is full or less than full and can occur in a period of recession, in a period of stagnation, or in one of recovery. It can appear, as well, during a period when prices are also rising as a result of excessive demand.

This type of inflation may be initiated by management in an effort to widen profit margins and could then be properly called "profit-push" inflation. It could also be initiated by labor in an effort to obtain unwarranted wage increases which would, in turn, be called "cost-push" inflation. To avoid any implication of its specific source, it will be called here "administrative inflation," leaving the complex issue of the initiating source open for further investigation in each specific case.

The first clear example of administrative inflation in the United States occurred in the 1950's. In the five years from 1953 to 1958, there was an 8% increase in the wholesale price index, while at the same time, unemployment of both men and machines was excessive and higher at the end than at the beginning of the period.

The present writer brought this new phenomenon to the attention of the Senate Anti-Trust and Monopoly Committee in July 1957, and in January 1959, presented the committee with Chart III (below). It covers all items in the wholesale price index grouped into seventeen industries. The height of each column shows the change in the index for the respective industrial group from the average for 1953 to October 1958. The width of each column indicates the relative weight the group carried in the total wholesale index. This chart shows that the bulk of the increase in the wholesale price index was in the more concentrated industries (indicated in black) while prices in the more competitive industries (indicated in white) went down or rose little. This finding was confirmed by the investigations of the Joint Economic Committee.[4]. If all whole-sale prices had behaved like those in classically competitive indus-tries, there would have been no inflation. If all had behaved like the more concentrated prices, the administrative inflation would have been nearly twice as great.

It is clear that in this period the major source of the inflation was the 36% rise in steel prices and the substantial price increases in the steel-using industries. Together these accounted for more than half the rise in the total wholesale price index. Subsequent information has made it clear that the steel price rise involved a very considerable widening of steel profit margins, so that this particular administrative inflation was initiated as a profit push.[5]

The administrative inflation from 1953 to 1958 was clearly not due to an excess of aggregate demand. It did not involve either of the other two classical types of inflation—or a reflation. It could not have taken place if administered prices had behaved in the classical manner.

Administrative inflation appears to be endemic under the condi-tions of modern industry. It occurs in periods of full employment when there is no excess in aggregate demand. It occurs when there is excessive unemployment. And it even occurred in the recession of 1969-1970 when administered prices rose, while those prices subject to market forces and the level of employment both dropped.

Unlike reflation, administrative inflation presents major problems of economic theory and economic policy. Why do administered prices rise in a period when there is no excess in aggregate demand and classical market prices are not rising? How can it be that administered prices rise when aggregate demand is declining? And most important, how can administrative inflation either be prevented or kept to a minimum during a period of expanding demand leading to full employment, as well as after full employment has been achieved?

EFFORTS TO CONTROL ADMINISTRATIVE INFLATION

Much light can be thrown on administrative inflation by consider-ing the six qualitatively different attempts at inflation control which have been employed in the United States in the last twenty years.

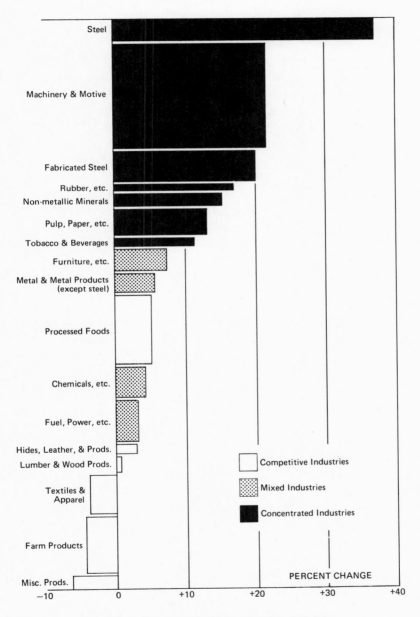

Chart I-III

ADMINISTRATIVE INFLATION
Wholesale Price Changes by Product Groups 1953 to October 1958
Average Increase 8.1 Percent

Steel

Machinery & Motive

Fabricated Steel

Rubber, etc.

Non-metallic Minerals

Pulp, Paper, etc.

Tobacco & Beverages

Furniture, etc.

Metal & Metal Products
(except steel)

Processed Foods

Chemicals, etc.

Fuel, Power, etc.

Hides, Leather, & Prods.

Lumber & Wood Prods.

Textiles &
Apparel

Farm Products

Misc. Prods.

Competitive Industries

Mixed Industries

Concentrated Industries

PERCENT CHANGE

−10   0   +10   +20   +30   +40

Source: B.L.S. Width of column represents weight of item in the Index.

Monetary Contraction

The first attempt came in 1956-57 when the Federal Reserve Board sought to control the *administrative inflation* of the 1950's through a tight money policy. This more than halted the growth of the nominal stock of money and produced a 10% drop in the *real* stock of money.⁶ It also precipitated the recession of 1957-58.

This effort to control administrative inflation was a complete failure. Farm and other market-dominated prices fell with the recession and rose with the recovery when the tight money policy was reversed. But industrial prices continued to rise and, by 1959, were 5% above their 1956 level. The 13% decline in industrial production and the extra two million persons out of work had little effect in reducing the administrative inflation.

The failure of this effort at controlling inflation arose from the fact that while a sufficiently tight money policy can control a demand inflation, it cannot control an administrative inflation. This was acknowledged by the chief economic advisor to the Federal Reserve Board, Dr. Woodlief Thomas, when he wrote to the *Washington Post* in March, 1959:

> "Recent discussion of the influence of administered prices, stimulated by . . . the Kefauver Committee, has made a significant contribution to a better understanding of the problems of inflation and fluctuations in economic activity and employment. This contribution is in pointing out that there are unstabilizing forces in pricing actions of the private economy—on the part of both management and labor—that cannot be effectively controlled or corrected by governmental actions in the area of fiscal and monetary policies."

The Kennedy Guideposts

The second major attempt to control administrative inflation was the Kennedy guidepost program which was the first to directly face this problem. When the program was being drafted in 1961, unemployment was above 6%. The problem was recognized as one of preventing administrative inflation while expanding demand through fiscal and monetary measures so as to achieve full employment.

The guidepost program was both an outstanding success — in holding down administrative inflation while expanding demand through fiscal and monetary measures—as well as a partial failure. By the end of 1965, full employment had been substantially achieved, while unemployment fell to 4%. Labor had adhered to the wage guideposts so closely that the labor cost per unit of manufacturing output was down 3%. Management had not adhered as closely, and industrial prices rose a little. This in itself was not serious and alone might have been corrected. Nearly full employment had been achieved with a total four year rise of less than 0.6% a year for wholesale prices and close to 0.4% for industrial products.

But this goal had been achieved at the expense of a serious distortion in the relation between prices and wage rates because the guidepost program took no account of the *reflationary* rise in the prices subject to market competition which was appropriate for a period of recovery. The increase in demand which reduced unemployment from above 6% to a level of 4%, in conjunction with only a small increase in the most administration-dominated prices, could have been expected to raise substantially the average of farm prices and other flexible market prices. And in fact this is what happened, creating some overall increase in the average of prices and living costs. Between the end of 1961 and the end of 1965, the wholesale price index for processed foods rose 8%, while the index for industrial products rose only 2%. In the same period, the consumer price index rose to an intermediate degree. Yet the wage guideposts took no account of this appropriate rise in living costs.

As the result of the failure to include a cost-of-living factor in the wage guidepost, the program suffered a partial breakdown. By 1965, the rise in living costs had absorbed more than a third of labor's legitimate productivity gains. During the same period, industry had significantly widened profit margins. When this unfairness in the guideposts became obvious, labor refused to cooperate any longer and forced wage increases larger than gains in productivity in order to catch up with living costs. Management, striving to maintain the widened profit margins, passed along the increases in labor costs. This struggle lifted the wholesale index of industrial products by another 4% from the end of 1965 to the end of 1967, but also brought wages and profits more nearly in line with each other.

Even with the partial breakdown of the wage guidepost, nearly full employment was maintained throughout 1966 and 1967 without signs of excessive demand prior to the fall of 1967. The average unemployment in each of these years was 3.8%. Farm prices did not rise, a normal indication that excess demand was not building up.

Profit margins in industry, which had increased substantially over the long run, declined somewhat, but were still abnormally high. It is clear that the immediate source of inflation in 1966 and 1967 was administrative and came primarily from the effort of labor to realize its share in the productivity gains generated during the whole guidepost period — gains which the guideposts had denied to labor.

When the whole period from 1961 to the end of 1967 is taken into account, it is apparent that most of the inflation was a reflation. In moving from a 6.8% rate of unemployment in the first quarter of 1961 to the 3.8% level of 1966 and 1967, a normal reflation would have been expected to lift the wholesale index substantially. The actual increase in prices—under 6% for the total six years—does not indicate much administrative inflation. Instead, it primarily indicates a delayed reaction of wage rates to the normal reflationary rise in living costs. One must give high, though not perfect, marks to the guidepost program.

It seems likely that with an appropriate living-cost provision in the wage guidepost, the full recovery and reflation could have been accomplished by 1965 and held for another two years with negligible administrative inflation. Whether or not full employment could have been maintained for a much longer period without further inflation is another matter. But the many claims that the guidepost program was a failure—because the total index of prices rose—fail to take account of the reflation which was a necessary part of the recovery.

War Inflation

The third recent attempt to control inflation arose out of the Vietnam War and was an effort to prevent a *demand* inflation. In calendar year 1966, the federal budget was in balance according to the National Income Accounts. But military expenses were expected to increase rapidly and produce a heavy deficit unless taxes were raised. With the economy already at full employment, the extra demand for military supplies could have been expected to produce an excess in demand, causing a demand inflation unless nonmilitary demand was restricted.

This danger of demand inflation was well recognized by the administration. In January 1967, President Johnson recommended a 6% surtax to be made effective by mid-1967. But the Congress failed to act. The President repeated his request in the summer of 1967, raising the requested surtax rate to 10%, but again the Congress took no action. And again in January 1968, the President repeated his request. It was not until mid-1968 that a 10% surtax was finally passed, a year-and-a-half too late. It brought the budget into balance by the last quarter of 1968 and insured a substantial surplus in calendar 1969. A prime source of demand inflation was thus finally removed.

In the meantime, demand inflation had pushed the wholesale price index up more that 3% from the 1967 level, with the increase approximately equal for the market-dominated and the administration-dominated indexes. It seems probable that if the surtax had been passed in early 1967 and the guidepost policy stressed, full employment could have been maintained and the war program financed without either demand inflation or serious administrative inflation.

Planned Stagnation

The fourth recent attempt to control inflation began in 1969 and was a complete failure due to a faulty diagnosis. On taking office, President Nixon announced that prices and wage rates would be left to be controlled by the free market, and inflation would be controlled in the classical fashion by fiscal and monetary means, thus rejecting *any* price-guidance program. A large budget surplus was maintained throughout 1969 as a result of the surtax imposed the year before, and such a tight money policy was adopted that expansion in the money stock was halted. Throughout 1969 there was no clear evidence of an excess in demand. Yet in the same year, the wholesale price index rose 4.8%, twice the annual rate of the years from mid-1965 to the end of 1968 when guidelines were to a greater or lesser degree in operation.

In his 1970 Economic Report, President Nixon explained the price rise by saying, "The inflation unleashed after mid-1965 had gathered powerful momentum by the time this Administration took office a year ago." He designated *the growth of total spending* as "the driving force of the inflation" and outlined the plan being followed to "slow down the rapid expansion of demand firmly and persistently." The actual program being followed was set forth in the body of the President's Economic Report. It was to take the heat out of the inflation by creating two-and-a-half years of planned stagnation. This is clearly shown in Chart IV which reproduces, on an enlarged scale, the relevant part of Chart 8 in the President's report. The chart shows the actual growth of GNP in constant prices from 1967 to mid-1969, then the halting of growth in the last half of 1969 and the planned halt to mid-1970 followed by two years in which GNP was, *by plan,* to be kept some $30 billion a year below the estimated potential of the economy. This called for an increase in unemployment by two million persons in an effort to increase the rate of unemployment to around 6%.

Chart I-IV

PLANNED STAGNATION

Actual Gross National Product Through 1969
Planned and Potential Gross National Product After 1969

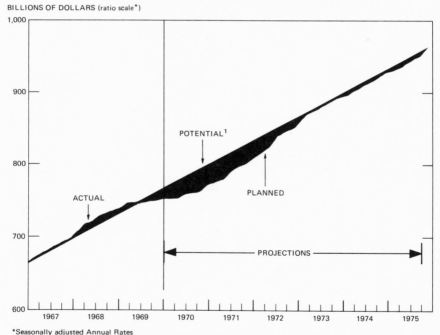

BILLIONS OF DOLLARS (ratio scale*)

*Seasonally adjusted Annual Rates
[1]Trend line of 4 percent from 1965 IV to 1969 IV, 4.3 percent from 1969 IV to 1970 IV, 4.4 percent from 1970 to 1971 IV, and 4.3 percent from 1971 IV to 1975 IV.

This brutal plan was indeed successful in creating stagnation. The continued budget surplus became a restraining force, and the money stock, measured in constant purchasing power, was reduced. Real aggregate demand declined, industrial production started down in the summer of 1969, and unemployment increased as planned. By the end of 1970, the goal of 6% unemployment had been reached and a recession had been achieved.

But stagnation did not halt the inflation. The reason is simple. The driving force of the inflation in 1969 was not "the growth of total spending." Rather, the President had unleashed the forces of administrative inflation by pointedly rejecting the guidepost program. The inflation in the 1969-70 recession was almost entirely administrative inflation.[7] It was the kind of inflation that Dr. Woodlief Thomas had said could not be controlled by fiscal and monetary measures.

The administrative character of this inflation-in-recession is easily shown by examining the main sources of the rise in the wholesale price index. Chart V makes clear the parallel to the administrative inflation of the 1950's. As in Chart III, the more concentrated groups are shown in black, the most competitive in white, and the mixed groups in light gray, while the height of each column indicates the price change, and the width shows the weight which each group carried in the total index.

As can be seen, the great bulk of the increase in prices during the recession was contributed by the concentrated industries. In the more competitive industries, prices went up little or went down. The only exception to this tendency was the fuel and power index which rose 11% largely because of the scarcity of pollution-free fuels.

The dismal failure of this attempt to control administrative inflation by the planned creation of stagnation was acknowledged by the New Economic Policy of August 1971 which froze prices and wages after the stagnation plan had already cost the country nearly $50 billion in lost GNP and promised more loss until reflation could restore full employment. But no apology was given to the millions who suffered unnecessary unemployment or to the stockholders whose profits were reduced. Nor was there acknowledgement that the crucial presidential decision to create planned stagnation was in direct conflict with the Employment Act of 1946.

The New Economic Policy

The fifth effort at controlling inflation, the President's *New Economic Policy,* involved a return to price-wage guidance and was more successful. It directly faced both the problem created by the

Chart I-V

ADMINISTRATIVE INFLATION IN RECESSION
Wholesale Price Changes by Product Groups June 1969 to December 1970
Average Increase 4.0 Percent

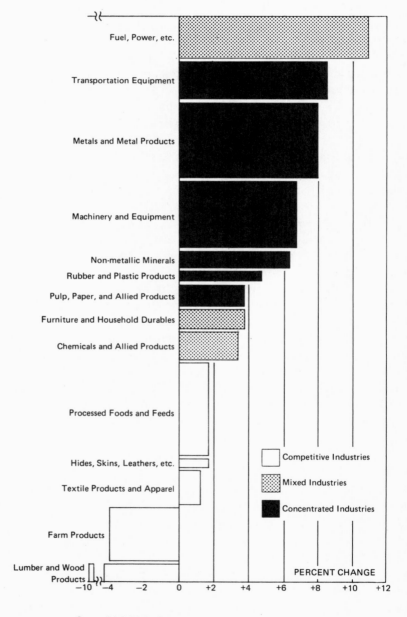

Source: B.L.S. Width of column represents weight of item in the Index.

lack of an adequate market control of prices and the necessity of reflation as the stagnation mistake was corrected. The new guidelines introduced in Phase II were a distinct improvement over the Kennedy guideposts in two respects. The wage guideline included a factor for the rise in the cost of living which would accompany the process of reflation. The price guideline focused on the holding of profit *margins* which allowed enterprises to increase their profits by producing more, but not by increasing prices relative to costs except in special cases. In addition, both guidelines were backed by legislative authority to exercise and enforce controls.

In its first sixteen months up to December 1972, the price-wage program was quite successful in preventing *administrative* inflation. The weighted index for the six most concentrated industrial groups in the wholesale price index rose at the annual rate of only 1.8%, while the index for the three mixed groups went up at an annual rate of 2.5% as shown in Table II. Both of those increases could have been expected as a part of the normal reflation. The cost-of-living factor meant that the labor cost, per unit of output, increased by around 2%.

Competitive prices went up more than would have been expected on the basis of reflation alone. The partial recovery in this period could have been expected to raise market-dominated prices by perhaps double that of the mixed groups, or around 5%. But the weighted index of the five most competitive groups of the B.L.S. index went up at an annual rate of 10.3% to December 1972. A severe drought in Texas and the destructive corn blight in 1970 broke the cattle cycle, so that less meat and fewer hides were available in 1972. Then drought in other parts of the world forced up grain and feed prices and, in turn, produced abnormally high prices for hogs, poultry, eggs, and an added increase in beef prices. The floating of the dollar in August 1971 and its devaluation in May 1972 also contributed, particularly for the flexible market prices. If the special restrictions on supply are excluded, the wholesale price index would have increased during these sixteen months at an annual rate of around 3%, instead of 5.3%, almost all of it an appropriate reflationary response to the partial recovery of the period.

It should also be noted that unlike the guideposts of 1961-65, the effects of Phases I and II were substantially fair to both labor and capital. In the last half of 1972, the division between capital and labor of the income generated by nonfinancial corporations was almost exactly the same as it was in 1969 and in the eight years of the Eisenhower administration: 87.6% to labor and about 12.4% to capital.[8]

Table I-II

WHOLESALE PRICE BEHAVIOR
UNDER PHASES I AND II

Average Increase

Concentrated Industries	Percent Change August 1971 to December 1972	Annual Rate
Rubber and Plastic Products	0.0	
Machinery and Equipment	+ 2.1	
Non-Metallic Minerals	+ 2.5	
Metal and Metal Products	+ 2.6	
Transportation Equipment	+ 3.2	
Pulp, Paper and Allied Products	+ 4.1	
Weighted Average	+ 2.4%	+ 1.8%
Mixed Industries		
Chemicals and Allied Products	+ 0.4	
Furniture and Household Durables	+ 2.0	
Fuel, Power etc.	+ 6.1	
Weighted Average	+ 3.3%	+ 2.5%
Competitive Industries		
Textile Products and Apparel	+ 5.2	
Lumber and Wood Products	+11.1	
Processed Foods and Feeds	+12.0	
Farm Products	+21.1	
Hides, Skins, Leathers, etc.	+24.3	
Weighted Average	+13.8%	+10.3%
Total Wholesale Index	+ 7.0%	5.3%

The success of Phases I and II in preventing administrative inflation suggests the efficiency of this type of control in a period of recovery. How long the controls could be effective once full employment is achieved still remains a central problem of economic analysis and economic policy.

COMPOUND INFLATION AND THE PROBLEM OF DIAGNOSIS

A particular period of inflation may be dominated by a single major source—such as a general excess in demand, as in 1967-68, or by the exercise of market power in the administrative inflation of the 1950's. Diagnosis is a relatively simple problem once the different possible sources of inflation are recognized. But inflation in a particular period may reflect a compound of several different sources. Then diagnosis becomes difficult.

Such is the case with the hyper-inflation from June 1973 to June 1974. In this single year, the wholesale price index rose 14%, in part from the Arab-created rise in fuel prices, in part from the effects of inflation abroad, and in part from administrative inflation at home. But how much should be attributed to each is not easy to determine.

What is easier to determine is the possible sources which did *not* contribute to this inflation.

Clearly there was no general excess in demand. Aggregate demand went up less than prices, and real national income went down. Unemployment increased from 4.8% to 5.2% of the labor force, and the proportion of manufacturing capacity utilized declined from 83.3% to 80.6%. The economy had unused reserves of manpower and plant that could have supplied at least another $50 or $60 billion of demand without establishing the conditions for inflation.

Likewise, there was no element of reflation in the price rise since production declined and unemployment rose.

The rise in farm prices as a result of previous crop failures had come to a practical end with the index of farm prices down more than 7% from June 1973 to June 1974 and the wholesale food and feed index up only 3.7% during the year — together contributing nothing to the 14% rise in the wholesale index.

Finally, it is clear that wages followed, rather than initiated, the price rise. In the twelve months from June 1973 to June 1974, the average hourly earnings for the private nonfarm economy went up 8.0%, but prices went up so much faster than wages that the real income per worker-hour went down 2.8%. Thus wage rates lagged substantially behind the rise in living costs.

The Compound and Three Major Sources
This leaves three sources to account for the 14% price rise: the

energy crisis, the domestic effects of foreign inflation, and administrative inflation coming from the side of management.

The direct contribution of the energy crisis is evident in the 57.8%
rise in the wholesale index for fuels, related products, and power.
This alone accounted directly for nearly a third of the rise in the
wholesale index. The rise in fuel and power prices also added to costs
of production in nearly every field, and the raw materials for other
industries such as chemicals and plastics became more expensive.
Perhaps half the year's rise in the wholesale index, seven percentage
points, should be attributed to the direct and indirect effects of the
energy crisis.

Another part, but probably small in the total, should be attributed
to the domestic effects of the rapid inflation in the leading foreign
industrial countries. Throughout the year, the U. S. economy was to
a considerable degree protected from foreign inflation by the floating
exchange rate — but not as completely as traditional theory would
lead one to expect. Traditional theory assumes that general demand
inflation will lift all prices in about the same degree in the inflating
country. In such a case, it could be expected that a floating exchange
rate would largely insulate one country from demand inflation in
another. The decline in the real value of money in the inflating
country would be just offset by the decline in its exchange value. But
in modern industrial countries, a general demand inflation operates
first and most extensively on market-dominated prices so that they
advance ahead of prices dominated by administration. As a result, a
floating exchange rate does not give a country complete protection
from the effects of foreign inflation. It is in this way that the flexible
market prices of many imported raw materials such as lead, zinc, and
copper have been raised in the United States, thus adding to domestic costs and contributing to the 14% inflation.

How much of the 14% rise should be attributed to this foreign
inflation is difficult to say, but *total* imports in that period
amounted to only 8% of GNP, and only a part would be involved in
the wholesale index. Even taking account of the indirect as well as
the direct effects of these flexible-priced commodities, it is doubtful
if they accounted for anything like half of the 14% rise in the
wholesale index.

The third claimant, administrative inflation from the side of
management, appears to have been a much more important element.

First, most of that half of the 14% price rise still to be accounted for came in the more concentrated industries. This is shown in Table III which classifies the fourteen B.L.S. group indexes in the same fashion as in Charts III and V and shows the percentage increase from June 1973 to June 1974.

Table I-III

INFLATION FROM JUNE 1973 TO JUNE 1974

A Breakdown of the B.L.S.
Wholesale Price Index to Reflect the Relative Role of Market-Dominated and Administration-Dominated Prices

Competitive Industry Groups	Percent Change in Price Index	Weighted Change in Price Index
Farm Products	−7.5%	
Hides, Skins, and Leather Products	+3.6	
Foods and Feeds, Processed	+3.7	+1.9%
Lumber and Wood Products	+5.0	
Textile Products and Apparel	+14.7	
Mixed Industry Groups		
Furniture and Household Durables	+9.5%	
Chemicals and Allied Products	+29.3	
Fuels and Related Products and Power	+57.8	
Concentrated Industry Groups		
Transportation Equipment	+6.8%	
Nonmetallic Mineral Products	+16.3	
Rubber and Plastic Products	+20.4	
Pulp, Paper, and Allied Products	+20.9	21.9%
Machinery and Equipment	+21.9	
Metals and Metal Products	+31.3	
All Commodity Index		+14%

Source: U.S. Bureau of Labor Statistics

Of the five more competitive groups, only textiles went up as much as the total index; and the five groups taken together increased less than 2%. On the other hand, of the six more concentrated groups, all but transportation equipment went up more than the total index, and the weighted average for the six went up nearly 22%.

This table reinforces the evidence already given that there was no general excess of demand to account for the inflation of the period. The prices most sensitive to rising demand rose little at the same time that fuel and the administration-dominated prices rose sharply. An outstanding example of the latter is the 31% rise in the index of iron and steel prices. In the year from August 1973 to August 1974, the index for finished steel prices rose a total of 44%.

How much of the 22% price increase in the concentrated industries came from increased fuel and raw material costs, how much from the wage increases which averaged 9.6% per man-hour for all manufacturing, how much from the increase in interest rates, and how much from widened profit margins can only be determined from an industry-by-industry analysis. But corporate profits increased substantially in this period, while real production did not. The reduced profits of the more competitive industries, which could not raise their prices as easily, tended to cover up the greater increase in the more concentrated industries within the total industry figures. The tentative conclusion is justified that a substantial part of the 14% inflation at the wholesale level arose from the excessive widening of profit margins.

A similar compound inflation occurred in the galloping inflation of the two months following June 1974. In that period, the wholesale price index rose 7.5%, or at an annual rate of 45%. This inflation reflected not only the continued rise of fuel prices, but also a renewed rise in farm and food prices as a result of drought and crop damage in the mid-West. But the price indexes for the other three competitive industry groups went up little or went down, and the bulk of the remaining price increase was in the more concentrated industries whose combined index went up 5.8%, an increase at an annual rate of 35%. Again, the figures point strongly to a further widening of profit margins in those industries in which there is such a degree of concentration that management can exercise substantial market power.

In these two months of galloping inflation, the rate suggests that *the expectation* of further inflation may have played an important role. As traditional theory has explained, the pure speculator can stimulate inflation, pushing up prices through buying a part of the supply. When the speculator unloads, the price is pushed down, and the speculator has no *net* effect on price, once adjustment to the cause of price change has been made. But where an industry is concentrated and management has a substantial degree of market power, there is usually little room for the pure speculator. A speculator outside the auto industry could expect a rise in auto prices and buy, say, 10,000 cars; but it would require more than just a sell order to dispose of them. Thus the independent speculator is not a problem in the concentrated industries.

However, an expectation of inflation can introduce a quite different effect in the concentrated industries — an arbitrary price increase by management. Once there is a *general* expectation of continued inflation, the market controls of cost and demand become even less restrictive in the concentrated industries than they would be in more normal times, and prices can be raised by sizable amounts. Astute management seeks to "beat the gun" on inflation by raising prices more in relation to costs than if there were no general expectation of inflation. Again, only detailed industry studies would show how much this factor contributes to an inflation once it has started. What is important is that this factor can operate when inflation occurs under conditions of stagnation.

INFLATION AND PUBLIC POLICY

Once the source or sources of a given inflation have become clear, the appropriate public policy is reasonably clear, except in the case of administrative inflation.

When inflation comes from a *general* demand in excess of what can be met with available resources, traditional theory correctly calls for a tight monetary-fiscal policy to limit demand.

When prices rise for particular market-dominated commodities because of a crop failure or oil crisis, traditional theory again correctly offers the alternative of rationing through price increases or, where the damage through price increases would be great, the alternative of price control and government rationing. Indeed, whether the high price of imported oil calls for rationing through greatly increased prices or calls for domestic price control and government rationing would be a legitimate matter of debate under traditional theory. In either case, the short-run answer to reduced supply is belt tightening, while the longer-run answer is the increase in supply and more efficient use.

Domestic price increases arising from inflation abroad present a more complex problem. Domestic policy would call for a floating exchange rate. Then it might simply treat the increases which bypassed the floating exchange rates in the same fashion as other temporary limitations on supply. Or policy could be aimed at helping other countries to control their own inflation.

The latter course seems indicated by the fact that much of the foreign inflation can be linked to the uncontrolled expansion in eurodollars — dollar deposits held in foreign commercial banks — which have already reached the magnitude of $185 billion. They have arisen in part from imbalances in U. S. payments abroad with the backing of dollars in the U.S. But in substantial part, they have been created abroad and are not in any way an obligation of the U.S. Traditional theory does not concern itself with the effect from the deposit currency of one country when it is created in another. But foreign inflation is likely to continue as long as the stock of eurodollars is allowed to expand without control, and there is an increasing recognition that the effect is inflationary. A eurodollar may have a low velocity of use in a foreign country, but as a liquid store of value, it can take the place of the country's own currency and force a rise in its velocity. This presents a problem, along with that of oil, which requires international cooperation.

Limiting Administrative Inflation

The really immediate issue is that of limiting the abuse of market power in concentrated industries. Because traditional theory does not envisage administrative inflation, it can give little guidance in its control. Indeed, traditional theory could not even provide a basis for setting up the principles to guide management in adjusting its prices to changed conditions. The principle of equating marginal cost and marginal revenue would have no relevance.

The first essential is to provide management with a clear set of guidelines which would define what use of market power is consistent with a national policy to achieve high employment without inflation and what actions constitute an abuse of such power. An effort to "beat the gun" on inflation is obviously such an abuse, and until management is provided with clear guidelines, it cannot be expected to act responsibly.

Labor has shown that it will abide by price-wage guidelines when it believes (1) that the guidelines are fair and (2) that management will also abide by them. This is partly because labor has a greater interest than management in avoiding inflation and partly because management will tend to act as enforcer of wage guidelines.

In the case of management, there is no possible enforcer in sight except the government. Suppose that a fair set of price and wage guidelines had already been set up. Some more responsible enterprises might abide by them, and most could be expected to enforce them on labor. But most businesses could be expected to continue to abuse their market power, and the result of a simple publication of such guidelines would clearly be unfair to labor.

Yet, consider the advantages to management if all enterprises with significant market power were to abide by a fair set of guidelines. If a given enterprise with market power were offered a contract that would make everyone else adhere to the guidelines providing that it would agree to do so in turn, the signing of such a contract would usually be an excellent piece of business. A small diminution of discretion would promise to remove the headaches of this type of inflation, both with respect to wages and the constant need to readjust to changing prices and the accounting problems this generates. And if it would allow an expansion of real demand, operations under a prosperous economy would yield larger profits.

But only government could enforce such a contract. The problem is to work out a program of enforcement which would interfere minimally with business discretion in the carrying out of its productive activity.

It would probably be sufficient to limit the enforcement to the few hundred largest manufacturing corporations. This is where most of the significant market power resides. It seems likely that, if the abuse of market power were prevented in the more concentrated industries, and for their more important products, administrative inflation could be kept to an acceptable minimum.[9]

It may be said that such government interference with the private administration of prices by the big corporations is an invasion of individual freedom. It should be recognized, however, that the market power of big enterprise is only possible as the result of the power to operate as corporations, and the power to operate as a corporation is a grant of power from the government, not a "natural right" of individuals. This grant of power does not entitle corporations to abuse their market power. And their very size vests them with a public interest.

An alternative approach would be to reduce or eliminate market power through the more stringent enforcement of the antitrust laws and the breakup of big business. The antitrust laws have been outstandingly successful in preventing actual *monopoly*, the industry with only one seller. There are very few industries in which there are not at least several competing producers. But these laws were never designed to prevent *oligopoly* — the current source of market power. A substantial reduction of market power will, in any case, take time.

Public policy might well combine the short-run course of guiding the use of market power with longer-run measures to reduce it, waiting on the success of each to determine the subsequent weight to be given to each.

CONCLUSIONS

Simultaneous inflation and stagnation or recession is a relatively new phenomenon which lies outside the framework of traditional theory and traditional policy. It has plagued the American economy for a score of years and clearly cannot be controlled by the traditional measures of fiscal restraint and tight money. In the United States, it has arisen primarily from the abuse of market power by big business, while the compensation of labor has lagged behind the rise in prices. Its essential character can be summarized in the simple Chart V, which shows the anatomy of this inflation from September 1973 to September 1974. In this period of stagflation, the weighted index for the concentration-dominated industries rose 27%, accounting for half the rise in the wholesale index, while average hourly compensation to labor in manufacturing during the same period rose only 10%. The index dominated by competition rose less than 5%.

In the short run, it is likely that this new form of inflation can be substantially controlled by government through the guidance of pricing of a few hundred of the largest manufacturing corporations. To what extent it can be controlled in the longer run by reducing market power through antitrust action or the break-up of enterprises remains to be seen.

Chart I-VI

THE ANATOMY OF THE RECENT STAGFLATION
September 1973 to September 1974

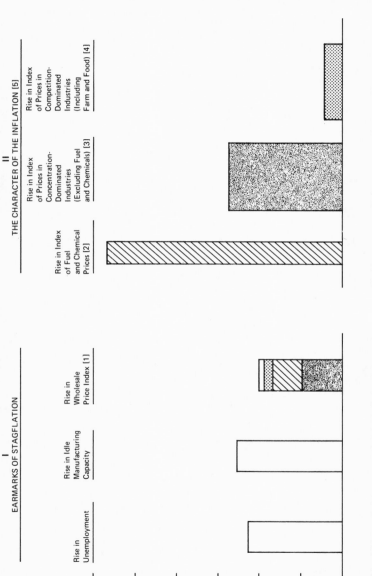

II
THE CHARACTER OF THE INFLATION [5]

Rise in Index of Fuel and Chemical Prices [2]

Rise in Index of Prices in Concentration-Dominated Industries (Excluding Fuel and Chemicals) [3]

Rise in Index of Prices in Competition-Dominated Industries (Including Farm and Food) [4]

I
EARMARKS OF STAGFLATION

Rise in Unemployment

Rise in Idle Manufacturing Capacity

Rise in Wholesale Price Index [1]

60 50 40 30 20 10

(1) In addition to the industry groups included in II, the wholesale price index includes B.L.S. groups "Miscellaneous" and "Furniture and House-hold Durables" which cannot be attributed as primarily concentrated or primarily competitive and account for 5% of the increase in the whole-sale index.

(2) Weighted Average of Wholesale Indexes for Fuel, etc. and Chemicals, etc.

(3) Weighted Average of Wholesale Indexes for Metals, Machinery, Non-Metallic Minerals, Rubber, Paper, and Transportation Equipment.

(4) Weighted Average of Wholesale Indexes for Farm, Food, Leather, Lumber, Textiles, and their products.

(5) Width of columns indicate relative weight of groups in the wholesale price index.

Source: B.L.S. and F.R.B.

II
INFLATION IN THE UNITED STATES
A SHORT-RUN TARGET RETURN MODEL

John M. Blair

With macroeconomic analysis having forged the tools needed to prevent unemployment, inflation has become the Number One unsolved economic problem of the day. Since World War II, economic thinking on inflation has largely revolved around three concepts, each with its own implications for public policy: "demand-pull," "cost-push," and the "Phillips curve." The view that inflation is "everywhere and always" the result of an excessive increase in the money supply resulting in excessive demand has been put forward repeatedly by Milton Friedman.[1] Translated into public policy, the idea that inflation can be restrained by reducing demand was largely responsible for the recessions of 1957-58 and 1969-70 as well as for much of the retardation in economic growth during the intervening years. More recently, it has certainly been a contributing cause of the decline in industrial activity in 1974.

The "cost-push" concept, usually associated with labor costs, regards inflation as the inevitable consequence of increases in wages (and other fringe benefits) in excess of the increase in labor productivity. Translations of this doctrine into public policy include the voluntary wage restraints of the Kennedy "guideposts" and the mandatory wage-price controls of Phases I and II of the Nixon stabilization program. The Phillips curve poses the dilemma of a seemingly inevitable trade-off: inflation can be arrested, but only at the cost of high unemployment; unemployment can be kept low, but only at the cost of a high rate of inflation.

One obvious effect of this dilemma in the realm of public policy was President Ford's reluctance in 1974 to call for anything more than a modest 5% tax surcharge since, while dampening inflationary pressures, a really substantial tax increase would have accelerated the rise in unemployment.

There can be little question but that during particular periods and under particular circumstances inflation has been due to "demand-pull," or to "cost-push," or to both. Advocates of both, however, have sought to transform them from specific into general explanations through the use of "time lags." Thus, increases in the price level during particular periods when wages were *not* rising more rapidly than productivity have been explained in terms of the time required to transmit through the economy increases in unit labor costs occurring in prior years. Similarly, the upward trend in prices during recessions has been attributed to the time required to translate into an effect on the price level the tight money policy instituted earlier. However, the idea that the price level will be influenced by reduced demand only after a lengthy period of time is contradicted by the behavior of products sold in competitive markets which usually respond to a falling-off of demand with an almost immediate reduction in price. Through its effect on costs, a reduction in demand can have a delayed reaction in concentrated industries, but, as will be seen, the direction of price change will be opposite to that presumed under the demand-pull doctrine.

To the extent that they have empirical bases, "demand-pull," "cost-push," and the "Phillips curve" have been derived from studies involving the use of measures of the general price level. But, as Gardiner C. Means showed some forty years ago,[2] the distribution of the price structure is U-shaped: that is, the movements of the overall price series are *not* indicative of the movements of most individual prices which have *either* low amplitudes and frequencies of change *or* high amplitudes and frequencies. The average is the exception. Moreover, recent evidence indicates that in recession, different groups of price change in opposing *directions*, causing the overall series to conceal more than it reveals. The proper study of prices, therefore, is prices, not the general price level.

This analysis will thus be addressed to the behavior of specific prices: prices of concentrated versus unconcentrated products, with concentration measured as the share of shipments accounted for by the four largest producers. The unconcentrated products (those in which the four largest firms made less than 25% of the shipments) have been found to behave more or less in accordance with the expectations of traditional theory. But for the concentrated products (those where the four largest made 50% or more of the shipments), the price behavior is anamolous. Hence, a model will be proposed to explain the seemingly paradoxical behavior of prices in those industries where a few firms have substantial discretionary pricing power.

PERVERSE PRICE FLEXIBILITY

Postwar Recession Price Behavior

The unique feature of the price behavior in the postwar recessions has been a difference in the *direction* of change in concentrated and unconcentrated industries. During the depression of 1929-33, the direction of price change of concentrated industries was downward, although the decreases were much more limited than the declines of unconcentrated industries—and have thus been referred to as "rigid," "inflexible," "sticky." In contrast, during the postwar recessions, the direction of price change in concentrated industries has been upward, a phenomenon which I have referred to as "perverse price flexibility."

This anomaly first revealed itself during the recessions of 1954 and 1958 when a number of indirect measures appeared to show a general decline in demand to be accompanied by a tendency for prices to rise in oligopolistic industries.[3] One of these measures consisted of a distribution of the prices in the U.S. Bureau of Labor Statistics wholesale price index classified by quintiles according to the frequency of price change. At least an indirect relationship can be inferred between industry concentration and frequency of price change on the grounds that concentration has been shown to be related inversely to amplitude of change and amplitude directly to frequency.

But of more importance are the economic realities involved. In most of the major concentrated industries (e.g., steel, automobiles, aluminum), it is a known fact that price changes are normally made once or, at most, only twice a year and seldom followed during the year by more than one "revision." The typical oligopoly is thus not likely to have more than two changes a year which would encompass quintile I (with a median of .3 changes a year), quintile II (1.2

changes) and quintile III (2.0 changes). Rarely would it have as many as 3.7 changes a year—the median of quintile IV—and virtually never would it have 8.5 changes a year—the median of quintile V. There are thus good *economic* grounds to assume the price behavior of oligopolistic industries to be reflected by the movements of the first three quintiles. And in view of their relative importance and known infrequency of change, it is probable that the movements of these three groups are determined largely by the price changes of the major oligopolistic industries. In contrast, the behavior of quintile V can be taken to represent the movement of unconcentrated or competitive industries, while that of quintile IV reflects the movements of an intermediate grouping which is both partly oligopolistic and partly competitive.

During the 1958 recession, prices of farm products moved contrary to the behavior expected of unconcentrated products. This was because of bad weather and a poor growing season for some crops and the low year of the two-year corn-hog cycle for others. Together with processed foods, farm products made up 64.4% of the value of quintile V. The problem presented by the atypical behavior of farm products can be obviated by focusing on the movements of the different quintiles *within durable* goods, which also provides a better basis for examination, in that durable goods suffered a greater reduction in output (14%). In each of the recessions, the three quintiles which represent industries with inflexible prices (I-III) moved upward, while the quintile representing flexible prices (V) registered a noticeable decline.

This contrasting behavior within durable goods casts a serious cloud over both the cost-push and the demand-pull rationalizations. If the upward movement of the inflexible-price products of concentrated industries is to be explained on the basis of cost increases, is it to be assumed that in the flexible-price durable goods industries costs declined? Similarly, while the fall in the flexible-price products can be explained by a decline in demand, would this same fact explain the tendency for the inflexible-price products to rise?

This same tendency for prices of products in concentrated industries to rise during recessions while prices of products in unconcentrated industries decline (or register a considerably smaller increase) has been revealed by four other studies, the results of which are brought together in Table I. At the top are the results of a comparison of price

Chart II-I

ANNUAL AVERAGE PRICE INDEXES OF DURABLE
MANUFACTURED COMMODITIES, BY PRICE FLEXIBILITY
QUINTILE, 1947-1960

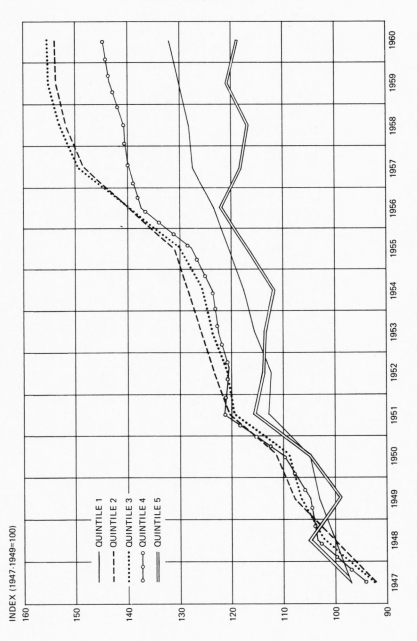

INDEX (1947-1949=100)

QUINTILE 1
QUINTILE 2
QUINTILE 3
QUINTILE 4
QUINTILE 5

movements for sixteen pairs of products during the 1957-58 recession. The two members of each pair are in the same major industry group and subject to similar expansions or contractions in demand, but one member is a concentrated product, while the other is unconcentrated. Of the seventeen concentrated products, twelve registered increases, three remained unchanged, and two declined. Conversely, of the sixteen unconcentrated products, all but one showed declines.

Another study by George J. Stigler and James K. Kindahl of prices actually paid by buyers provides for forty-two products "transaction" prices which can be matched to Census Bureau concentration ratios. Between January 1957 (the earliest month for which the price series are available) and April 1958 (the bottom of the recession), fifteen of the twenty-four concentrated products rose in price, two remained unchanged, and seven declined. Three of the latter were aluminum products which were affected by a short-lived invasion of the United States market by French and Norwegian producers. Although coverage was quite small, it is still interesting to note that three of the four unconcentrated products declined.

For the 1970 recession, 347 "industry-sector" products of the B.L.S. have been matched in the third study with their appropriate "5-digit" Standard Industrial Classification Census concentration ratios. Between December 1969 and December 1970, ninety-one of the concentrated products rose in price, while less than half that number (44) declined. In contrast, only nine of the fifty-two unconcentrated products registered increases, while more than twice that number (21) recorded declines. The ratios of increases to decreases were better than two to one for concentrated products, and less than one out of two for unconcentrated products.

Finally, in a study of 235 (4-digit) industries, figures presented by J. Fred Weston and Stephen H. Lustgarten show that during the recession of 1969-70, the annual price change for concentrated industries was an average increase of 4.2%, as contrasted with an average of only 2.8% for the unconcentrated industries.

The B.L.S. "Industry-Sector" Prices

A relatively new body of data, the "industry-sector" prices of the Bureau of Labor Statistics, makes possible a more precise analysis of the behavior of prices according to differing levels of concentration than has hitherto been available. These series are prepared on the

Table II-I

COMPARISONS OF PRICE CHANGES DURING RECESSIONS
BY (4-Company) CONCENTRATION RATIO INTERVALS

Direction of Price Change	Concentrated (50%+)	Intermediate (25%-49%)	Unconcentrated (−25%)	Total
	"Pairs of Products" Comparison[*]			
1957-58	(No. of Products)			
Increase	12		1	13
No Change	3		0	3
Decrease	2		15	17
	Distribution of "Transaction" Prices[**]			
Jan. 1957-Apr. 1958	(No. of Products)			
Increase	15	5	1	21
No Change	2	4	—	6
Decrease	7	5	3	15
	Distribution of Industry-Sector Prices[†]			
Dec. 1969-Dec. 1970	(No. of Product Classes)			
Increase	91	34	9	134
No Change	95	23	22	140
Decrease	44	8	21	73
	Avg. Ann. Change of Industry-Sector Prices[††]			
1969-1970	(No. of Industries)			
No. of Industries	81	89	65	235
Avg. Ann. Change	4.03%[a]	4.22%	2.81%	3.80%

[*] John M. Blair, *Economic Concentration,* New York, Harcourt, 1972, p. 458. One comparison contrasts two concentrated products with one unconcentrated product.

[**] Computed from George J. Stigler and James K. Kindahl, *The Behavior of Industrial Prices,* National Bureau, Economic Research, 1970, pp. 108-71.

[†] Blair, *op. cit.,* pp. 546-547.

[††] J. Fred Weston and Steven H. Lustgarten, "Concentration and Inflation," Columbia Law School Conference on Industrial Concentration, March 1974 (Forthcoming).

[a] Average of 22 industries with concentration ratios of over 75% and an avg. annual price change of 4.39% and of 59 industries with concentration ratios of from 50% to 75% and an average annual price change of 4.03%.

basis of the product and industry definitions of the Standard Industrial Classification (the 5-digit product classes) used by the Census Bureau, thereby making possible an exact match between the price indexes and the concentration ratios. Thus far, the B.L.S. has compiled some 347 "industry-sector" price indexes representing more than a third of the number of all product classes and more than half of their total value. In addition to these 347 manufactured products, the analysis that follows includes 22 farm products and three scrap materials (wastepaper, iron and steel scrap, and nonferrous scrap) — all products of low concentration.[4]

In the past, some studies of concentration and price changes have been made on what might be referred to as an "aggregate" basis, while others have been on a "selective" basis. The former include all the products (or all of those within a large sample) for which data are available[5]; the latter exclude those products where the concentration ratios, for one reason or another, are not comparable with the price indexes.[6] In this analysis, distributions of price change by concentration category will be made on the selective basis, since there is little to be said for including those products whose domestic concentration ratios are clearly not comparable with their price series.[7]

Since the economic issue is whether there is a significant difference in price behavior between concentrated and unconcentrated (competitive) industries and *not* whether there is a tendency for prices to show progressively smaller declines (as in the Great Depression) or progressively larger increases (as during the postwar recessions) with progressive increases in concentration, the empirical data are presented here in terms of discrete classes—either a trichotomy or dichotomy. The former is used for all products; the latter for the major product groupings, which are either the "2-digit" major industry groups or combinations of such groups. The reason for the difference is the insufficient number of product classes with low concentration ratios in most of the product groupings.[8]

Table II shows the weighted average price change by concentration category during (a) the recession of December 1969-December 1970, (b) the reflation of December 1970-December 1971 and (c) the period encompassed by both the recession through the reflation, December 1969-December 1971. The changes are based on the 296 product classes that remain after the deletion of (a) products sold in subnational markets, for which "average market shares" based on regional ratios are not available, (b) those stabilized by governmental market intervention, (c) those affected by unusual climatic conditions, and (d) those with prices determined in international markets.

Table II-II

MAJOR PRODUCT GROUPINGS: WEIGHTED AVERAGE PRICE CHANGE IN RECESSION, REFLATION AND RECESSION THROUGH REFLATION

Major Industry Group	4-Co. Concentration Ratio	No. of Products	Recession 12/69-12/70	Reflation 12/70-12/71	Recession Reflation 12/69-12/71
Farm, Food &	50+	18	6.8%	1.0%	7.9%
Tobacco	−50	89	−7.9	12.4	1.6
Textiles, Apparel	50+	12	−4.0	4.5	0.4
& Leather	−50	22	0.5	1.5	2.0
Lumber, Furniture	50+	7	4.4	2.9	7.5
& Paper	−50	17	−2.8	13.0	9.5
Chemicals &	50+	11	6.3	−0.9	5.3
Petroleum	−50	6	−0.4	−3.1	−3.4
Stone, Clay &	50+	9	5.8	5.6	11.7
Glass	−50	6	5.7	3.9	9.5
Primary Metals	50+	25	6.0	8.1	14.6
	−50	17	−1.8	1.5	0.1
Fabricated Metal	50+	22	5.6	3.9	9.8
Products & Machinery	−50	29	4.7	2.9	7.7
Elec. Machinery	50+	22	4.4	−1.0	3.3
	−50	14	2.8	2.0	4.8
Transp. Equip. and	50+	11	6.3	2.5	9.0
Other Products	−50	9	3.2	1.5	4.7
All Products	50+	137	5.9	2.7	8.7
	−50	159	−3.0	6.7	2.5
	50+	137	5.9	2.7	8.7
	25−49	110	−1.0	6.0	4.6
	−25	49	−6.1	7.8	−0.1
TOTAL		296	1.6	4.7	5.7

The 1970 Recession

During the recession of 1969-70, concentrated and unconcentrated products changed by nearly the same extent, but in opposite directions. As can be seen at the bottom of Table II, between December 1969 and December 1970, the weighted average change for products with concentration ratios of 50% and over was an increase of 5.9%. For those with ratios of less than 25%, the change was of the same magnitude, but in the opposite direction, a decrease of 6.1%. The intermediate group showed an intermediate change, declining about 1.0%.

Similarly, all but one of the nine major product groupings used in this analysis was characterized by either a price increase for the concentrated items accompanied by a decrease in the less concentrated products, or by a greater increase in the concentrated than in the less concentrated products. In such dissimilar areas as farm, food, and tobacco products; lumber, paper, and furniture; chemicals and petroleum; and primary metals — the average weighted price of the concentrated products rose, while that of the less concentrated items declined.

In four other areas — stone, clay and glass; fabricated metal products and machinery; electrical machinery; and transportation equipment and other products—the average price increased in both categories, but increased more in the concentrated products. All but the first are made up of products manufactured principally out of metals. The general tendency for hourly compensation in this (unlike earlier) recession to continue to advance as rapidly as in the preceding year probably contributed more to raising the cost base in metal-working industries than in industry in general because of the higher proportion of labor cost to price. Also contributing to cost increases in the metal-working industries were the substantial price increases for steel products. But while affecting both, there is no reason to assume that either factor would have any lesser effect on the unconcentrated than on the concentrated industries. As can be seen, the concentrated industries were more successful in translating these higher costs (and perhaps other factors) into higher prices.

Only one product grouping (textiles, apparel, and leather) registered a decline in the concentrated products and an increase in the less concentrated products. The explanation for the former, a decline, appears to lie in the fact that the principal concentrated items are synthetic fibers of one type or another which, despite the apparent control of the market, have been characterized by intense price competition; for the slight rise in the latter, the explanation appears to lie in the apparent price stability of unconcentrated "price-line" apparel items.

The influence of concentration as contrasted with other determinants of price change can be examined in greater detail by comparing the behavior of concentrated and less concentrated *individual* product classes within the same major product grouping. This type of analysis is severely limited by the lack of sufficient unconcentrated products to provide a meaningful basis for comparison — only forty-nine in the entire study. One way of increasing the number is to raise the upper limit of the concentration ratio for the unconcentrated products from 25% to 39% and, to maintain a clear distinction, to raise the lower limit for the concentrated products from 50% to 60%.

Farm, Food and Tobacco — Within this grouping there are six individual food and tobacco products in which the four largest producers accounted for 60% or more of the sales. During the 1970 recession, five showed price increases, all over 5%. In contrast, three of the six products with ratios under 33% registered price decreases, and of those with increases, the largest was less than 5%.

Table II-III

SELECTED FARM, FOOD AND TOBACCO PRODUCTS

S.I.C.	Product Class	Concen. Ratio	Change 12/69-12/70
21110	Cigarettes	90%	7.1%
20873	Flavor. Extract for use by Bottlers	90	2.9
20991	Desserts (ready to mix)	90	0.0
20952	Concentrated Coffee	85	6.2
20730	Chewing Gum	81	14.6
20521	Crackers & Pretzels	71	6.8
20136	Pork	20	−23.0
20137	Sausage	22	−12.3
20111	Beef	26	−2.4
20980	Macaroni, Spaghetti & Noodles	31	3.9
20341	Dried Fruits & Vegetables	32	2.7
20361	Frozen Packaged Fish	32	4.5

Neither cost nor demand factors would appear to explain these differences in price behavior. Labor costs are highest among the items which registered actual price decreases (meat products) and of relatively minor importance among the products that recorded the largest price increases (chewing gum, cigarettes, crackers and pretzels, and concentrated coffee). Nor can the price increases of the former be attributed to expansions in demand, since the demand of such products as cigarettes, concentrated coffee, and chewing gum is highly inelastic with respect to both income and price.

The 7.1% increase for cigarettes, incidentally, compares with an advance of only 1.3% for leaf tobacco, while the 6.2% rise for concentrated coffee compares with a rise of only 3.3% for the product class, green coffee, cocoa beans, and tea (of which coffee is by far the most important component).

Lumber and Paper—During the 1970 recession, the weighted average price for the broad industry grouping, lumber, furniture, and paper, remained almost unchanged, rising 0.2%. This overall stability

Table II-IV

SELECTED LUMBER AND PAPER PRODUCTS

S.I.C.	Product Class	Concen. Ratio	Change 12/69-12/70
26471	Sanitary Napkins & Tampons	95%	6.3%
26551	Paperboard Fiber Drums	90	8.7
26541	Milk & Other Beverage Containers	79	3.0
26542	Cups & Oth. Liq-Type Food Containers	76	4.8
26472	Sanitary Tissue Health Products	64	5.0
26100	Wastepaper	n.a.	−20.6
26111	Unbleached Kraft Pkg. & Indus. Paperboard	35	−3.6
26543	Other Sanitary Food Cntnrs.	37	1.8
24992	Pallets and Skids	8	−1.8
24262	Hardwood Dimension Stock	9	1.1
24212	Dressed Lumber	14	−4.8
24314	Doors, Wood, Interior & Ext.	15	0
24316	Finished Wood Mouldings	15	−2.9
24313	Wood Window and Door Frames	20	−3.7
24261	Hardwood Flooring	29	−13.8

was largely the result of a composite of price declines in lumber products which were offset by price increases among paper products. In five of the seven lumber products (all unconcentrated), prices declined, while in the five concentrated paper products, prices rose. The falling-off of building activity in 1970 resulting from restrictive monetary policies would help to explain the general decrease in lumber prices; it would hardly explain the tendency for concentrated paper prices to rise.

Within paper goods alone, there is a recognizable difference between the price behavior of the most and the least concentrated products. All of the five concentrated items registered price increases, three of which were 5% or over. In contrast, of the three less concentrated paper products, two recorded decreases, and the third, an increase of less than 2%. From a cost standpoint, all of the paper products would benefit to a greater or lesser extent by the 20.6% decline in the price of a raw material — wastepaper. Of particular interest are the differences in price between similar products affected by virtually identical demand factors. Thus, an 8.7% price increase for concentrated paperboard fiber drums compares with a -3.6% decline for unconcentrated Kraft paperboard; a 4.8% increase for concentrated cups and other liquid-type food containers compares with a rise of only 1.8% for unconcentrated other sanitary food containers.

Primary Metals—The broad area of primary metals provides three types of concentration-price comparisons: (a) between steel and nonferrous metals, (b) between different raw materials used in metal-making, and (c) between primary and secondary products. The first involves a contrast between products whose domestic prices have long been established through a pattern of price leadership in an asymmetrical oligopoly with items whose domestic prices have been determined in an international market, responsive to supplies produced in scattered areas of the world under widely varying conditions. Moreover, competition in nonferrous metals is enhanced by secondary refiners (who use scrap as their raw materials) and by custom smelters (who operate on the basis of a fixed margin between the ore price and the refined metal price).[9]

One of the most striking and persistent contrasts is between two materials used in the production of steel — pig iron and iron and steel scrap. While pig iron is produced almost entirely by the major integrated steel producers, the gathering, segregation, and assembly of steel scrap certainly places it within the less concentrated products. Whereas the price of steel scrap declined by 5.0%, the price increase for pig iron, 17.0%, represented one of the most extreme cases of perverse price flexibility recorded in any manufacturing industry.

Table II-V

PRIMARY STEEL AND NONFERROUS METAL PRODUCTS

S.I.C.	Product Class	Change: 12/69-12/70
	Steel Products	
33122	Steel Ingot and Semifinished Steel	5.4%
33124	Hot Rolled Bars	6.0
33128	Cold Finished Steel Bars	4.3
33123	Hot Rolled Sheet and Strip	8.2
33126	Steel Pipe and Tubes	4.4
	Nonferrous Metals	
33312	Refined Primary Copper	1.1
33323	Refined Primary Lead	−8.8
33334	Refined Primary Zinc	−3.2
33572	Copper and Copper-Bars Alloy	−3.6

A third comparison is between largely interchangeable nonferrous metals—those made by integrated producers from ore (primary producers)—and the same metals made by "secondary producers" from scrap. Both nonferrous scrap and secondary copper reacted to the decline in demand by registering pronounced price decreases. In

Table II-VI

PRIMARY AND SECONDARY NONFERROUS METAL PRODUCTS

S.I.C.	Product Class	Concen. Ratio	Change 12/69-12/70
33312	Refined Primary Copper	79%	1.1%
33412	Secondary Copper	40	−19.2
33323	Refined Primary Lead	76	−8.8
33413	Secondary Lead	51	−1.2
	Nonferrous Scrap	n.a.	−30.6

contrast, primary copper was able to resist the decline in demand, registering a slight increase. Perhaps reflecting an unusually high level of concentration (51%) for a scrap-using industry, the price of secondary lead remained almost unchanged, while the price of the primary product dropped 8.8%.

Other products — The other groupings do not contain a sufficient number of unconcentrated products to permit this type of comparison on any systematic basis. Given the available data, the most that can be done is to offer selected examples of illustrative value only. Thus, nine comparisons of pairs of products have been drawn with

Table II-VII

SELECTED PAIRS OF PRODUCTS

S.I.C.	Product Class	Concentration Ratio	Change 12/69-12/70
34212	Razor Blades and Razors	90%	14.3%
35451	Small Cutting Tools	23	−3.8
35662	Taper Roller Bearings	92	5.0
34930	Steel Springs	34	2.9
36410	Electric Lamps (Bulbs)	88	11.9
36427	Residential-type Elect. Fixt.	17	2.0
36132	Power Circuit Breakers	81	7.2
36993	Resistors for Electronics App.	38	−4.9
35195	Outboard Motors	74	9.5
35227	Lawnmowers and Snowblowers	33	2.0
34110	Metal Cans	70	7.9
34911	Steel Shipping Pails	33	4.9
36240	Carbon & Graphite Pdcts.	84	7.0
39550	Carbon Paper	31	−0.2
32210	Glass Containers	60	8.3
20797	Plastic Dinnerware	37	0.0
29115	Residual Fuel Oil *	n.a.	73.5
29920	Lubricating Oils and Greases	37	2.9

*No concentration ratio is given for residual oil, whose market area, the Eastern seaboard, is served largely by Venezuelan imports, principally from Exxon and Shell.

one member a concentrated and the other an unconcentrated product. In each pair, both members are from the same product grouping; they experience cost changes that are certainly similar in direction and probably not greatly dissimilar in extent. And though generally not substitutable, most are subject to much the same expansions or contractions in demand. With concentration ratios of over 60% (and in all but two cases over 70%), the concentrated products are outstanding examples of either asymmetrical oligopolies or duopolies.[10]

As can be seen, all of the concentrated products registered price increases in excess of 5%; three were greater than 10%. The increase of 73.5% for residual oil was the largest recorded by any of the industry-sector prices. Three of the unconcentrated products registered decreases in prices, and of those showing increases, all but one were less than 3%.

The individual product comparisons confirm the conclusion that during economic downswings, concentrated products no longer remain "rigid." They have become flexible — *upward*. This form of behavior, accompanied by the traditional downward flexibility of the unconcentrated products, has created a bifurcated price structure whose average change in time of recession is merely a happenstance composite of the opposing movements of its components. Moreover, the recession behavior of concentrated products implies a Phillips curve in reverse: the greater the importance of concentrated products in an economy, the greater the likelihood that rising unemployment will be accompanied by rising prices.

REFLATION

The 1971 Reflation

It has long been observed that during the recovery following a downswing (or "reflation" to use Means' term), prices of concentrated products rise less rapidly than competitive prices. By December 1971, the level of economic activity had nearly returned to the pre-recession level, the index of industrial production having risen to only 1.6% below its level of December 1969. As can be seen from Table II, the weighted average price for the concentrated products rose only modestly (2.7%), while for the unconcentrated products, the increase was three times as great (7.8%). Again, the changes for the intermediate category (6.0%) was between the extremes. The same pattern was displayed by three of the major product groupings: farm, food and tobacco; lumber, furniture and paper; and electrical machinery. A contrary pattern was displayed by five groups, but in two, the difference in price change (one percentage point) is so small as to be of little significance. But textiles, apparel, and leather continued to constitute an important exception. Just as the prices of its concentrated products rose less than its competitive items during the recession, so also did they rise more during the reflation. Unlike the concentrated textile products which fell in recession and rose in recovery, the other conspicuous exception, primary metals, rose substantially in *both* the 1970 downswing and the 1971 upturn— 6.0% in the former and 8.1% in the latter.

Recession Through Reflation

If, as compared to competitive prices, oligopolistic prices decline less in recession but also rise less in reflation, the logical inference would be that the long-run change in the two types of prices would be about the same. And this would be, and indeed has been, cited as a reason for regarding oligopoly, and the type of price behavior associated with it, as a problem of *de minimus* importance. But this argument falls if the proper comparison is between one group of prices which moves downward and upward, cyclically, with another which never falls but rises (though at different rates) in both stages of the business cycle. Here, the logical inference would be that the long-run change in the two types of prices would be quite dissimilar: little change in competitive prices over time in contrast with a substantial and continued upward movement of oligopolistic prices.

The interval for which new data on concentration-price behavior offered here, December 1969-December 1971 (Table II), while not a long-term period, does encompass both a recession and an ensuing recovery to about the pre-recession level. For products with concentration ratios of under 25%, the recessionary decline was almost exactly offset by the reflationary rise. In contrast, for those with ratios of 50% and over, the net effect of increases during both stages was an overall rise of 8.7%. Again, the change for products with ratios of 25-49% was intermediate (4.6%). The price increase over the two-year period was greater for the concentrated than the less concentrated products in six of the nine industry groupings. Textiles and apparel was again a conspicuous exception, as was lumber, furniture, and paper, where an unusually sharp price rise in lumber accompanied the 1971 revival of the construction industry. But in general, the showings suggest that with the passage of time and the recurrence of the business cycle, the divergence between the levels of oligopolistic and competitive prices will tend to widen.

THE EFFECTIVENESS OF PRICE CONTROLS

The data brought together for this analysis can also be used to shed light on the question of the effectiveness of the government's program of price-wage controls during Phases I and II, which had been necessitated by the failure of restrictive monetary and fiscal policies in arresting, or even moderating, the pace of inflation. The analysis, here, has been extended to September 1972, the latest date — four months before the program was eviscerated by executive order in January 1973 — for which data were available for incorporation into the tabulation on which this analysis is based.

In evaluating the control program, the relevant issue, in the words of the Council of Economic Advisors, involves an inherently speculative question: "What would the inflation rate have been without controls?" [11] The council ventured only a qualified and tentative answer: "We believe it is probable that the controls did reduce the rate of inflation, but the magnitude of the reduction is uncertain." [12] It is the difficulty in arriving at a definitive answer to this hypothetical question that permits unsupported clichés to gain wide currency; that is, that "controls never work," or that the inflation following their removal is due to the "distortions" occasioned by their existence. The council cited an econometric study showing the projected inflation rate to have been higher than the rate actually experienced in 1972, suggesting that "the controls reduced the inflation rate"; on the other hand, "the poor record of this technique in predicting the rate of inflation prior to controls does not inspire confidence in their use, and evidence from this source must be regarded as inconclusive." [13] But a "poor" record is almost inherent in any study that fails to distinguish between the types of price behavior at different stages of the business cycle associated with different types of industry structure.

That the Council did, in fact, indulge itself in an excess of caution is suggested by the movements of the various overall price series. The

following table derived from the Council's report shows the annual
rate of change in the wholesale price index and the implicit GNP
price deflator for the 1970 recession, the 1971 reflation, and under
price controls. The last is in turn broken down into three intervals:
the price freeze of Phase I (from August to November 1971); the
"bulge" in prices which took place as a result of selective relaxations
of the freeze (from November 1971 to February 1972), and the
subsequent "post-bulge" period of Phase II (from February to
December 1972).

Since no attempt was made to control farm prices and since food
processors were generally permitted to pass on the cost of higher
farm prices, the most significant series for the purpose of determining the effectiveness of price controls are the "industrial commodities" of the B.L.S. wholesale price index and the "nonfarm"
products of the GNP deflator. And since the "post-bulge" interval of

Table II-VIII

ANNUAL RATE OF CHANGE IN OVERALL PRICE MEASURES, 1969-1972
(Seasonally Adjusted)

	Recession	Reflation	Freeze	Price Control Bulge	Post-Bulge
Wholesale Price Index					
All Commodities	2.2%[a]	5.2%[b]	−.2%[c]	6.9%[d]	6.5%[e]
Farm and Food	−1.4 [a]	6.5 [b]	1.1 [c]	14.7 [d]	14.7 [e]
Industrial Commodi-ties	3.6 [a]	4.7 [b]	−.5 [c]	4.0 [d]	3.4 [e]
Implicit GNP Deflators					
Total GNP	5.3 [f]	5.1 [g]	2.2 [h]	5.1 [i]	2.3 [j]
Private Bus. GNP Farm	−7.3 [f]	12.1 [g]	16.3 [h]	20.1 [i]	21.5 [j]
Nonfarm	5.1 [f]	4.3 [g]	1.2 [h]	3.6 [i]	1.5 [j]

[a] December 1969-December 1970   [f] 1969 IV-1970 IV
[b] December 1970-August 1971   [g] 1970 IV-1971 II
[c] August 1971-November 1971   [h] 1971 II-1971 IV
[d] November 1971-February 1972   [i] 1971 IV-1972 I
[e] February 1972-December 1972   [j] 1972 I-1972 IV

Source: *Annual Report of the Council of Economic Advisers*, January 1973, p. 57.

Phase II controls was a period of rapid economic expansion, a more appropriate comparison is with another period of economic growth— the pre-control reflation of 1971. It will be noted that between the reflation and the Phase II period, the annual rate of change of the B.L.S. industrial commodities fell from 4.7% to 3.4% while the GNP deflator for nonfarm products registered a very sizeable drop — from 4.3% to 1.5%.

It must be recognized, however, that economic activity was expanding more rapidly in 1972 than in 1971 (the index of industrial production rising 8.5% in the latter period as compared to 3.7% in the former). Based on the considerations set forth in this analysis, this greater increase in output should have had an ambivalent effect depending on the level of concentration. By tending to bring about reductions in both unit fixed costs and unit labor costs, the greater expansion of production would have tended to increase profit margins, thereby lessening the need for price increases in the concentrated industries. At the same time, however, prices in the unconcentrated industries would have reacted to the increase in demand by rising sharply.

Some light can be shed on the question of whether the Phase I and II controls reduced the increase in price below that which would have taken place in their absence by comparing the actual with the expected 1972 price change, with the latter calculated by deriving the ratio of price change to production change in a benchmark year and applying that ratio to the production change in 1972. What this approach would be implying is that, in the absence of controls, the expected price change would have borne the same relationship to the actual production change in 1972 as the actual price change had borne to the actual production change in the base year. On the basis of the data used in this study, such an approach can be employed for the 296 commodities as a group. It must be recognized, however, that this approach necessarily involves the considerable assumption that the concentrated, unconcentrated, and intermediate industry groups were all characterized by the same change in production.

If•in 1972 the price change for concentrated products had borne the same relationship to the production change as had been true in 1971, the expected price increase would have been 6.2%, or nearly double the actual weighted average price change (3.3%). Reflecting the greater influence of the uncontrolled "free market" prices, the estimated 1972 increase for the unconcentrated products (17.9%) was only moderately greater than the actual increase (14.3%). The greatest contrast between the expected and the actual increases was in the intermediate group of products with concentration ratios of 25-49%. Here an estimated advance of 13.8% is contrasted with an actual increase of only 4.2%. These are products which, on the one hand, did not enjoy the freedom (to rise) of the unconcentrated, free market prices, but which nevertheless recorded a considerably greater reflationary increase than the concentrated products during the base period.

Table II-IX

296 PRODUCT CLASSES
EXPECTED* AND ACTUAL** WEIGHTED AVERAGE PRICE CHANGES
UNDER PHASE I AND II CONTROLS

Production Change 1971 1972	Concentration Ratio	Price Change		
		Actual '71	Expected '72	Actual '72
	50%	2.7%	6.2%	3.3%
	25-49%	6.0	13.8	4.2
	−25%	7.8	17.9	14.3
3.7% 8.5%	TOTAL	4.7%	10.8%	5.7%

* Expected on basis of ratio of changes in price and production in reflation (Dec. 1970-
Dec. 1971) to change in production under price control (Dec. 1971-Sept. 1972)
**Dec. 1971-Sept. 1972

Since the relative importance in the economy of the concentrated and intermediate groups is greater than the unconcentrated manufactured products, the 1972 price rise that would have been expected on the basis of the change in production (10.8%) was nearly double the actual advance.

Additional evidence of the effectiveness of Phase I and Phase II controls in the area where they have a chance at success — in industries where sellers have significant discretionary power over price — is provided by a chart comparing price movements of oligopolistic and competitive industries presented on February 6, 1974, before the Senate Banking Committee by John T. Dunlop, then head of the Cost of Living Council. Although cited as proof of the absence over the entire fifteen month period of any relationship between concentration and inflation, closer examination reveals the following:

1. For the recession (quarter IV 1969 to quarter IV 1970), a price *increase* for the oligopolistic industries, accompanied by a *decrease* for the competitive industries.

2. For the reflation (quarter IV 1970 to quarter III 1971), a *slower* increase in the oligopolistic industries than during the preceding recession, accompanied by a rapid increase for the more competitive industries.

3. For the Phase I-II period (quarter III 1971 to quarter IV 1972), a slower increase for the oligopolistic industries than during either

Chart II-II

"OLIGOPOLISTIC" VS. "COMPETITIVE" INDUSTRIES
CHANGE IN WHOLESALE PRICE INDEX

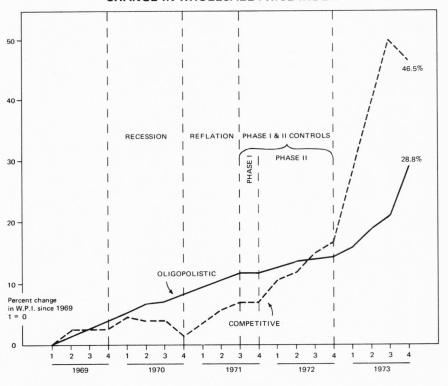

Note: Definition of oligopolistic and competitive W.P.I. groups based on Eichner, Alfred S., "A Theory of the Determination of the Mark-Up Under Oligopoly." *The Economic Journal* (Dec. 1973)

the preceding reflation or recession, accompanied by a continuation of the rapid increase in competitive prices that had begun in the first quarter of 1971 and was interrupted in quarters III and IV only by the general price freeze of Phase I.

Except through a general price freeze — which by its nature cannot be long maintained — prices in unconcentrated industries during an inflationary period usually defy stabilization. Because sellers, as well as buyers, are numerous, the result of enforcement efforts range from poor to disasterous. If the products are "free market" items whose prices are determined in an organized exchange, efforts to set maximum prices below what buyers are willing and anxious to pay would merely result in a circumvention of the exchange. Failure also usually attends any governmental attempt to restrain competitive sellers from at least "passing through" increased costs since, otherwise, those with higher costs tend to disappear, thereby diminishing supply at the very time it needs to be increased. This limitation applies with particular force to the numerous smaller manufacturers in such fields as foods, textiles, apparel, lumber, furniture, and many building materials whose raw materials are supplied by competitive industries, the prices of which would be on the rise.

Recognizing these and other inescapable economic facts of life, the price regulations under Phase II abounded with exemptions for unconcentrated industries. Completely exempted were raw agricultural and import prices. Pre-notification of price increases was not required for firms with annual sales of under $100 million, and quarterly price reports were not required for firms with sales under $50 million. Firms with sixty or fewer employees were completely exempt from the entire program.[14] In view of the exemptions and the expansion of the economy, it should not be surprising that the prices of competitive industries rose rapidly throughout the duration of Phase II.

One effect of this sustained rise coupled with the slow advance of oligopolictic prices has been to cause studies on the effectiveness of the price control program based on overall price series (consumer price index, wholesale price index, implicit GNP price deflator) to understate the effectiveness of the program in the area to which it could be actually applied. Paul H. Earl has made a compilation of twelve studies that have thus far been made on "The Impact of Price

Controls," all but one of which are based on such overall series.[15] Summarizing the findings of these studies, Robert Lanzilotti writes that "according to the results of econometric models used to appraise Phase II the estimated effects of six quarters of controls include . . . an annual reduction in the annual rate of inflation of about 2.0 percentage points."[16]

When allowance is made in these studies, however, for the industries to which price control was never effectively applied, this not negligible accomplishment can be seen, then, to understate the ability of government to control those prices that can be controlled.

A SHORT-RUN TARGET RETURN MODEL

Recognition of an anomaly is one thing; its acceptance by a scientific community is something else. Before the latter takes place, there must be offered some sort of theoretical rationale which (a) provides a logical explanation for the phenomenon and (b) permits predictability. Thomas S. Kuhn, in his study of scientific discovery, points out that " . . . a scientific theory is declared invalid only if an alternate candidate is available to take its place."[17] Scientific discovery starts with "the recognition of anomalies that cannot be explained by the existing paradigm"; i.e., a model or pattern that "for a time provide[s] solutions to problems of concern to a group of practitioners." The "characteristic feature" of these anomalies is their "stubborn refusal to be assimilated into existing paradigms. This type alone gives rise to new theories."[18] Discovery then "continues with a more or less extended exploration of the anomaly. And it closes only when the anomalous has become the expected."[19]

The possession by the leading sellers of sufficient market power to give them substantial discretionary authority over price must serve as the starting point in gaining an understanding of what makes an otherwise inexplicable phenomenon comprehensible. Unlike competitive markets, a producer in a concentrated industry is not restricted to the price that equates marginal revenue with marginal costs; rather, he can elect one of a number of alternative prices. It is submitted that the price elected will usually be governed by the considerations developed in studies of "full-cost" pricing; i.e., that price will be the sum of "full-costs" plus an allowance for profit at some assumed volume of output, or "standard volume."[20] As long as actual output remains at or near the standard volume, price will usually be changed only under two circumstances: (a) if the firm elects to alter its target return, or (b) if, as a result of a new labor contract, higher prices for materials, etc., the company experiences cost increases which significantly narrow its profit margin at the standard volume. This allowance for profit will be the margin on sales required to attain the company's "target return," usually expressed, or at least thought of, in terms of a rate of return on investment. The thesis set forth here is that the company will seek to attain its target objective not simply over the long run, with good and bad years averaging out around the target, but in *each year.* Hence, the term, "short-run target return model." As originally conceived, the target return was thought of as a long-run profit objective. Attempting to attain the target return in the short run appears to be a fairly recent development that may have been facilitated by the advent of computers.

In most manufacturing industries, however, demand and thus volume of production do not remain unchanged over any length of time. An explanation of oligopolistic pricing must therefore be based on something more than a simplistic adjustment of price to changes in cost at a constant volume. The model outlined here reflects the effect of changing volume on costs, thereby on the profit margin, and thus on price.

Materials costs per unit of output are assumed to remain constant up to a high level of output. As production approaches capacity, the general expansion of the economy will lead to shortages of needed material and components, premium prices, inferior quality, tie-in requirements, "grey markets," and other factors which raise costs directly or indirectly. Below the level of capacity operations, materials costs will probably decline with falling demand if the supplying industry is unconcentrated (e.g., lumber) but rise if it is concentrated (e.g. steel). To simplify exposition, however, the assumption here is that through most of the range of output, unit materials costs remain unchanged.

One of the two determinants of unit labor costs, namely wage rates (plus fringe benefits), are also assumed to remain constant up to a high level of operations. In a tight labor market, employers will often have to pay premium wage rates to secure labor or, what amounts to the same thing, "full" wages for inferior workers. Union contracts do not prohibit the employer from making above-normal

Chart II-III a

RELATIONSHIP BETWEEN YEAR TO YEAR

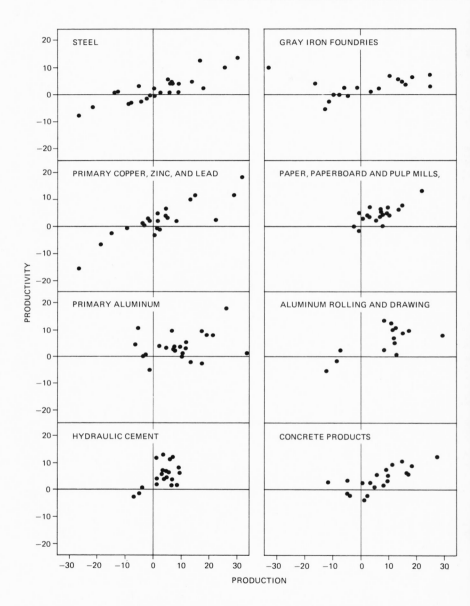

The coefficients of correlation (R) for the various industries are as follows: motor vehicles and equipment (.91), primary copper, lead and zinc (.89), steel (.83), paper and paperboard and pulp mills (.81), manmade fibers (.80), metal cans (.79), concrete products (.75), gray iron foundries (.72), tires and inner tubes (.72), footware (.67), aluminum rolling

Chart II-III b

CHANGES IN PRODUCTIVITY* AND PRODUCTION

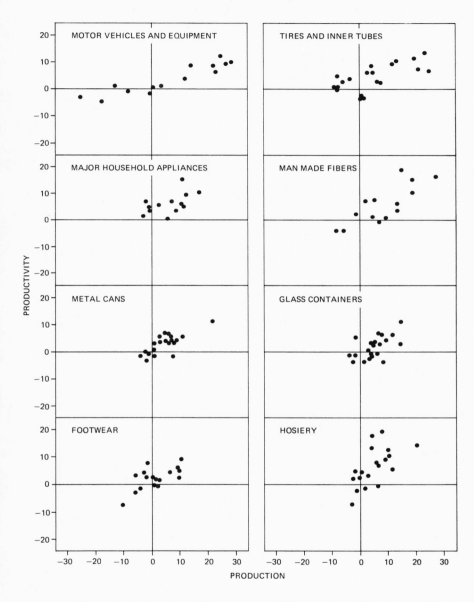

and drawing (.64), major household appliances (.56), hydraulic cement (.53), glass containers (.50), hosiery (.46), primary aluminum (.25).
(Source: Bureau of Labor Statistics)   *Output per all employee manhour

payments in a tight labor market, but they do prevent him from reducing wages below the level specified by the contract in a surplus labor market. Changes in the other determinant, productivity, are assumed to be directly related to changes in output — an assumption for which there exists a strong empirical basis. For sixteen manufacturing industries, the relationship between changes in industry output and output per employee man-hour, as compiled by the Bureau of Labor Statistics, is shown in Charts IIIa and IIIb. These constitute the industries for which comparable series are available, except for extractive industries, in which no such relationship is to be expected, and food and related industries which, by their nature, are characterized by very small annual changes in demand and thus offer little opportunity to provide evidence of a relationship between changes in production and other variables.

The relationship is particularly strong in such mass-production, capital-intensive industries as steel, primary nonferrous metals, paper and pulp, motor vehicles, man-made fibers, and metal cans. It is weakest in industries with a smaller scale of operation, notably footware and hosiery. Paradoxically, the relationship is weak in capital-intensive primary aluminum and strong in labor-intensive concrete products. A tendency for productivity gains to be smaller (or actually register decreases) with declining production has been attributed to a belief on the part of employers that, in the long run, it is cheaper to keep superfluous skilled workers on the job when demand falls than to try to locate and rehire them in a tight labor market or train unskilled workers to take their place when demand expands. With wage rates assumed to remain constant per unit of output (up to near-capacity operation) and labor productivity rising with increasing production, unit labor costs will tend to decline as output rises and increase as it falls.

The final cost component, unit fixed costs, will also vary inversely with output, as total overhead expenses are spread over a larger number of units. It is quite possible, however, that during a marked expansion of economic activity, some of the "fixed optional" overhead costs (insurance premiums, advertising expenses, interest rates on new borrowings, etc.) will tend to increase, thereby offsetting the savings associated with greater output. But such a departure from the general tendency will occur only at a high level of output.

The effect of these cost changes is illustrated in the accompanying

Chart II-IV

MODEL OF OLIGOPOLISTIC PRICING UNIT COSTS, PROFIT AND MARGIN PRICE

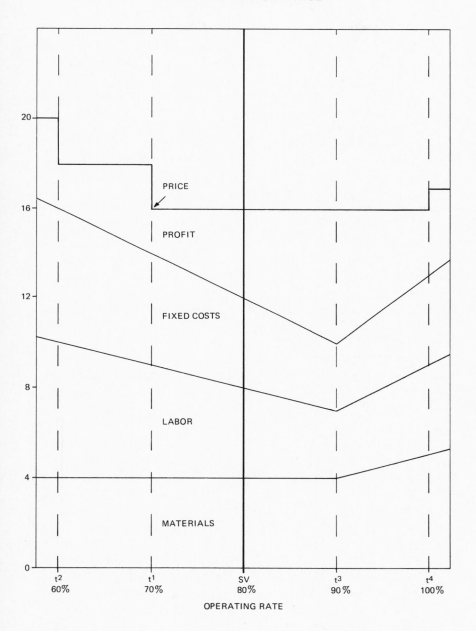

chart (IV). Contrary to customary practice, the starting point in reading the chart should not be the left side, but the center, represented by "standard volume" or SV (assumed for illustrative purposes to be 80% of capacity). If the producer's output begins to fall below the SV level (i.e., moves to the left of SV on the diagram), he will experience increases in two of his cost factors. Because of the smaller number of units over which his overhead will be spread, his unit fixed costs (f) will rise. And because of a decrease in labor productivity (or slowing down of its rate of increase below that assumed when his last wage contract was entered into) his unit labor costs (L) will rise. At point t^1 (70% of capacity), the increases in L and F will have so narrowed the profit margin (P) as to compel the producer to raise his price in order to restore his profit margin to the dimension existing at SV. If output continues to decline to 60% of capacity, a further price increase will be required at t^2. These increases, it should be noted, come only after the producer has become convinced that the decrease in output (and accompanying increase in costs) is not a transitory phenomenon but requires an upward price adjustment if his profit showings for the year are not to be significantly impaired. The result is that changes are made only at discrete intervals, with price moving in a "rachet," or "stairstep," manner instead of following the smooth curve of classical theory.

The model also provides an explanation for the price-determining firm's behavior during periods of expanding demand. Starting again at the middle of the diagram as output expands from SV toward 90% of capacity (t^2), unit labor and fixed costs will initially tend to decline. Overhead is spread over a larger number of units, and better use is made of the labor force. But while the cost changes (and reasons therefore) are the same (except in reverse), the behavior of price will not be the obverse of its movement when demand was falling. Although his costs are decreasing, the producer will not lower his price since, when what is being contemplated is a price reduction, the logic of imperfect competition theory comes into play. He will abstain from lowering his price since, because his output is large enough to affect the market, he would assume that any price reduction on his part would immediately be noted and matched by rivals whose production is sufficiently large to deprive him of the benefit of a lower price, resulting only in decreased revenues for all.

Nor will the producer take advantage of the increase in demand by raising his price. For one thing, the expansion of output makes it possible for him to achieve his predetermined profit margin without an increase in price. Moreover, exceeding that objective will not result in anything like a corresponding increase in managerial compensation which has been found to be determined far more by corporate size and growth than by profitability. At the same time, a price increase might have undesirable consequences such as an influx of newcomers, greater resistance by oligopsonistic buyers, an acceleration in the use of substitutes, etc. Today, the large corporation in a concentrated industry tends to be "profit satisficing," rather than profit-maximizing. Hence the result at t^3 is price stability.

As output continues to expand, however, costs will tend to rise owing to the complex causes mentioned above. Shortages of supply develop, and the cost of obtaining, training, and paying additional workers in a tight labor market will come to exceed the increase in revenues resulting from their employment. Certain of the "fixed optional" category of overhead costs will rise. At some point, these increases in costs will reach such proportion as to narrow the profit margin below the dimensions assumed at SV. When this occurs, say at 100% of capacity (t^4), prices will be raised.

What has been set forth above is nothing so ambitious as a "general theory"; it is merely one "model" or "pattern," (i.e., a "paradigm") to explain an otherwise inexplicable form of behavior. This model would appear to offer an explanation for:

1. The tendency for oligopolistic prices to rise during recession.
2. Their tendency to show a lesser price increase during reflation.
3. Their failure to decline at any stage of the business cycle.
4. Their tendency to manifest their changes at irregular intervals in a "ratchet" or "stair-step" manner.

It thus meets the two essential requirements of a paradigm — providing a logical explanation for what is clearly anomalous under existing theory and establishing a basis for predictability. Other and probably better explanations will, or at least should be, developed, since the observed behavior appears to be not only very real, but possesses far-reaching implications for public policy. Indeed, such explanations may well play a role in the formulation of public policy before they are accepted by the academic community. But this is to be expected since, according to Kuhn, efforts are customarily made "to force" an observed anomaly "into the preformed and relatively

inflexible box that the [existing] paradigm supplies; . . . indeed those
that will not fit the box are often not seen at all."[21] Efforts will be
made to modify the existing theory in order to assimilate the
anomalies. "They will devise numerous articulations and ad hoc
modifications of their theory in order to eliminate any apparent
conflict."[22] Whether the troublesome phenomenon does in fact
present an anomaly will also be questioned: "Only when these
attempts at articulation fail do scientists encounter the recognized
anomalies whose characteristic feature is their stubborn refusal to be
assimilated into existing paradigms. This type alone gives rise to new
theories."[23]

Price Followership

Thus far the discussion has proceeded in terms of the price leader.
Any understanding of the phenomenon of perverse price flexibility
requires an explanation as to why the lesser oligopolists who, by
definition, also possess substantial monopoly power, join in the price
advance. When the direction of change is upward, rival oligopolists
would have apparently much to gain by refusing to participate. By
keeping their prices unchanged (or making a smaller advance), they
would attract business from those who raise prices, thereby reducing
their unit fixed and labor costs and increasing their profit margin.

Upward price-matching is certainly to be expected where the
largest firm (and customary price leader) is the most efficient
oligopolist. Being less efficient, the smaller producer would welcome
a price increase even more than the leader. Moreover, if in the face of
an increase by the leader, a lesser oligopolist keeps his prices stable
(or makes a smaller advance), he may anticipate, at best, that the
leader will come down to his level or, worse, even go below it. The
latter could touch off a price war from which the leader, because of
his greater efficiency, would inevitably emerge victorious.

More common in the United States, however, are concentrated
industries in which the largest producer is not the most efficient
oligopolist. Here, the danger of touching off a price war should not
be a matter of particular concern to the lesser but more efficient
oligopolists. In such cases, the explanation for upward price-
matching may be found in the possession by the leader of substantial
monopoly power covering a wider range of products, industries, or
market areas. Despite his lesser efficiency, the leader could wage

competitive warfare in the particular product or market areas important to the noncooperating oligopolist, subsidizing his campaign with monopoly profits made elsewhere. The awareness by the lesser oligopolists of this possibility would make them reluctant to touch off a price war whose outcome would be determined, not by considerations of efficiency, but by the leader's greater ability to engage in cross-subsidization.

It is also possible for upward price-matching to be the result of some sort of collusive arrangement, either express or implied. As the U.S. antitrust laws have been interpreted, the problem for the antitrust agencies is not the uncertainty of the law, but the quantum of evidence required to establish a violation. The Supreme Court has repeatedly emphasized that conspiracy is a "crime of darkness" and can therefore be established by indirect or circumstantial evidence of its operations and effects. The Court, however, has never been given an opportunity to rule on the question of whether a showing of price *increases* of the same extent, to the same level, made at or about the same time by different producers with different costs when demand is falling constitutes, in and of itself, sufficient evidence to establish either a conspiracy in violation of Section 1 of the Sherman Act or a "planned common course of action" in violation of Section 5 of the Federal Trade Commission Act. And until and unless it makes such a ruling, producers (or at least their legal counsel) will continue to regard upward price-matching as permissive, assuming, of course, the absence of direct or overt evidence of agreement.

Implications for public policy flow from both the empirical evidence and the theoretical model presented in this study. From the former, the more obvious is the futility of efforts to restrain inflation in the concentrated sector by reducing demand through restrictive fiscal and monetary policies; the only result is that bizarre hybrid, "stagflation" — rising prices accompanied by rising unemployment. Less obvious, but equally important, are the implications suggested by the behavior of the less concentrated products. During the 1970 recession, the restrictive macroeconomic policies achieved their intended objective by bringing about a substantial price reduction of unconcentrated products and price stability in the intermediate group. Dissolution actions which would move an industry out of the concentrated sector into the less concentrated groups would therefore improve the prospects of controlling inflation through fiscal and monetary measures alone. Moreover, the stimulus to competition resulting from deconcentration would improve the performance of the economy in other ways: by exerting a constant downward pressure on costs, providing a continuing incentive for invention and innovation, and allocating resources out of declining and into expanding industries.

But until and unless such deconcentration takes place, inflation in the concentrated industries can be restrained only by the imposition of direct price and wage controls. The data presented earlier suggest that, apart from the unconcentrated industries, the imposition of Phase I and II controls substantially reduced the increases in prices that would have taken place in their absence. Given the prevailing asymmetrical structure of American oligopolies, much can probably be achieved with a more limited intervention by the government aimed at industry leaders, since an industry's lesser firms will rarely try to exceed the leader's price.

A few additional implications are suggested by the method of pricing portrayed in the model. Through an appropriate instrument of government, the public interest should have some influence in determining the target return of dominant firms in important concentrated industries. Restraints should be imposed on sudden and substantial increases in the target rate of return (as were made by the steel industry in the 1950's[24] and the oil industry in 1973). As was originally intended, the target return should be regarded as a long-range objective, not a goal to be achieved in each individual year. In particular, price increases to meet the target rate during a recession should be prohibited. And in industries subject to such restraints, wage and salary increases should also not be allowed until economic recovery is underway.

As a further principle, it is suggested that the desireability of any form of regulation should be considered directly proportionate to its ability to bring about the same type of economic behavior that would prevail if the industry were competitive. For example,

Earnings above a specified return on investment or greater than those earned during a base period [in World War II] had to be returned to the Treasury. The purpose of the excess-profits tax was to prevent corporations from profiteering through high prices made possible by war-induced excessive demand and by excessive prices on war contracts. The same principle can be applied to prevent corporations from profiteering through high prices made possible by the possession of substantial monopoly power.

While there can be no question of its workability, such a policy would, in itself, benefit the consumer only by lightening his tax burden. Its scope, however, could be broadened through a "forgiveness" feature under which the tax owed would be forgiven *to the extent that price reductions were made*. With such a feature the objective of the tax would be to return monopoly profits to the public either through tax revenue or lower prices at the corporation's discretion. Any corporation involved could obtain "forgiveness" of all or any part of the tax owed by the simple means of reducing the prices of its products in the following year. That is to say, if a corporation's proposed price reductions in the following year, as applied to its physical output in the taxable year, represented an amount equal to all of its monopoly profits tax, it would owe no tax and pay no tax. If its proposed price reductions, as applied to the physical output in the taxable year, represented an amount equal to part of its tax, its tax would be reduced by that amount. The corporation would have full discretion in determining whether it simply wanted to pay the tax or whether it wanted to obtain "forgiveness' through price reductions on all or any part of its output.[25]

III

STAGFLATION IN GREAT BRITAIN
THE ROLE OF LABOR

P. Sargant Florence

Ever since World War II, Britain has had a far lower rate of economic growth than other European countries, though a rate not far below that of the United States. Like those countries, however, Britain has suffered from increasing prices; and until recently, this inflation has been associated with extremely low rates of unemployment which, between the years 1947 and 1966 inclusive, never exceeded 2.5%.[1]

Since 1967, however, the rate of British unemployment rose considerably and was coupled with a much steeper rise in prices. For this unusual coupling of stagnation and inflation, so puzzling to economists believing in the empirical and theoretical basis of the Phillips curve (a coupling evident in the United States too), the convenient term "stagflation" has been applied.

THE FACTS OF BRITISH STAGFLATION

The month by month course of British retail price inflation between 1963 and August 1973, together with contemporary changes in wages and earnings, is shown graphically in Chart I.[2] Bearing in mind that the vertical scale is logarithmic (e.g., from 150 to 165, a rise of 10%, is marked out the same distance as 100 to 110), four features stand out:

(1) The rapid rise in retail prices, during the period (1963 to August 1973), from 100 to 173;

(2) The still more rapid rise in wage rates during the same ten years, from 100 to 222;

(3) About the years 1969 and 1970, a distinct upward thrust in

Chart III-I

EARNINGS, WAGE RATES, RETAIL PRICES, WAGES AND SALARIES PER UNIT OF OUTPUT: MONTHLY INDEX NUMBERS PERCENTAGE OF UNEMPLOYED: YEARLY AND HALF YEARLY (1965-1973)

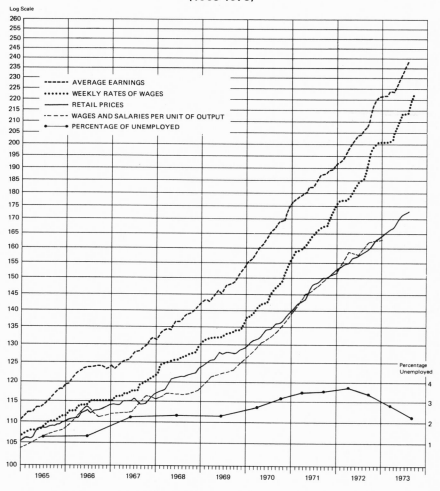

Sources: United Kingdom, Department of Employment Gazette; Table II, column 1, below.

workers' earnings and in wage rates, indicating that the *rate of rise* was accelerating;

(4) The great difference in the trend of wage rates which stood, in August 1973, at 173% of the 1963 level, and earnings, which stood at 240%.

To indicate the contemporary changes in unemployment, I have added at the bottom of Chart I a curve joining the official percentages of all workers unemployed in the years or half years between 1965 and 1973 as given in Table II. These percentages are the original data, not index numbers with a base in some particular year, and only the shape of the curve is significant. From this shape, the peculiarity of the "stagflation" of 1967-71 leaps to the eye. Unlike the previous years of rising inflation since the war, unemployment rose steeply in 1967, and still more steeply in 1970-71. Not until 1973 does unemployment fall back, though not to the usual low level associated with inflation.

Table III-I

FIVE-YEAR PERCENTAGE CHANGE IN PRODUCTION, PRICES, WAGE-RATES, LABOR EARNINGS AND POPULATION U.K. 1958 - 1973*

| | Three Five-year Periods 1958-1973 | | |
	1958-63 1958 = 100	1963-68 1963 = 100	1968-73 1968 = 100
(1) Volume of Total Industrial *Production*	119.0	119.8	112.9
(2) Total Retail *Prices*	111.7	120.7	142.0
(3) Weekly Wages *Rate*	117.8	126.3	168.3
(4) Weekly Labour *Earnings*	127.5	136.8	171.2
(5) Total Industrial Net Output per Person Employed (Productivity)	116.0	121.7	120.1
(6) Population	103.9	103.3	100.9**

*Source: Index numbers in Appendix of National Institute *Economic Reviews,* November 1967, 1971, May 1974.   **Estimated.

British inflation since 1963 is presented summarily in Table I based on the official "retail prices" and "consumer prices" indexes.[3] The last column of the table shows the faster upward trend in prices since 1968 when we compare the 1968-73 price change with that for 1963 to 1968. In this latter five-year period, retail prices rose 42.0%, as compared with the five-year rise of 20.7% in 1963-68 and 11.7% in 1958-63.

To bring British inflation into perspective, comparison may be drawn between the change of consumer prices in the United States and Britain in the ten-year period 1963-73.[4] For the period 1963 to 1970, consumer prices in the United States rose 26.7%, and from 1970 to 1973, 14.4% — a total of 41.1%. For the United Kingdom, they rose in the same two periods by 35.3% and 26.8% — a total for the ten years of 62.1%.

Stagnation, the second dimension in stagflation, is measurably indicated today by a number of statistical series. The most often quoted is the rate of unemployment. More fundamental measures, however, are the physical volume of industrial output or the value of gross national product at the prices prevailing on some fixed date. But to correspond more closely with prosperity, this total product should be divided by the population, which continues to grow. The relevant figures measuring percentage changes, including that of population, appear in Table I.

The volume of all industrial production (line 1) increased steadily, but slowly, until 1968 at the rate of 19% to 20% every five years. But after 1968, as the last column shows, the increase fell to the rate of 12.9% per five years.

Comparison of stagnation in Britain with that in America is difficult, since the timing of the cycles has been different in the two countries. Table II gives the officially recorded rates of unemployment year by year between 1964 and 1971. Stress should not be laid on the different levels of unemployment shown in the two columns, since definitions and methods of calculation in the two countries were different. The significant point is the amplitude of the swings within each column.

It will be seen that there has been a clear upswing in unemployment during recent years — after 1967 in Britain, and after 1969 in the United States. If we compare the half-yearly rates of unemployment for the years 1970, 1971, and 1972 with the four lowest yearly rates between 1964 and 1969, the British upswing appears considerably more violent than the American. From the low rates averaging 1.62 in 1964 to 1967, the British swing rises (half-yearly) between 1970 and 1972 to 2.75, 3.16, 3.50, 3.58, 3.75 and 3.45 (averaging 3.35) — an increase between the two averages of 107%. From the low rates averaging 3.7 in 1966 to 1969, the American swing rises half-yearly to 4.5, 5.5, 5.0, 5.9, 5.8, and 5.5 (averaging 5.5) — an increase between the averages of 49%.

Table III-II

UNEMPLOYMENT RATES IN U.K. AND U.S.A. 1964-1973

		U.K.*		U.S.A.**	
1964		1.56	⎫	5.2	
1965		1.32	⎬ 1.62	4.5	
1966		1.38		3.8	⎫
1967		2.21	⎭	3.8	⎬ 3.7
1968		2.35		3.6	
1969		2.32		3.5	⎭
1970	1st half	2.75	⎫	4.5	⎫
	2nd half	3.16		5.5	
1971	1st half	3.50	⎬ 3.36	5.0	⎬ 5.4
	2nd half	3.58		5.9	
1972	1st half	3.75	⎭	5.8	
	2nd half	3.45		5.5	⎭
1973	1st half	2.80		5.0	
	2nd half	2.34		4.7	

Sources: *U.K. Dept. of Employment   **U.S. Dept. of Labor: all workers

The statistics of unemployment and price increases presented in Tables I and II form together a useful summary of the course of British stagflation from available official sources. Britain has experienced, clearly, a more severe increase than America, both in stagnation and in inflation. But, as so often happens with summary statistics, they do not tell the whole story.

A COST-PUSH INFLATION

The Impact and Background of Wage Increases

We must resist the common temptation to look for a single cause of the current British inflation and stagnation. As is usual in human affairs, there is a multiplicity of causes. Yet, we cannot just list all probable or possible factors involved and leave it at that. Where large changes have been observed, such as the recent rise in prices, we must look for similarly large changes associated in time and place for which a reasonable theory or working hypothesis as to causation can be advanced.

In the opening words of his introduction to the series of *Cambridge Economic Handbooks,* J. M. Keynes wrote that "The theory of Economics does not furnish a body of settled conclusions immediately applicable to policy. It is a method rather than a doctrine, an apparatus of the mind, a technique of thinking, which helps its possessor to draw correct conclusions."[5]

Following this technique, economists have grouped theoretical interpretations of inflation into those on the "demand," and on the "supply" side—in short, into a "demand-pull" associated with increased monetary circulation, and a supply or "cost-push." The costs involved, again following the economists' "apparatus of the mind," are grouped into the various "factors of production" — labor, capital, management, etc.

A large change associated with the considerable price rise in the period 1968-71 was the large rise in wage and earnings costs described above. Since there was only a small rate of quinquennial increase in labor productivity of 20.1%, compared with the sizeable increase in wage rates of 68.3% and in labor earnings of 71.2%, labor costs rose very considerably.

The difference between wage rates and earnings has long been observed in British industry under the name of "wage drift" and is due mainly to the working of more overtime hours, the up-grading of individual workers (more being placed in the higher grades), and the movement of workers into higher paid occupations and industries.[6]

Whatever the reasons, earnings are the out-of-pocket expenses of an employer (as well as the in-pocket "take-home" income of workers), and the quantity by which they rise is more significant in the market than the rise in wage rates.

On the demand side, both Tables I and II show that the volume of production rose only 12.9% in the same period, 1968-73, as against 19.0% and 19.8% in the two previous five-year periods, and unemployment was rising more rapidly. So there is little sign of any demand-pull. Rather the opposite: demand was falling, causing stagnation as well as inflation.

The height of the rise in prices in the period 1968-73 can only be matched, then, by the height of the rise in workers' incomes. But the question remains: which of the two is a main cause, which is effect? And the seriousness of inflation is precisely the vicious circle which can continue indefinitely, whereby price rises cause workers to seek wage rises, and wage rises cause employers to seek price rises. In the present British situation, one can point, however, to *prima facie* evidence. At the outset, in the earlier period of the price rise in 1958-63, prices rose considerably less than wages and earnings, as they did, similarly, in the next period 1963-68; and (in Chart I) the curve of wage rates, and still more of earnings, runs ahead of prices from the beginning of the period.

The causes, then, of the British stagnation today would seem to include steeply rising costs of the supply of labor, and not insufficient demand, as diagnosed by Keynes in the long drawn out unemployment of the depression of 1929-35.[7] The percentage rise in wage rates, and particularly in labor earnings, more than match the rise in prices — an experience which has quantitatively no precedent.

In the 1969-72 period, unlike 1929-34, a price rise occurred concurrently with a rise in unemployment, contrary to received theory and contrary to any movement along the empirically discovered Phillips curve. The sheer quantitative intensity of the rise in labor costs is the significant factor. The increase in the wages and earnings of labor is so fast that employers must, if only because of the cash flow shortages, get rid of some of the expensive labor (some perhaps unnecessarily hoarded in the past) as well as raise the price of products.[8] Demand may increase to some extent because of the increased earnings of labor, thus absorbing some of the unemployed — but only after a considerable lag. Demand, moreover, will not always increase exactly where there is a gap in employment, and much of it will disperse into imports from abroad.

What factors can explain this steep upward wage trend? An economist naturally would look to an increased level of demand or a failing supply of labor. But judging by the percentage of the unfilled job vacancies (to the total labor force), the unsatisfied demand for labor in 1967-71 was less than in 1964-1966, and judging by population figures,[9] with no changes made in the school-leaving age, the supply was higher.

I am driven back then to the possibility, if not the probability, that the unprecedented recent rise in British wages and earnings is due not so much to economic circumstances as to (1) the particular philosophy and leadership of the British labor movement, which has always been particularly independent of the current mainstream of economic thinking and even oblivious of many contemporary economic and technological trends.

The conceding of higher wages may be due, as well, to (2) a new phase in capitalist organization in which the top decision making is made, in the first instance, by managers keen on the job itself, but who are not primarily owners of capital and receivers of the profits that would suffer from increased wages.

Another factor in rising wages is (3) the raising of supplementary benefits — an increase in social security — to the dependents of strikers, which makes a strike less forbidding to workers. In the bargaining process, the balance of power has shifted in favor of labor. Its side is strengthened by greater determination to seek substantial wage increases and by less deterrence from striking. The employers' side is weakened by less determination in resisting wage claims and by greater frustration when strikes stop men getting on with the job — stop, in fact, growth.

It is not possible to gauge the likely extent of the wage claims and the success of trade unions in getting their claims accepted on purely economic grounds. To put the case bluntly, the British labor movement has been independent, parochial, generally oblivious to modern economic thinking, and, moreover, apparently unaware of what policies will serve its own long-run interest, much less that of the general economy. To illustrate my point, we must get to know the social and ideological background of British industrial relations. Without such knowledge, policies cannot be put forward with any chance of being effective; nor, in particular, can policies involving radical changes in the structure of government, such as were introduced in the short-lived Industrial Relations Act of 1971, be realistically assessed for a solution to stagflation in the short or long run. The relevant background is mainly sociological; but after all, realistic economics can seldom be abstracted from social history, attitudes, and structures.

In their contribution to *Do Trade Unions Cause Inflation?* Jackson and Turner quote Henri Aujac, writing in 1950, "that stocks and flows neither exist nor move by themselves,"[10] emphasizing that the economy could not be seen simply as a set of economic flows, but must be considered as a set of flows manipulated by the pressures of different social groups.[11] The main sociological points that bear upon stagflation are the continued existence of a class system, the present relations between the "working" and other classes, and within the working-class world, the use of the weapon of the strike and its likely power in the future.

The British Class System

The late Professor R. H. Tawney spoke of a "horizontal" stratification, "as between those who occupy a position of special advantage and those who do not. The degree to which such horizontal divisions exist varies widely in the same community at different times, and in different communities at the same time. They are more marked in most parts of Europe than in America and the British dominions, [more] in the East of America than in the West, [more] in England than in France; and they were obviously more marked in the England of half a century ago than they are in that of today." Later, Tawney speaks of the "blend of a crude plutocratic reality with the sentimental aroma of an aristocratic legend — which gives the English class system its peculiar toughness and cohesion. It is at once as businesslike as Manchester and as gentlemanly as Eton."[12]

Undoubtedly the so-called "public schools," with Eton at their head, are mainly responsible for the continuing English class differentiation. The adjective "public" is confusing to Americans, as these schools are in fact highly exclusive. It indicates that the schools are not run privately for profit, but endowed and supervised by elected trustees. During their formative years, usually from eight to nineteen, upper and middle-class boys, whose parents can afford the expense, are segregated into boarding establishments. The system includes "preparatory" schools that prepare, often for four to six years, for the public schools.[13]

We are not here interested in the upper class in itself, but in its relation to the working class with its separate philosophy and, if you like, separate "culture." The upper classes with their segregated schools grow up knowing little of the working class, but have some concern as part of the establishment for the country as a whole. In contrast, the working classes, being the poorly paid underdogs, are inclined not to see the whole. Workers are more readily alarmed by slowly mounting unemployment than by the faster mounting inflation in the whole economy. When its many middle-class supporters seek to draw attention of the labor movement to national needs, they are liable to be dismissed as "intellectuals."

The peculiar independence of the British working class (which combined with the separation of the public school "gentlemen" makes for a class "system" rather than a mere stratification) has many roots in British history and British character. Three that affect wage claims more than others may be singled out:

(1) Horrifying working and living conditions were imposed on a large proportion of the population by the industrial revolution. They were described at the time by Friedrich Engels and have been vividly recounted more recently by the Hammonds[14] and others. This experience is still kept fresh by such often-told history as the Tolpuddle martyrdoms, the Peterloo massacre, and other labor hagiology. A hundred years later, labor was forced to experience fresh horrors in the long unemployment queues and "life on the dole" in the great depression of 1929-35.

(2) Education spread very slowly — much slower than in America or Germany. Compulsory education was not introduced until 1871 and did not extend beyond the age of fifteen until 1972. The number of boys and girls of seventeen at school as a percentage of all aged seventeen shows England and Wales with 14% (or 18% including full timers in college of further education), as against the United States, with 75%. And up to the late nineteenth century, there were in England only two main universities, Oxford and Cambridge.

(3) An enterprising organizing spirit has always appeared throughout British society fostering the formation of innumerable private societies for a variety of purposes — educational, social, aesthetic, sporting or political. Of such societies, the most important for the country's economy generally, and in particular for working-class claims and ambitions, were three founded by the working class itself: trade unions, cooperative societies and the Labour party. The reliance which the workers placed on trade unions and "direct action"

tended, and tends today, to increase with the political frustrations of the political Labour party. A peak was reached around 1912 when "workers' control" and "syndicalism" was the vogue in Europe, which a few years later developed in England under G. D. H. Cole as guild socialism.[15]

The World of Labor

The "World of Labour," the title used by G.D.H. Cole for his first book, best expresses the characteristic independence, solidarity, and self-containment of the British labor movement with its own methods of organization and its own outlook. The same methods and outlook can be observed in each of its three main wings, with a philosophy confined to the distribution of its wealth, rather than to the growth of the total wealth of the nation.

Where the methods and organization of the world of labor differ from that of the world at large is in the stress on democracy, rather than meritocracy, in making appointments (university graduates are not appointed to cooperative positions because this is considered unfair to boys climbing up the ladder after leaving school at fifteen); the stress on security of tenure for officials, rather than pruning for efficiency; and conservatively respecting traditional rights, rather than embarking on radical enterprise.[16] This stress can also be observed in the shunning of possibly expert intellectuals who might apply economic thought to given circumstances. These characteristics were borne in upon me quite traumatically during a detailed analysis of the cooperative organization in 1936-38.[17]

When discussing wages costs, it is trade union organization that is of chief interest, and here the lag behind general economic thought is particularly noticeable. It took time for the cooperatives to learn from Keynes that to reduce unemployment they should not hoard, but should reinvest out of surplus,[18] and thus increase the demand for labor. Having learned Keynesian principles, the trade unions now seem to think a rise in wages of whatever size will automatically create the market to prevent unemployment in spite of the inevitable rise in costs and prices.

The Trade Union Congress, furthermore, is powerless to coordinate the individual unions, and some large individual unions are, in turn, powerless to control shop stewards. There is no agreed differentiation of wage rate claims between industries and occupations to balance the arduousness of the work they entail. Wages structure remains the result of *ad hoc* and sectional bargaining, and the need, in a socialist plan, of a national wage policy is ignored.

This lack of coordination and plan is brought forcibly home to the national economy in the multiplicity of trade unions with which employers often have to bargain, even within one single plant. It is understandable that the various occupations or crafts (clerks, pattern-makers, etc.) that appear and reappear in a number of industries should have separate unions, though to be sure, in the early twentieth century, industrial unions covering all the occupations in one industry were being advocated. But in the end, it was neither industrial nor craft unions that developed fastest in Britain, but general unions incorporating all trades. The Transport and General Workers Union amalgamated, between 1922 and 1947, fifty-eight different unions ranging from dock workers to vehicle, coal, quarrying, and glass workers and, in Ireland at least, hospital workers, textile workers, butchers, and bakers.[19] This trade union, and others such as the National Union of General and Municipal Workers, might fittingly be called "conglomerates."

While faced with a multiplicity of unions in settling wage claims, the employer is also faced with a certain multiplicity of authorities and procedures within a single trade union. The British unions are peculiar in their low proportion of full time officers to members. The (Donovan) Royal Commission of 1968 calculated that there was one union official for every 3,800 union members in Britain, as compared with but one for every 1,400 in the United States, and one for every 800 in West Germany.[20] The deficiency is made up by the part time shop stewards which accounts for the informality of many union decisions. British trade union leaders have in the past taken pride in this unsystematic, decentralized nature of their movement and complained that the new Industrial Relations Act was imposing, with its Industrial Relations Court, a legal straitjacket.

Living in a "world of one's own," however, suggests a certain blindness to external events and facts outside that world. This is indeed true of labor. Mr. Feather, then secretary of the Trade Union Council, spoke in April 1972 of his resentment at "the suggestion that there is a trade union movement on the one hand and a public interest on the other — we are not only representatives of the public interest, we are the public interest."[21] One is strikingly reminded of the view that "what is good for General Motors is good for America."

Other statements of union leaders are significant, if not positively symptomatic, of the medievalism of much trade union thinking—a resemblance that has not escaped foreign observers.[22] Medieval economic thought revolved around certain static points: the "just" price, the "right" rate of interest, and the "right" work for men of given status involving demarcation rules. During the miners' strike of 1972, Mr. Jack Jones, the leader of the largest British trade union, argued for a "just" wage for the miners in view of their arduous work, whether or not it resulted in their own or other workers unemployment or in inflated coal prices. At present, individual unions speak as judges of justice in their own cause, and inevitably, each of them wants to promote that cause.

Today, the "right to work" is perhaps the main static point of the trade union position, a point that has been conceded by most Western states in their postwar declaration for a policy of full employment. Unfortunately the average trade union member's interpretation of the "right to work," in many actual situations, is the "right" to go on working at the same job or in the same firm, regardless of changes in technology or consumer demand.

On paper and in theory, trade union leaders applaud "modernization," and the word was, indeed, one of Mr. Harold Wilson's slogans in the 1966 Labour party campaign. Modernization of industry usually involves the substitution of machines for men, or more efficient organization (such as containerization), or the abolition of traditional featherbedding practices. When this modernization is actually carried out, however, workers often strike against elimination of the "redundancy" naturally involved. Labor has not, in short, realized the contradiction between its own proclaimed socialist slogans and the policies involved in applying them in industry at large.[23] Continental European observers such as Ferdynand Zweig are always surprised how "the core of British socialism" is not Marx, but the trade unions; the core can be defined just as "defending the interests of the workers against the boss class."[24]

The precise impact of trade union ideas comes in the confrontation of collective bargaining with employers and its possible outcome in a strike. Strikes have greatly increased in recent years, and because of their effect in boosting the cost of production as well as in their power to influence wage negotiation, some comparison must be drawn of recent strike experience between Britain and America.

The Strike Weapon and Its Cost

It has long been pointed out that the proportion of total man-days of work lost by strikes tends to be lower in Britain than the United States. One such comparison was that drawn from the International Labour office by the Devlin Royal Commission, covering the years 1964 to 1966, and gives the United Kingdom's days lost by strikes annually per 1,000 persons employed as only 190 compared to France's 200, Italy's 1,170, and the United States' 870.[25]

One must question, however, whether this apparently sophisticated measure is really the correct indicator of the costs involved. Does not every strike cause a certain quantum of disturbance to management, regardless of duration or even of the number of workers involved — and particularly the unforeseeable wildcat strike? I do not refer to the direct immediate loss of production which reduces the profits and dividends of shareholders, so much as the loss of time, frustration, and additional worry of business managers — eventually leading to the need for more and more highly paid managers.

A strike of a few craftsmen or maintenance workers may result in a whole plant having to be shut down. Recently, for example, a large loss of work in an English automobile component factory was due to the strike of less than a dozen lavatory attendants. And with the modern interdependence of one factory or one firm on another, a strike involving however few in one plant may affect its total production and that of many other factories.[26]

In short, the bare number of strikes is significant, and its rate per total workers employed should be placed side by side with the now conventional rate of hours lost per possible total of hours worked.

Comparing the United Kingdom with the United States between 1958 and 1968, I have found that in the average (median) year, man-days lost by work stoppages were 23,300 in the United States, 3038 in the United Kingdom — or 7.75 to 1. But the actual number of stoppages was, in spite of a U.S. labor force from three to four times as large, 3,694 to 2,449 or merely 1.5 to 1. The number of stoppages per thousand employees ranged in the United Kingdom in these eleven years as high as between 0.8 and 1.8; in the United States, only between 0.48 to 0.64.

If we may believe the official statistics comparing the duration of strikes, the contrast between the two countries comes out still more strongly. In the three years 1966, 1967, and 1968, the number of short (one to six day) strikes outnumbered the long strikes respectively by 13.5, 3.5, and 11 times in Britain; but in the United States, it was the longer strikes that were more frequent.

Probably the chief cause of the more frequent but, on average, shorter and smaller scale strikes in Britain is the greater proportion of unofficial wildcat strikes not called by the central trade unions. N. Harman has estimated that 95% of British strikes are unofficial.[27] This high proportion is, in turn, largely due to the lower degree of authority and discipline exercised by the official trade unions. Just as the British trade unions function independently of the national economy, so, too, within the national unions, the part time, unpaid shop stewards often go their own way independently of the union full-time hierarchy.

This independence was brought home forcibly when, in June 1972, the Transport and General Workers Union appealed (and won) against the Industrial Relations Court's fine imposed because the Liverpool dock stewards "blacked" (embargoed) container vehicles that dispensed with their labor. Although, subsequently, the Law Lords sitting in the House of Lords reversed the Appeal Courts decision, the case illustrates that independence is often the natural reaction from the enormously large and conglomerate unions that have evolved. Mere size entails decentralization of control and adds to the strike power of shop stewards, relatively to full-time trade union officials.

Carried to its logical conclusion, workers' control based on strike power leads to an odd distribution of wealth between workers in different industries and often to the opposite of justice according to degree of arduousness. If strike success is to determine wage levels, workers in industries that immediately affect the public, such as the electrical heating supply, passenger transport, and other service industries, are likely to secure higher wages than workers in industries more arduous, but more distant from the consumer. Workers in consumer services can count on a nuisance value in their strikes.

Coal mining, for example, is "distant" from the consumer, until it affects the power supply. In the course of the British coal strike in the winter of 1971-1972, Mr. Joe Gormley, the miners' union leader,

pointed out that "public sympathy is often only as strong as a tele-
vision signal, and when the pictures fade along with coal stocks, so
will support. And support will be practically nonexistent when the
cookers go out."[28] During the strike of the less distant power workers a year earlier, irate housewives were reported to have thrown
bricks through strikers' windows. The mere report printed in the
newspapers was, apparently, an eye-opener to the strikers as to their
unpopularity. The world of labor, with its own moral standards,
condemns "scabs," "blacklegs," and "rate-busters," but is blind to
the general community condemnation of absenteeism, strikes, and
going slow.

Loss of public support works both ways. It will strengthen the
public demand for an end to the strike and will bring in government
intervention toward coming to terms; but whether the terms are
more favorable to strikers or to employers mainly depends on political maneuver. The point is that industries far distant from the final
consumer are less likely to be considered urgent, and the strike may
well be allowed to peter out, thus shifting the income distribution
against that industry. This was certainly the result of the British
postal strike in the winter of 1971. The public found it did not
require the postage of letters so long as a sufficient supply of telephone workers remained on the job, and the workers finally had to
accept the employer's offer. Yet distant from the consumer market
though they are, industries such as coal-mining, supplying fuel, and
building business premises, may be fundamental to the economy in
the long run.

Given these economic circumstances of supply and demand, we
may perhaps look a little under the surface at the social structures
— the organizations of employers and workers that confront one
another — and study their behavior and attitudes. In this regard,
employers currently at the point of confrontation in Britain are
mainly nationalized enterprises. The most severe strikes in the years
1969-1972 involved the Coal Board in February 1972, the Post Office Board in February 1971, the British Electricity Authority in
November 1970, municipal authorities employing the "dustmen" in
October 1969, and British Railways at various times.

It seemed probable at the time of nationalization that the government, whether Labour or Tory, with their declared policy of greater
equality in distribution of income and high employment would be

more liberal in granting wage increases than the capitalist employer. But to the surprise of some socialists, and as evidence that British socialism means little more than trade unions theory, the workers seem to make no distinction between a capitalist employer liable to "grind the faces of the poor to increase his profit," and the state aiming at no profit, but with prices just to cover costs. The capitalist employer is predominant in British manufacturing, although not in public utilities and mining.[29] Here inflation may be caused not only by increased costs such as more generous wage payment, but also by other factors such as monopoly exploitation.

THE IMPACT OF NONWAGE COST FACTORS

Changes in the Industrial Structure and Concentration

We turn from labor to the employer, the other possible main source of increased cost inflation. Within an industry, and within the firms composing an industry, the British employer structure has, like the American, been changing fundamentally in two respects. There are fewer, but larger, employers, so much so that just a few large firms often employ a majority or near majority of workers in an industry.[30] This fact, first statistically measured by Gardiner Means, is popularly known as concentration and academically discussed as oligopoly. Its economic significance is that prices may then be "administered" and held for a considerable period by the few sellers producing the bulk of the output — regardless of the immediate market forces of supply and demand — instead of responding to these forces from day to day.

But there is a second sort of concentration less well known and less completely measured. The industrial employer today is almost invariably of corporation form (in English terms, a "company"), as Gardiner Means again pointed out for the United States, and I, following in his traces, showed for England.[31] Corporations today differ widely in the distribution of their ownership. Some closely held firms have just a few shareholders (out of the tens of thousands that are quite usual in large companies) who own a majority of shares and, thus, of votes; others have no single shareholder owning more than 1%. These "open" firms would require perhaps a thousand shareholders to agree before an actual majority of votes could be secured. Effective control would then be concentrated probably in the directors and top managers, most of them owning few shares and paid by salary — at which point a managerial revolution has been accomplished.

Recently in Britain, however, the so-called "take-overs" by yet larger firms have loomed large, and directors and managers are frightened that if they do not pander to their shareholders, or at least to their larger shareholders, they in turn will sell out their shares to some other company offering a bid higher than the shares' current market price. Before crucial decisions are made, directors are now inclined to consult a few leading shareholders who might be tempted to sell out, particularly if they are institutions and not business-shy, individual shareholders.

It is important, therefore, to analyze the structure of the largest companies to discover how far a few shareholders hold a large proportion of the capital and, also, who they are — whether companies, institutions, or private persons. I attempted such an analysis for the years 1936-1951[32]; and, in 1951, identified 30 of the largest 98 industrial companies as owner-controlled. Half of these companies had five or more institutions among their twenty largest shareholders; three had twelve or more. Only two had none.[33]

Since the time Means and I first wrote, more companies have certainly had their control concentrated in a practically shareless management, possibly consulting a few leading shareholders. Thus a double concentration of power has been taking place: concentration within an industry in a few firms; and within these firms, concentration of power in the hands of the management. A question relevant to the present inflation of prices thus arises whether the substitution of a few firms under certain management power in place of a multitude of competing owner-managers has not radically changed the pricing mechanism and the attitude to cost, especially wages, and thus inflation, as envisaged in economic textbooks.

Economists have made some return toward the more comprehensive and integrated approach of Adam Smith and Alfred Marshall.[34] Attention is gradually being paid to the differential effect of different types of structure upon prices and employment. In concentrated industries, these matters may be decided by the administration of a few firms with relatively inflexible decisions which are infrequently changed. By contrast, in the more competitive market structure normally assumed in pure theory, prices are determined quasi-automatically day by day, not by any "personal" decision, but by the "forces" of demand and supply. In those circumstances, there appeared no need to trace the particular procedures and policies of institutions or structures such as the firms within the market. Not until the notion that prices were administered, not determined by market "forces," was it considered necessary to analyze an administering firm's policies and to identify the actual seat of control. Consequently, it is hard, as yet, to be conclusive how far the recent jump in prices is attributable to the recent changes in employer structure (the growing size of firms and the concentration of market power) or in motivation (payment of management by salary, not profit). In fact, only a few attempts have been made in Britain to gather empirical evidence on pricing procedures, in spite of the pioneer work of P. W. S. Andrews in 1949.[35]

One reasonable possibility should be tested, connected as it is with the rise in wages already described. It applies in those many companies where the top, or, as I like to call him, the prime manager, holds few shares, and management is divorced, generally speaking, from ownership. This situation may be critical, since pure economic reasoning leads us to suppose that managers are not directly motivated toward a maximum profit in which they do not share, but instead hate the disorganization injected by strikes, particularly in modern technologically developed industries.

Several modern economists believe, indeed, that management's main motive in such companies is the smooth *growth* of the company. This hypothesis could be tested if these management-ruled companies were identified and compared with other companies in their wage negotiating behavior in order to see whether the wages of their employees rise faster. Conceding wage demands without raising prices will cut into profits, but does not necessarily check growth. Thus the shareless managers are easier game for the trade union leadership. Unless constrained by their leading shareholders, such firms may not resist wage claims so strenuously as the classical owner-manager entrepreneur.

Though the danger of concentration has loomed larger in the thoughts of American economists than in those of Britain, concentration appears, in fact, a greater threat in Britain.[36] British economists are, however, more alarmed by the much faster increase in the *general or aggregate* concentration of British firms regardless of particular industries. This poses problems in the distribution of power in the whole community, rather than problems of price inflation due to monopoly exploitation.

The sequence in the percentages held by the hundred largest firms in the two countries, as revealed by various surveys, may be set out in Table III.

Table III-III

SHARE OF LARGEST HUNDRED FIRMS IN MANUFACTURE GENERALLY.

	U.K. (Output)*	U.S. (Shipments)	(Assets)
1947	———	23.0%	39.3%
1948	20.5%	———	———
1963	38.0%	33.0%	———
1967	———	33.0%	———
1968	———	———	49.3%
1970	51.0%	33.0%	———

* Private communication from Professor S.S. Prais, National Institute for Economic and Social Research. The Institute's Report for 1973 mentions that, on average, the hundred largest firms owned 26 plants in 1958, but an estimated 70 each in 1972.

On the whole, the largest firms tend to be the most "manager-controlled," with a greater proportion of shareless, or almost shareless, directors not paid by a share of profits.[3] Their motivation must often, in fact, be sought elsewhere than profits. English economists such as Robin Marris have been impressed by the broad surveys of the problem of motives undertaken by their colleagues in America. Curiously enough, however, it was English experience that led me to point to the strength of noneconomic motives such as rivalry, pursuit of power and public recognition, loyalty, camaraderie and *esprit de corps,* and being keen on one's work.[3t] None of these motives, however, leads directly to keeping wages down, per unit of output.

In so far as the alarming increase in general concentration is due to more management-controlled conglomerate firms, costs may rise not only because of the unwillingness of management to exert the utmost control of costs in the absence of a personal profit motive and of competition, but also because of the lack of specialization. All too many conglomerate firms include incompatible industries and at-tempt to manage activities in which they are inexperienced or which have little connection in markets or sources of supply with their original activities.

Where size of plants, not firms, is concerned, Joe Bain's conclusion, as quoted by Ricard Caves, "that large U.K. plants run almost one quarter smaller than their U.S. counterparts,"[39] is misleading (it has misled Caves) because he selects, as an index, the average number employed in the twenty largest plants, not in all plants. A smaller country is likely to have absolutely fewer plants both large and small and, naturally, sizes will taper off more rapidly from largest to small-est. Counting all manufacturing plants, the average British plant, though commonly thought to be smaller, is in fact larger than its American counterpart.[40]

The only important exception to the similarity of British and American *structure* is the British nationalization of public utilities and one manufacturing industry — iron and steel.[41] While this nation-alized segment will be considered later, the immediate importance of nationalization is to put the control and direction of industry more into the hands of professional managers and away from capital owners.

To sum up, then, the trend toward concentration of production within a few large firms in an industry, and also toward the concen-tration of power in the management, rather than private owners, within the firm seems to have occurred about as strongly in Britain as in America. But Tables I and II have shown a more severe rise in British prices and, relatively to previous years, a more severe rise in British unemployment.

Are there any facts apart from the attitude of labor already con-sidered that might account for this difference? High prices or high unemployment can often be attributed to concentration by reason of exploitation of the consumer or restriction of output so as to obtain high profit. But concentration, with its tendency to monopoly, may also involve an unnecessarily high price in restricted employment, also because of too high a *cost*. Having no fear of competition, monopolists may well become slack in controlling the cost of materi-als,[42] equipment, and salaries, as well as wages of labor.

We have as yet no statistics to show whether concentration in-creased in the later years (1971-73) of the acute rise in prices, but the increased concentration recorded during 1968-70 may affect the costs and prices of today. It is not the *process* of concentration that might make management slack, but the fact of being concentrated.

Functioning and Performance of the Structure

Although the general growth of British industry is slower than in other industrially developed countries, this growth rate is not very far below that of the United States. Differences occur, however, in three other ways in which the two national structures have been acting, which may involve different costs.

(1) Foreign trade is a far higher percentage of British gross national product than of American. I have always to remind others, and also myself, of the great difference between the two countries in this respect; and I have found the most telling way of bringing the difference home to be a diagram (Chart II) of the value of different countries' trade relative to their total product. Arrows inward and outward each show 1% of the total national production, imported and exported, of both Britain and America.[43]

The question of competition from foreign countries is more urgent in Britain than the United States; and the chart shows that the higher British proportion of foreign trade to national product applies to manufactures as much as to fuel, food, and raw materials. It is a genuine functional difference between the two countries and has changed little in recent years.

This dependence upon a high proportion of exports and imports has resulted in balance of payments difficulties. And the need to pay for an excess of imports over exports has led the government to a stop-go, or rather a go-stop, policy, which has cut across any pursuit of planned expansion.

(2) The productivity of labor is between 1.5 and 2.5 times higher in United States than in British manufacturing. This difference is very largely accounted for by the difference in mechanization. The year 1951 was the last census when figures were available in the United Kingdom for the horsepower of machines per worker, which was then 3.1. In the United States it was 6.5 as early as in 1939, and 9.6 in 1954.

This lower level of mechanization has predisposed the British economy to a greater dependence on the supply of labor. British industries are certainly more labor intensive, and a given wage concession is more likely to result in a greater loss of profit.[44]

Chart III-II

IMPORTS AND EXPORTS AS PERCENTAGE
OF NATIONAL PRODUCT*

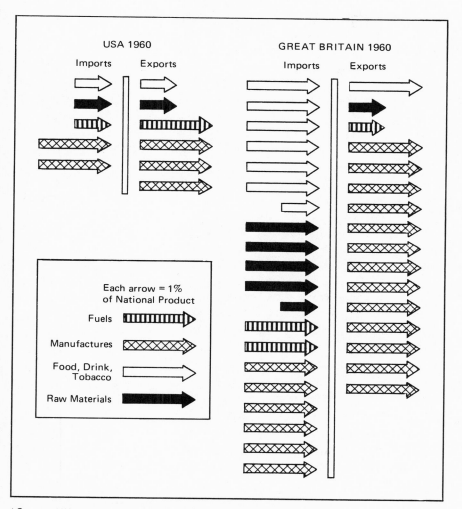

*Source: UK Abstract of Statistics, U.N. Series P 1964.

(3) America's higher labor productivity may be due not only to greater mechanization, but to more efficient business organization. An important factor here is the relative ability of the persons who are in business as against persons in the different professions. Assuming the same general proportions of ability among the two populations, that line of activity will obtain the higher ability which has the greater prestige. In America, business has certainly greater prestige than most professions; in Britain, less prestige as compared to the law, the civil service, even politics or university work. In consequence, the ablest young people are attracted away from business. Indeed, careers advisors and tutors at Oxford or Cambridge, before 1939, used to advise their brightest pupils to avoid jobs in industry.[45] Then, in a vicious circle, business not being so ably performed, became less and less prestigious. It is only fairly recently, too, that undergraduate business education has been undertaken in British universities, and only *very* recently, post-graduate education.[46]

The lower management ability involves lower powers of adaptation and resourcefulness to meet the new impact of high wage claims and to avoid a loss without rising prices. Moreover, continuing low labor productivity involves lower wages, nearer to bare living standards, which may in turn impel labor to ask for more.

These differences in the proportion of output exported, in labor productivity and mechanization, and possibly in management ability and education, though present throughout the twentieth century, may all have indirectly favored the chronic increase of inflation and unemployment in Britain in the recent years. They were, like a patient's constitution, the conditions predisposing to the impact of infection.

We must conclude that no particular *new* impact appears on the British scene in the period 1969-72 heavy enough to account for the exceptional stagflation of this period, except the increased wages and labor earnings, mentioned previously, taken in conjunction with concentration as high as in America, and with the constitutional weaknesses in management.[47]

BRITISH GOVERNMENT POLICY

Policies to curb inflation but avoid stagnation fall naturally into two types; short-run policies for immediate direct control of prices and wages, and long-run policies to affect prices and wages by changing the structure of the controlling organizations. This distinction will be familiar to economists brought up on Alfred Marshall's *Principles*. His "short" periods refer to what can be produced "with the existing stock of plant"; his long (but not secular) periods, to what can be produced with plant, which "itself can be produced and applied within the given time."[48] Substituting "structure" for "plant," the long period involves changing or adding to industrial structures, the short period "making do" with existing structure.

Short-Run Policy

The existing industrial structure in both Britain and America consists normally of competing profit-making firms of a great variety of sizes — although in several industries, a few larger firms produce the bulk of the output — together with independent trade unions bargaining collectively with firms or associations of them over wages, hours, and working conditions generally. Short-run government policy is limited to this existing normal apparatus. When, abnormally, monopoly appears, government policy is to restore competition; when, abnormally, collective bargaining breaks down, it is government's role to conciliate and mediate between the parties. In the United States, the emphasis was historically on restoring competition; in Britain, on mediation. But since 1948, Britain has passed laws largely on the American pattern.

In 1948, the Labour government passed the Monopolies and Restrictive Practices (Inquiry and Control) Act which set up a special Monopolies commission to investigate and take action and granted it powers to take evidence and make recommendations to Parliament. In 1956, under a Conservative government, largely on the initiative of Mr. Heath, the Minister for Trade, a judicial tribunal was set up under the Restrictive Practices Act, a revolutionary step in British institutional history and economic life. Agreements to restrict supply so as to keep up or raise prices were found in many industries and were made illegal, or voluntarily abandoned, as was retail price maintenance by manufacturers. However, price inflation continued, and after the Labour government took office in 1964, a new structure was set up going beyond mediation, in the form of the Prices and Incomes Board, to which the government would refer cases and whose decisions on "ceilings" it would enforce.[49]

The practical question is how far the Prices and Incomes Board reduced the rise in prices and wages below the levels they would have reached if no board had existed. Wages, if not prices, seem in fact to have increased rather faster over the years since the board was broken up following Mr. Heath's electoral victory in 1970.

Once the aim of full employment is accepted, cost inflation probably cannot be checked without some sort of national wage plan. Logically, such a plan is not out of keeping with socialism — rather the contrary — and the Labour party might be expected to support it. But many Labour members of Parliament rely for support on the trade unions, and we know by the experience of the 1969 Bill put forward by the Labour government that the trade unions will block any attempt to apply sanctions against deviations and deviators from the nationally planned wage. Mrs. Barbara Castle, who, as Minister for Employment and Productivity in the Labour government, had to steer this bill through Parliament, could not convince her back-bench colleagues that, ultimately, a national plan would not have to be enforced by fines, if not imprisonment. In short, a Conservative government, in spite of its traditional *laissez-faire* leanings, would be the more likely to sponsor a national wage plan backed by legal sanctions.

Meanwhile control of wage inflation will have to consist in somehow restraining the particular trade union or group of workers which is setting the pace by its claims. Such a claim-leading group will not necessarily be in an industry or occupation which is in the greatest demand or shortest supply, present or prospective. Success will, rather, crown a union possessing the greatest potential for creating a nuisance to the community by striking and the greatest bargaining strength by enrolling the highest proportion of the total of workers in the industry or occupation. This high proportion seems to depend in turn upon three main points: (1) a high proportion of *wage-earning* employees among the total occupied (that is, where there are few self-employed or small proprietors); (2) upon close localization of the industry, allowing employees to meet together easily; and (3) upon a low proportion of women among workers. The system of awarding "points" marked mining as easily the top sector in union strength, and sure enough, it is the British mining industry which has shown how strong a union can be. Early in 1972, the government's temporary guideline of an 8% rise in wages was shattered, and after a short enquiry by Mr. Justice Wilberforce, 18% was granted. Mining was declared to be a "special case" because of the arduous and hazardous character of its work.

It did not require, however, a long and costly strike and a judge of the high court to discover the arduousness and hazards of the mining industry. Since the government could have recognized the special case in the first instance, it is difficult to escape the conclusion that it was the cohesion of the mining union along with help from other sympathetic unions, its disciplined siege of coal and coke stocks, together with its picketing of power stations (whether they used coal or not) that brought the government to its knees.[50] The "special" case of the miners has been, in fact, denied by a whole series of other industries, particularly those that were, like the coal mines, nationalized. Railwaymen obtained almost as high an increase three months after the victory of the miners. And soon after that, the already highly paid dockers.

To avoid immediate wage inflation in one industry after another, a national policy must prevent one particularly strong group from getting control through picketing and siege tactics. Legislative measures could limit more clearly the "peaceful" picketing now allowed and would deal with sympathetic strikes disallowed in the 1927 Act following Britain's general strike, and still not allowed in the United States.

In conceding almost as much as the miners' union had demanded, the government claimed mining was a "special case." But it was ominous to its policy that union leaders in other nationalized industries interpreted the "special case" to cover, not just arduous work, but all state-run industries such as road transport and even school teachers. In short, the policy of using the nationalized segment to anchor down wage rates for industries in all segments has failed.

By the Nationalization Acts of 1946-51, the public corporations are charged to avoid losses, and to strictly carry out this duty in present circumstances, they must either raise prices or keep wages below the general level, or do a bit of both. Wages below the general level involve large scale strikes; therefore the public corporations may have to resort to raising prices. What is likely to happen is a compromise: prices will be raised, but not sufficiently to cover the increased costs, and the losses will be subsidized out of government taxation. This has already happened in the railway and coal industries.

Long-Run Policies

The policies considered so far for fighting inflation directly, not by tackling monopoly, have been mainly "ad hoc" — all short-run in the sense of not involving radical changes in the structure and appartus normal to Western industry and consisting mainly of more or less competing firms bargaining collectively with trade unions. Individual arbitrators and tribunals were set up as adjuncts, rather than as parts of a new appartus, in order to conciliate or mediate between the parties. But they have not been very succesful so far.

Now we must consider the more radical long-run remedies. They may be broken down into four points of policy:

    (1) Nationalization to keep prices down;
    (2) Job comparability classification;
    (3) An adjudicating organ built up specially;
    (4) The use of legal sanctions.

Nationalization

One radical policy to control prices and unemployment by changing the industrial structure is the policy Britain adopted under the Labour government in the late 1940's — nationalizing the "natural monopolies," mainly public utilities. The control of prices, if not employment, was one of the aims of nationalization subsumed under the Labour party's statement of policy in 1950 that public ownership is "a means of ensuring that monopolies do not exploit the public."

This is not the place to describe in detail the procedures adopted in the British legislation of 1945-51, nor to analyze the logic underlying the choice of industries for nationalization. There was considerable logic, but not to the extent of ensuring full and stable employment in the industries nationalized or of immunizing them from inflation.[51] Changes in technology and in demand (the slump in coal and rail travel) have been overriding.

On attaining office in 1970, the Conservative government declared against the control of private industry and in favor of its "standing on its own feet." Since private industry, in fact, gave way to trade union demands, this declaration placed the ball in the court of the nationalized industries if any direct action was to be taken toward stabilizing prices and wages.

But the government reckoned without trade union solidarity and their keen "keeping up with the Jones' " mentality. Trade unions in the nationalized segment did not see why their members should receive lesser increases in wages than the members of unions in the private sector. Indeed, the objectives of the Labour party in nationalizing these industries had been, they thought, to improve their lot compared to other industries, not the opposite. In short, the public authorities' offer of moderate wage increases was unacceptable, and the nationalized coal miners, helped by other nationalized workers such as the electrical power and transport workers, scored an undoubted victory in February 1972.

Job-Comparability Classification

The court of enquiry presided over by Mr. Justice Wilberforce, hastily summoned and hastily reporting on February 18, 1972, gave the strikers' victory a semblance of legal respectability by drawing a significant distinction in granting most of the increase in wages the miners had demanded. Part of the increase was to keep up with the cost of living and to maintain their relative position among other industries; but another part was stated to be an "adjustment" to put the miners in a more just position in view of the hazards and arduous nature of their occupation. This "comparability" criterion has long been appealed to by labor in attempts to classify jobs into grades for purposes of payment. Its most famous citation was at a tribunal on railway wages chaired by the Cambridge economist C. W. Guillebaud, a nephew of Alfred Marshall. The principle, indeed, has the sanction of Adam Smith[52]; but in spite of its revival by Marshall in his notion of the "net advantages" of different occupations, it has been strangely neglected in the social sciences. Yet the cooperation of industrial psychologists and sociologists with economists should have proved fertile; and is not merely academic. This very question of the comparability or, as it might be called, the relative cost benefit of different occupations [53] is the rock on which any fundamental wage policy is now splitting. Moreover, it was always a fundamental question in furthering the mobility necessary to a successful and dynamic economy where labor moves into those industries that are developing, and away from those that are decaying.

Unfortunately, *economic* grounds for paying high wages in any one industry or occupation do not always correspond with equity, or "justice," based on psychological and sociological grounds. Under competition from oil production and natural gas, coal mining, until recently, was not a developing, but rather a declining industry. It is, on the other hand, as hazardous and arduous as any industry and therefore should, on the comparability criterion, earn a very high wage. But an economist must ask whether men should be attracted into the industry, and kept at the industry, by top rank wages? If they are, and the industry continues to decline, increases in unemployed or underemployed seem inevitable. It is a sad and unpalatable truth that wages cannot always be equitable and fair if the economy is to remain viable and dynamic.[54]

Building an Adjudicating Organ

The short-run problem in fighting inflation is largely one of periodically putting on the brake for everyone to slow down to some fixed speed of wage increase, or even stopping increases completely by a freeze or standstill. This policy, particularly the complete "wage standstill," is relatively acceptable as fair, at least temporarily, especially if it is accompanied by price and dividend freezes. This does not call for an adjudicating body.

But in the long run, wages and the earnings of labor get out of line, new types of jobs arise and old types decay, and some adjudicating structure must be built into the economy to adjust the comparative wages of different industries and occupations. In Britain, with its horror of imposed authority, the most congenial body of this sort would be some joint committee of the Trade Union Congress or Council (the T.U.C.) and of the Confederation of British Industry. And although the T.U.C. did, in 1965, start an internal review of the wage structure of its own constituents, the matter was not later pursued.

The T.U.C. has little control over the individual trade unions, some of which are very large. At the end of 1970, the Transport and General Workers counted 1,639,000 members, the Amalgamated Engineers and Foundrymen, 1,270,000, and the National Union of General Municipal Workers, 853,000.[56] Each of the two largest unions have fairly recently elected militants as their general secretaries, men who proclaim the injustices of the present wage structure, but failed to reach agreement of what the review was to change.

Repugnant as imposed authority is to her traditions, Britain will, in the long run, have to rely, for want of democratic cooperation, on recommendations made in the first instance by some civil service organ with expert staff on what is essentially a large scale job evaluation combined with market research. If persuasion of both employers and employees proves impossible, some government department or agency will have to administer these recommendations, partly at least, with certain legal sanctions. Voluntary persuasion by the Confederation of British Industries did, in fact, succeed for fifteen months in 1971-72 in getting a large section of manufacturers to limit price rises to 5%. But the trade unions did not respond, pleading that other products beside manufactures enter into the cost of living.

It became obvious that the Prices and Incomes Board (P.I.B.) broken up by the Conservative government in 1970 would have to be revived in some form, possibly with wider membership and stronger powers. Some of its activities and staff had already, early in 1972, been resurrected; the acceptable offer by Wilberforce to the striking miners could not have been put forward so rapidly and successfully without the aid of the former P.I.B. files and staff. Some of the staff had, in fact, been transferred to the Office of Man-Power Economics which had been set up to deal with changes in the salaries of professional workers.

Experience of the Prices and Incomes Board certainly makes clear the need for resort to some such organ if there is to be any intelligent government control over the course of incomes.

The Conservative government, which on attaining office in 1970 had originally proclaimed that employers and employed should "stand on their own two feet" without government intervention, had come to realize the strength of the trade unions and did a U-turn back from reliance on voluntary agreements to statutory control of prices and wages of the type proposed previously by the Labour government but abandoned under trade union pressure. By November 1972, the "tripartite" attempt of the Trade Union Congress, the Employers Confederation, and the government to reach voluntary agreement in the fight against wage and price inflation had broken down, and the government set out on a policy of inflation control in several stages, first *without*, then *with* a special organization set-up.

Stage 1: — On November 6, 1972, the Counter Inflation Bill was introduced in Parliament by the Prime Minister, decreeing a ninety day statutory standstill on most increases in pay, prices, rents, and dividends. This "freeze" was extended later to March 31, 1973.

Stage 2 — On January 17, 1973, the next stage was inaugurated by a Bill to set up a Price Commission and a Pay Board and again to limit all increases in prices and wages from April of that year. The limits to wage and salaries increases finally fixed were 4% plus a £1 bonus. The flat "bonus" was intended as a move toward greater equality of incomes, benefiting particularly the lowest paid wage earners.

By the middle of 1973, this second stage in statutory control seemed to be succeeding. In the first six months, unemployment had fallen nearly 2.50%, and the rise in prices seemed to be slowing down. Moreover, productivity per worker took on a spurt which slowed down the increase of wage costs.

Stage 3:— By the end of 1972, however, stagflation threatened again, with Britain leading not only in price and wage rises, but also in unemployment and an adverse balance of payments. The details of Stage 3 in government policy were put before Parliament on October 8, 1973. It limited rises in wages to a basic 7% plus an addition (which the *Economist* called "fuzzy"[57]) to make a total increase of 10% to 12% plus a "threshold" agreement triggered only when the retail price index should rise by a full 7% above its October 1973 level. Many industries conformed to this pattern, but the National Union of Mineworkers demanded wage increases far beyond the statutory limit, partly because of price rises, but also because miners felt they had lost their "pecking order" rank in the contest for the highest wages since the Wilberforce award in 1972.

The other main alternative besides state control to the present system of *"laissez collectives faire"*[58] would be that of slipping back into the original policy or nonpolicy of "laissez *individuals* faire," where economic considerations reign and where the different classes of individual workers are just commodities subject to market demand and supply. Their price (i.e., wages) will rise with increasing demand (involving normally an expansion of money stock) or to a decreasing supply of available labor. If neither occurs and yet workers claim and obtain a rise in wages, less of them will be bought; that is, some will remain unemployed. Some British economists, indeed, consider unemployment the only effective sanction against such claims and advocate reduction in the money stock which, though feasible enough technically, would in all probability restrict employment to the extent of suicide for any political party.

The Use of Legislation and Legal Sanctions

The most prickly question for the future is, perhaps, that of applying legal procedure to trade union activities. To the British unions, the intervention of law and government into the conduct of their affairs is tantamount to sacrilege. Their feeling for "laissez collectives faire" is quite as strong as that of the employers for the original "laissez capitalists faire" some 150 years ago. Yet hated as it is, government intervention seems almost as necessary now as then.

The coal miners won their strike in February 1972 by a certain degree of unpeaceful picketing of some premises that were not coal workings, by many workers who were not coal miners. A union in any industry, provided it had enough pickets and sympathizers locally, could repeat the performance. Any government not supported by the trade unions is unlikely to leave the law, or absence of law, in this position; and from the Minister for Employment's replies in the House of Commons on March 2, 1972, a review was expected of the law on picketing, likely to allow and protect picketing only on a site of the pickets' own industry.

The Conservative government in 1973 got its Industrial Relations Bill on the statute book, but the Act proved a failure as far as the reduction of inflation was concerned. In the two main national strikes of 1971-72 for wages higher than those offered (the miners and the railway drivers), the employer was a nationalized public corporation. The history of the miners' strike has been told. The railwaymen, "working to rule," were ordered, according to the Act, a "cooling off" period of two weeks. When that was finished, they did not change their demands. A ballot of trade union members was then ordered, according to the Act, but this supported the railwaymen's leaders five to one. Finally, the men got a rise in wages very close to their demands, namely 15%.

CONCLUSIONS

The question has been raised in responsible quarters whether Britain was becoming ungovernable. The main cause why industrial anarchy is threatening more severely in Britain than in other industrial countries is that which I pointed to at the outset — the peculiar independence of British trade unions. The unions are independent of the government and do not concern themselves over the dangers of inflation to the whole national economy. In addition, the unions are independent of one another. The Trade Union Congress cannot, ultimately, control its individual affiliated unions. Each union has its own policy. Some, particularly those of skilled craftsmen, aim to maintain or increase the wages differential; others believe in greater equality of income. Even within a single industry, one union such as the engine drivers may strike, while another such as the National Union of Railwaymen, open to all grades, may not. But it takes a strike of only one union to hold up the whole railway system.

This is perhaps the most ominous feature of the British scene: the power of one, possibly quite small, group of workers deciding the value of its services, as judge in its own case, to hold up an entire industry and ultimately the entire national economy until its claims are met. If all sectional claims were met either in full, or even after bargaining, by the traditional part-way compromise with employers, the total is likely to add up considerably higher than the total national monetary value of the product to be distributed, unless money is lavishly printed.

The immediate question is whether the voluntary social compact between the trade unions and the government can be really made to stick and whether the unions' future wage claims are likely to be reasonable enough, in the light of the workers' relatively stagnant productivity, to leave industry with sufficient profit to permit its expansion or even its continuance. The technique of wage bargaining adopted by many of the larger unions (and the size distribution of unions is even more unequal than that of firms) is becoming quite a pattern. The unions propose some huge and economically impossible increases. Unless the employer, often a public corporation, responds with at least half that proposal, the offer is declared ridiculous. But half a proposed increase may still be impossible economically.

With the Labour party committed to full employment and no statutory restraints in the form of income boards, but largely dependent for funds upon the individual trade unions, and the Trade Union Council weakness in trying to coordinate these unions, it is hard to see how a Labour government can resist almost unlimited claims and eventually galloping inflation. Moreover, from the experience recorded earlier, it appears as though the Phillips curve breaks down, at least temporarily, when any rise in wages obtained is sudden and extreme and wipes out profit. Unemployment and stagnation will then, all too likely, combine with inflation to form a constantly renewed stagflation.

IV
THE PROCESS OF INFLATION
IN FRANCE

Joel B. Dirlam

In some respects the French inflationary experience has differed
strikingly from that of the other major Western European countries.
Most important, the French price level has risen faster over the long
run than those of its neighbors. French economists and foreign observers alike point out that inflation has become a part of the French
way of life. "A rhythm of sustained price increases is considered
more or less as normal."[1] Again, "What distinguishes the French
inflation from the inflation undergone by other developed capitalist
countries is its exceptional intensity."[2] In the sober language of the
Organization of Economic Co-operation and Development (OECD),
France is "the only large country among its members to have experienced such a large depreciation of its currency," reflected in the
exceptional number and magnitude of its devaluations. If one takes
the price deflator for gross domestic product as a measure, the
average annual rate of price increase for France was 3.5% for the
years 1958-1970 compared with an overall (weighted) average of
2.8% for Belgium, Germany, Italy, the Netherlands, Sweden, United
Kingdom, and the United States.[3]

Were it not for Max Peyrard's unsparing critique of an earlier version and the generous help
of Sylvie Bénard, Francoise Blanchon, Alexandre Combas, and Véronique Schloesing in
gathering and checking data, this chapter could not have appeared. None of these friends,
however, are responsible for, nor are they likely to be in agreement with, the views here
expressed.

Yet this inflation has been accompanied by substantial growth. Outpaced by Italy, West Germany, and Japan for the 1958-1970 period, France has pulled ahead of Germany during the past six years, both in per capita and total growth rates, while the Italian economy suffered from stagnation during 1971 and 1972.[4] Although a recession has been avoided, the French unemployment rate began to move up in 1970 and has remained at a level that has sustained it as a political issue.

One other characteristic distinguishes France from other Western countries less afflicted with inflation: she has adopted a more comprehensive array of price controls than can be found in any other nonsocialist economy.

It is not the purpose of this chapter to attempt a full-dress explanation of the origins of French inflation since World War II, if indeed an explanation of such a complex phenomenon were possible. The aim is much more limited in both time and scope. Rather, it is deemed of particular interest to examine those aspects of the French economy that may account for certain differences between the French and other inflations. It seems especially useful to examine those structural and behavioral characteristics that may have limited the vigor of competition, as well as other rigidities or domestic policies capable of being translated into upward price movements. The discussion will focus on the years 1968-1973, since it has been in this period that French inflation cannot be traced directly to excess demand originating in national budgetary deficits.

PRICE INDEXES

Before attempting to review the diverse influences that have served to give French inflation its special character, a word is in order on the statistical measures of inflation. France has no index of wholesale prices comparable in scope to the U.S. Bureau of Labor Statistics wholesale price index. The GNP deflator has interest for economists trying to determine the direction of movement of real national output. But it is only when the consumers price index advances sharply that governments are faced with the kind of unpleasant choices that have, almost uninterruptedly, plagued the French Ministry of Economy and Finances. Table I shows the yearly changes in the consumers price index from 1959 to 1973.

Table IV-I

COMPARATIVE PRICES, UNEMPLOYMENT AND GROWTH: 1959-1973

| | Consumers Price Index Yearly Change in Percentages | | Unemployment as a Percentage of Active Civilian Population | | Index of Industrial Production (excluding construction) Yearly Change in Percentages | Real GNP (French Definition) Yearly Change in Percentages |
	Paris (1)	France (2)	(French Definition) (3)	(U.S. Definition) (4)	(5)	(6)
1959	6.2	6.2	1.4	2.4	n.a.	n.a.
1960	3.6	3.6	1.3	2.2	n.a.	6.9
1961	3.3	3.1	1.1	1.9	n.a.	5.6
1962	4.8	5.0	1.2	1.9	n.a.	6.7
1963	4.9	5.8	1.4	1.9	5.0	5.4
1964	3.1	2.3	1.1	1.6	7.6	6.5
1965	2.8	2.6	1.3	1.8	2.6	4.5
1966	3.2	2.6	1.4	1.8	6.0	5.6
1967	3.1	3.1	1.8	2.3	4.0	4.9
1968	4.7	4.6	2.1	2.7	3.9	4.6
1969	6.6	6.4	1.7	2.1	12.0	7.3
1970	5.5	5.1	1.7	2.2	6.0	5.8
1971	5.7	5.5	2.2	2.7	6.3	5.3
1972	6.4	6.6	2.2	n.a.	6.5	5.4
1973	8.5	8.5	1.9	n.a.	6.3	6.0

Sources: Cols. (1) and (2): L'Expansion, February, 1971, p. 61; Conseil Economique et Social, Conjoncture Economique, Sept. 19, 1972, p. 580; I.N.S.E.E., Bulletin Mensuel de la Statistique, No. 1, 1974, pp. 34-36; No. 2, 1974, pp. 34-36.
Cols. (3) and (4): C. Sorrentino, "Unemployment in Nine Industrialized Countries," Monthly Labor Review, June, 1972, p. 30;
I.N.S.E.E., Enquête sur l'Emploi de 1972, 1973, p. 80, Enquête sur l'Emploi de 1973, 1973, p. 62.
Col. (5): Conseil Economique et Social, op. cit., pp. 499 and 536; I.N.S.E.E., Bulletin Mensuel de la Statistique, No. 2, 1974, p. 11.
Col. (6): I.N.S.E.E., Comptes de la Nation, 1973, Part 3, 1974, pp. 164-165.

The construction of the consumers price index has been changed
from time to time, the last two major revisions coming in 1963 and
1970. In order to reflect changing consumption patterns, less weight
was given in 1970 to food items, and more weight to services. In
1963, for example, food, not including restaurant meals, had a
weight of 41.8%, and services, including restaurant meals, 19.6%. In
1970, these weights were changed to 31.0% and 27.5% respectively.
The weight for manufactured products was raised from 35.6% to
41.0%. The new index is revised periodically when there are significant changes in consumption patterns, whereas the 1963 index
weights had remained unchanged until 1970.[5]

The 1963 index had come under justifiable suspicion of manipulation when the government deliberately froze the prices of certain
items so as to moderate demands for higher wages.[6] Nevertheless, it is
still alleged that the price control machinery could be focused on
certain retailers or specific products so that the new index, too,
might be biased.[7] Each of the three major trade union confedera-
tions, the C. G. T., the Force Ouvrière, and the CF. D. T., has compiled its own cost-of-living index. In disputing the accuracy of the
official index, the C. G. T., for instance, maintained that, in 1973,
rent should have been given a weight of 16.8%, rather than the 4.9%
of the official index. This difference and others accounted for the
fact that the C. G. T. cost-of-living index rose by 9.6% in 1972, while
the official index rose only 6.6%. Despite changes in weights in 1973,
the official index continued to lag behind that of the C. G. T.[8]

Until mid-1973, the manufactured goods component of the consumers price index rose less rapidly than other elements. In fact,
from 1958 through 1970, the average annual rate of increase of
manufactured products was only 3%, less than the overall annual rate
of 4.2%.[9] Thereafter, manufactured products prices leaped ahead,
and by April 1974, they were rising at an annual rate of 24%, compared with 10.5% for services and 11% for food. With this reversal in
the role of manufactured products in the consumers price index,
France was undergoing inflation in mid-1974 at a rate roughly double that of the preceding four years.[10] Table II shows the behavior of
the three major components of the consumers price index from
March 1970 to March 1974.

In France, as elsewhere, the food price component in the cost-of-
living index has tended to rise because of the greater degree of pro-
cessing and more costly packaging that accompanies supermarket

Table IV-II

CONSUMERS PRICE INDEX: MARCH, 1970 — OCTOBER 1973
(1970 Average = 100)

	Retail Food	Mfd. Products	Services	Total
Mar. 1970	98.1	99.	98.4	98.5
Dec. 1970	102.1	101.4	102.3	101.9
Mar. 1971	103.5	102.7	104.4	103.4
Dec. 1971	109.0	106.3	109.3	108.0
Mar. 1972	110.7	107.3	110.7	109.4
Dec. 1972	118.3	112.0	117.4	115.5
Mar. 1973	120.1	111.9	118.8	116.4
Dec. 1973	131.2	119.5	127.5	125.3
Mar. 1974	135.1	126.8	131.1	130.6

Sources: Conseil Economique et Social, *Conjoncture Economique au deuxième Semèstre,* 1972 Journal Officiel, Feb. 2, 1973, p. 106, and I.N.S.E.E., *Tendances de la Conjoncture,* June, 1974, p. 90.

merchandising. The rise has also been blamed, in part, on the 1969 devaluation, which brought in its train higher E.E.C. (Common Market) support prices measured in francs, and a 6.9% average annual increase in agricultural prices from 1968 to 1972, compared with a 1.5% annual increase from 1956 to 1968.[11] Because of the high priority all classes in France have placed on dining well, and because of the relatively larger proportion of food expenditures in the budgets of lower-paid workers, even a moderate percentage increase in food prices is likely to be soon followed by agitation and demonstrations for wage increases, whereas the public is more tolerant of a similar percentage increase for other items.[12]

ABSENCE OF EXCESS DEMAND 1969-1973

In 1961, a group of OECD experts concluded that inflation was caused by "very strong excess demand" originating in budget deficits of the governments of the member countries.[13] By December 1970, the experts were less sure of their ground. Nevertheless, the remedy they proposed was the adoption of "[f]irm fiscal and monetary policies," although price and incomes policies were recognized as supplemental solutions. In strong terms for an OECD document, the group suggested that ". . . governments should be prepared where necessary, to accept a temporary reduction in the rate of activity until there are signs that better price stability has been achieved."[14] By June 1971, however, an OECD working committee had given up the idea that restraints on government spending should be used to check the inflation then in progress among member countries. It concluded that no simple or constant relation could be found between rates of price increases, on the one hand, and the degree of demand pressure, rates of growth, and employment levels, on the other hand.[15]

Our examination of the French inflation since 1968 does not contradict the generalizations of the OECD working committee. Almost no evidence of excess demand appears in the national accounts. After realizing surpluses in 1969 and 1970, according to standardized national accounts concepts, the budget went only slightly into deficit in 1971, 1972, and 1973—on the order of 1% or less.[16]

It was on this account that the OECD, in trying to sum up the origins of the French inflation in 1972, found that cost elements had been more significant than demand elements. The National Institute of Statistics and Economic Studies (I.N.S.E.E.) concluded in August 1971 that "without what seems to be excessive demand, the French economy appears to be installed in inflation." More recently, I.N.S.E.E. blamed the accelerated pace of inflation in late 1973 and the early months of 1974 on rapid increases in the costs of imported fuel, food, and raw materials, as well as to inventory hedging spurred by the rising rate of inflation. These cost increases were translated, first, into prices of semifinished products, and, then, into prices of manufactured consumers goods, as shown in Table II. It seems fair to say that at least half of the annual inflationary rate attained by the middle of 1974 was attributable to a tidal wave of price increases in international markets, which France was no better equipped to hold back than any other Western country.[17]

This is not to say that opinion is unanimous in rejecting the view that the current inflation is attributable, ultimately, to excess demand. Using an approach developed at the Federal Reserve Bank of St. Louis, an economist on the staff of the Banque de France constructed a model that indicates, on the basis of certain lags, that increases in the money supply have been followed by increases in the price level.[18] And an American economist, after careful analysis, concluded that the system of government finance and credit controls has been "biased toward inflation" because, although the government has not borrowed in large amounts from the Banque de France, the preemption of the long-term market by Treasury financial institutions forces private business to resort to short-term borrowing from banks to finance long-term investments. The Banque de France, according to this view, has been unable to raise interest rates high enough to hold back an inflationary ballooning of the short-term credits and demand deposits.[19]

Another variant of the quantity of money and credit hypothesis sees the deficit in the United States balance of payments, used to finance acquisitions in Europe, as the major cause of French inflation. Although there were inflows of gold and foreign exchange amounting to over twelve billion francs in both 1970 and 1971, and seven billion francs in 1972, the trend was reversed in 1973, and France has continued to lose reserves without dampening the expansion of bank credit. Moreover, the government could have sterilized inflows by raising reserve requirements, as it did in 1971.[20]

There has been no exact correspondence between changes in the money supply and inflation. In 1969, when the money supply increased by 12.2%, the national consumers price index rose 6%. In 1972, however, the money supply expanded by 21.2% while the cost of living still increased at only 6.6%. Changes in the variables appear in Tables I and II.

It will be assumed, therefore, without more elaborate demonstration of the point that although an expansion of the money supply must have sustained the 1968-1974 inflation, the search for its origins cannot stop with the behavior of the banking system. Perhaps the matter can best be put in terms of public policy. No French government would attempt to impose a fiscal or monetary policy so as to produce a marked reduction in the rate of growth. Such a policy would immediately alienate not only the workers, but also *commerçants* (merchants) and other small businessmen who manage to survive because continued inflationary expansion creates profit margin storm shelters where they exist until their retirement. Nor would any French government permit unemployment to rise sub-

Table IV-III

MONEY STOCK AND GNP DEFLATOR IN FRANCE

Year	Money Supply in Billions of Francs* (1)	Percentage Annual Change in Money Supply (2)	GNP Deflator Percentage Annual Change (3)
1963	n.a.	n.a.	6.5
1964	179.2	n.a.	4.1
1965	197.2	10.0	2.6
1966	216.1	9.6	2.9
1967	241.6	11.8	2.9
1968	267.7	10.8	4.8
1969	300.3	12.2	7.0
1970	345.6	15.1	5.6
1971	406.3	17.6	5.6
1972	493.8	21.5	6.0
1973	567.6	14.9	7.3

*Defined as money in circulation, non bank demand deposits, and highly liquid savings, not corrected for seasonal variation. December of each year.
Source: Col. (1): Conseil Economique et Social, *Conjoncture Economique,* Journal Officiel, Sept. 19, 1972, p. 561; I.N.S.E.E., *Tendances de la Conjoncture,* Aug. 15, 1973, p. 98, January 15, 1974, p. 98.
Col. (3): I.N.S.E.E., *Comptes de la Nation, 1973, Part 3,* 1974, pp. 164-165.

stantially above the 1972 level. When credit restraints were imposed in 1969 and 1970, the rate of climb of consumer prices was reduced. But the slowdown in growth in industrial production, which fell from an annual increase of 12.0% in 1969 to 5.0% in 1971, led to fears of stagflation. The restrictions on bank lending were relaxed, and the government introduced some mildly expansionary fiscal measures. In 1972, France enjoyed the highest growth rate in Western Europe.[21] Faced in late 1973 by a 10% inflation rate, M. Valery Giscard d'Estaing, then Minister of Economy and Finances, relied on monetary policy only to the extent of moderately lowering the ceilings on bank credit expansion set for the next few months.

This conclusion is not equivalent to saying that French growth can be achieved only by inflation. Yet, growth and inflation appear to be Siamese twins. No economist has yet been able to think of a plan that would dispose of one without the other.

STRUCTURAL RIGIDITIES OF THE FRENCH ECONOMY

The structural aspects of the French economy to be analyzed here are those that appear most generally to limit supply, to impede the most productive use of resources, or to result in actual inefficiencies.

First among those handicaps has been the declining proportion of the labor force within the total population. During the postwar years, the population began to expand, reversing a previous decline. At the same time, the percentage of nonemployables rose — the young, the aged, students, and nonworking women. The share of the active population dropped overall from 48.5% of the total in 1946 to 43% in 1968, although the real numbers rose by 600,000.[22] For every 100 working Frenchmen in 1970, there were 139 who were not in the labor force, as against 111 in 1950.[23]

Secondly, France still has a relatively large agricultural sector compared with other industrialized countries such as Germany, England, and the United States. In 1969, about 15% of the active population was engaged in agriculture compared with 9.5% in Germany. In the same year, French industry (including manufacturing, mining, and construction) accounted for only 50.4% of gross national product, while in Germany the share originating in the same sectors was 56.6%).[24] Whether a relatively large, but shrinking, agricultural sector is a disadvantage cannot be easily determined. The number of persons active in agriculture fell from 7.4 million in 1946 to 3.1 million in 1968. In the course of the decline, younger agricultural workers shifted to other occupations, thus making it possible to increase output in the industrial and services sectors. In addition, agricultural production rose about 70% in the period from 1949 to 1967, reflecting an increasing efficiency on the farm.[25]

Entirely too many small holdings remain, however. Only 28% of the farms in 1967 cultivated more than 20 hectares (about 50 acres) of arable land, and the annual rate of disappearance of independent holdings was only 2.5%. In 1969, according to one estimate, there were between 250,000 and 400,000 peasants, mostly on small farms, with incomes below the official minimum wage.[26] It must be noted that France has now begun to import meat on a large scale, that domestic beef is produced under very inefficient conditions, and that productivity in the food manufacturing industries has risen less rapidly than elsewhere.

Thirdly, there is evidence to show that retail distribution in France is less efficient than it could be if it were restructured in larger units. Like agriculture, the distributive sector suffers from an excessive number of independent proprietors, but unlike agriculture, it has not benefited appreciably from adoption of new technology. Productivity in service and commerce combined rose 3.5% annually from 1959 to 1972, while productivity in industry rose 6.4%.[27]

There were six food retailers per 1000 inhabitants in France in 1968 compared with 1.5 in the United States. The average French shopkeeper had 87 customers; the average German, 123 customers. According to one informed estimate, some 200,000 retailers could have been dispensed with in 1971 without loss to the economy.[28]

This is not to deny that there have been improvements in the commercial sector. One source shows productivity in commerce rising by 5% annually in the period from 1959 to 1971.[29] Self-service food stores in 1972 accounted for about 38.8% of sales compared with 16.5% in 1967.[30] The number of supermarkets—defined as stores with a surface area of from 400 to 2500 square meters — increased at an annual rate of close to 20%[31] in the three years 1970-1972. While shopping centers and retail chains, both corporate and independent retailing associations, are present, the share of small, independent stores in all areas of distribution remains high, claiming 72.4% of the business in 1971.[32]

A fourth structural peculiarity of the French economy is that a high proportion of key decisions are made by officials in the public sector, although France is not, *en principe,* a socialist country. Government bureaucrats, or managers appointed by the government, directly determine prices, wages, purchasing, and investment for important economic sectors. The railways, electric power and gas, communications, coal, and large parts of the petroleum, airline, and aircraft industries are nationalized. In addition, the government exercises continuing control of financial markets by virtue of its ownership of the major commercial banks and insurance companies and a network of savings institutions.

In an effort to make France an influential world power as well as stronger economically, the government has used a variety of techniques to preserve, transform, or create industries in private sectors it believes to be of key importance.

Such a motive helps to explain the attempts to build a supersonic plane (with British cooperation), to create a wholly domestically owned computer industry to replace and compete with Machines Bull (currently controlled by Honeywell), to construct a nuclear power plant system based on a uniquely French technique, to accumulate vast petroleum reserves in Algeria, and to concentrate and reconstruct the steel industry. To embark on this ambitious program while renovating an antediluvian telephone system, easing the decline of the coal industry, and maintaining shipbuilding has consumed substantial savings with little immediate, and questionable future, returns.

The program for assuring France's independence in producing, refining, and marketing petroleum products, for instance, was not devised to lower the costs to the consumer. "The luxury of driving with Elf gasoline rather than Shell was at the price of billions [of francs] of investment by the State: couldn't these billions been better employed elsewhere?"[33] This question, first posed in 1969, is even more pertinent since the Algerian nationalizations.

One might inquire whether France, with an industrial labor force of about one-third that of the United States and income per capita at 60% of the United States level, can hope to establish itself competitively in so many different lines. Not enough can be spent on any single area to assure success. In 1971, for example, the state could devote only 718 million francs to national and bilateral space research and only 215 million francs to the computer project.[34] Although it is difficult to arrive at a total figure, expenditures on subsidies for all purposes save agriculture and housing reached approximately 11 billion francs, or $2.2 billion, in 1971. Over the years, of course, much larger cumulative totals could be identified as investments in questionable projects.

Fifthly, the French economy is more insulated from outside competitive pressures than other European economies. In 1969, French imports amounted to 15.7% of the GNP, and exports, 15.1%, a proportion (of foreign commerce as a percentage of total GNP) lower than all the other countries considered in an OEEC study in 1969, with the exception of the United States and Japan.[35] By 1971, French exports had climbed to 17.5% of GNP, and imports to 16.8%. The Italian percentages, on about the same level as the French in 1959, were somewhat higher in 1969: 20.5% and 18.2% respectively.

The relatively high French self-sufficiency can be attributed, in part, to the wealth and diversity of French natural resources as well as, in part, to the propensity of government bureaus to favor French products. Until recently, at least, "[t]he government firms 'buy French,' with decidedly few exceptions."[36] Thanks to the Common Market, however, Italian-made household appliances (Fanussi) invaded the French market temporarily in 1970, leaving only a handful of French firms still in production.[37] And imports of major steel products also account for 30% to 40% of the apparent domestic consumption.

Finally, there is much to indicate that French manufacturing has not only been characterized by units of production too small to achieve maximum economies of scale, but also, paradoxically, by other sectors which are excessively concentrated. In the latest study available, based on 1962 data, French manufacturing plants are shown to be smaller than their counterparts in other Common Market countries. The average number of workers per establishment was eleven in France, seventeen in Germany, and twenty-seven in Belgium and the Netherlands. In fact, 19% of French workers were employed in business establishments with less than ten employees, compared with 7% in Belgium, 8% in the Netherlands, and 13% in West Germany.[38]

A relatively small typical firm and plant size does not necessarily mean that numerous competitors regularly fight for the consumers' francs. A study by the I.N.S.E.E., again based on 1962 data, showed that of fifty-six major product groups, there were twenty-one in which the top four firms accounted for 50% or more of the shipments. "French industry, since 1962, appears to have a market structure more concentrated than American industry itself,"[39] according to Professor Maurice Parodi. Another analysis based on a finer classification, however, with 195 products, indicated a lower degree of concentration. In machine tools, cheese, and footwear, the number of French firms was quite high, rivaling or exceeding the United States numerical totals for these industries and reflecting the small size of the establishments and the artisanal methods of production.[40]

Hence, it is possible to conclude that French industry has been plagued by inefficiently small units and, at the same time, by too many concentrated markets.

LIMITATIONS ON COMPETITIVE RIVALRY

The Tradition of State Control

French acceptance of centralized control of business behavior slanted, not toward competition, but rather toward achieving a somewhat imprecisely defined goal of a stronger state can be traced as far back as the seventeenth century. De Toqueville, in his well-known work, the *Ancien Régime et la Révolution,* went to some pains to show how the representatives of the monarchy reviewed the details of local expenditure.[41] This tradition was so firmly impressed on the nation that the Revolution and subsequent restorations did little to change it. As has been aptly said, "Save for a momentary aberration from about 1860 to about 1880, France has always been, as it was in 1700, true in the main to the tradition of Colbert."[42]

Following this tradition, government policy has encouraged concentration, particularly in steel, electrical machinery, aircraft, and computers, and has not intervened to prevent mergers producing sharp increases in concentration in chemicals. In response, there has been a steady pace of mergers among French firms, including a few that have created companies of international importance, such as the 1971 union of Ugine-Kuhlman and Pechiney which turned an aluminum duopoly into a monopoly; the 1969 mergers resulting in Rhone-Poulenc, the fifth-ranking European chemical firm; and the 1972 union of B.S.N. and Gervais-Danone, now the fourth largest European food manufacturer. Although B.S.N. was unsuccessful in taking over St. Gobain in 1968, it was not because of government opposition. Under government pressure, the electrical machinery industry was restructured in 1970 to divide important markets between Compagnie Générale d'Electricité and Thompson-Brandt, the leaders in the field. There seems to have been little or no concern for the possible detrimental effects on competition within France which might result from the domination of a market by one of two individual firms.

But there are strong and highly placed advocates of competition in France. Otherwise the law would not have been strengthened to condemn such single firm, anticompetitive practices, and France would never have joined the Common Market in 1951. The Commissariat du Plan was one of the institutions supporting the latter move. And yet, uncritically equating size with efficiency, the 5th Plan for Economic Development (1966) called for the creation of giant firms capable of holding their own, not only in the Common Market, but worldwide. An interministerial committee was set up in May 1970 to see that concentration would proceed in electrical, textile, and other industries. Again the effect of such policy on competition within France was not considered.

Equally important, the very process of planning is dependent upon, or at least encourages, the cooperation of professional and trade associations that bring together business executives and planning officials in an atmosphere not usually favorable to innovative development or aggressive competition. Although published under a *nom de plume*, the conclusions of one economist have the ring of truth, indicating personal participation in the process:

> The Plan . . . has been often the scene of *ententes* and coalitions. The procedure assembles, in the same enclosure, the producers on the one hand and the *fonctionnaires* [employees of the ministries] on the other. The first have seen very quickly the benefit they can derive from a certain coordination of investments and production, permitting the development of their respective markets without price warfare and without objectionable cartels. The *fonctionnaires* have not succeeded in sufficiently stimulating conflicts among the various business interests to extract concessions. Instead, they have aimed at a conciliation by simply adding to the money supply.[43]

Thus, an official in the Commissariat du Plan has been quoted as telling members of an industry that he would refuse to plead their cause with the Price Control Office until they gave up price cutting.[44]

An elite corps of administrators, graduates of the Ecole Polytechnique or the Ecole National d'Administration, moves from top government posts to presidencies in nationalized and leading private firms and back again by a process known as *pantouflage*.[45] Most of this group share the convictions of one of the ablest, Lionel Stoleru, that the state must act to give direction to key areas in the economy because private firms lack the necessary insight, imagination, and vigor. It is possible that he is right, but deficiencies may just as likely result from the state maintaining its dominating role.[46] According to two management experts from Harvard Business School, "this cycle of professional training for top management has remarkably little relevance for a career in industry, except in the matter of making one's way when doing business with the State, and hence in negotiating with former colleagues in the civil service." [47]

Even when firms remain independent, traditions of live and let live, official obstacles to the entry of new firms (which the French refer to as "Malthusianism"), the enforced cooperation that has been required by earlier plans, and the role of trade associations in enforcement of price controls, have combined to create an atmosphere inimical to vigorous competition. Businessmen have become accustomed to having government officials, whether from the Commissariat du Plan, the Fonds de Développement Economique et Social, or the *tutelle* (a supervisory ministry), wield strategic power in setting prices, providing funds for investment, and making subsidies and other favors available.

Anticompetitive Practices of Government and Business

Many of the prevailing practices of the business and professional community are not conducive to vigorous and active competition. Prices of consumer goods are rarely competitively advertised. Continuous pressure is required to force shopkeepers to obey regulations requiring that prices be displayed. Fiscal (tax) fraud also impedes the effectiveness of competition, a practice that is acknowledged to be widespread among hotels and smaller wholesalers and retailers (particularly in fruits and vegetables, furniture, construction materials, footwear, and women's dresses). The failure of these smaller firms to pay their full tax burden (on profits as well as "value-added") permits the survival of marginal, inefficient firms. Their large and modern competitors who use standard and mechanized accounting systems cannot so easily evade taxes. [48]

Along with the "liberal" tradition which has proved sufficiently strong to provide private financing for an expansion of the telephone system and for private companies to build and operate (for profit) large segments of the French superhighway system, there persists an equally powerful philosophy and apparatus of protectionism. Summarized in the Armand-Rueff report to the National Assembly in 1960 and recapitulated in the report of the Committee on Competition of the 6th Plan, it embraces such regulations as the prohibition of bazaar trucks and single-price stores, adopted in 1936 and not repealed until 1960; the departmental prefects' power, conveyed as late as 1970, to prevent the opening of supermarkets; the commercial lessee's legally enforced right to the value of his clientele's patronage, which prevents a free market in retail shopping locations*; and the numerous state-enforced licensing restrictions (not a policy unique to France) designed to limit individual entry into the trades and professions. The strength of anticompetitive tradition was demonstrated by the adoption of the "Loi Royer," in 1973, which established local option for the expansion of chain stores." [49]

Influence of the investment banks, although not easily identifiable in specific circumstances, has been thought to have been be exerted to prevent disturbance of the status quo. Through their directorships — the Banque de Paris et des Pays-Bas has substantial holdings in over 200 firms, and the Banque d'Indo-Chine, an equivalent number of directorships — the investment banks are said to be the "orchestra leader" of the private sector. [50] Interlocking shareholdings are particularly numerous among leading firms in both the chemical and steel industries. [51]

Aggressive price competition in the provision of electronic equipment to the single most important customer, the Ministry of Postal, Telegraph, and Telephone Service, has been choked off. The Ministry has tried to preserve and encourage competitors of the ITT French subsidiary by assigning them quotas — with the result that prices appear to be about 20% above the world level for comparable equipment.

> "The division of orders among the five companies [making telephone switching equipment] was made up to 1970 according to a regime of extremely rigid yearly quotas; each company had the right to a certain percentage of the business. The price of each element had been calculated in 1961 and was reevaluated each year thereafter by a formula that took into account the increase in wages and supplies (including some discounts based on the quantity of sales). This rigid system was not displaced by competition. It was refashioned in 1970 by introducing a little competitiveness among the suppliers. The quotas were adjusted each year; a new price schedule brought down prices by 17% and strongly reduced the importance of annual price revisions . . . . The same concepts rule the relations between the administration and the suppliers of transmission equip-

---

*an unusual practice which provides for compensation to a merchant for the value of his clients' regular patronage in an established business location.

ment . . . . Here again, the price of each component, fixed at the time of the first orders, follows the evolution of wages and supplies cost according to a formula fixed in advance. What is more, each supplier obtains a fixed quota from the administration. . . . The administration rarely opens its notices of bids to outsiders. . . ."[52]

Weakness of Antimonopoly Legislation

Public policy toward overt anticompetitive behavior is ambivalent. Resale price maintenance, contracts with tie-in restrictions, refusals to sell, discriminatory practices, and retail sales below direct costs are illegal in most circumstances under decrees adopted in 1963, 1967, and 1969. Manufacturers do have, however, the protection of a "fair trade" policy and are not obliged to sell to retailers who employ their trademarked products as "loss leaders." Exclusive dealing can be permitted where the Ministry of Economy believes it necessary to protect the product quality.[53]

The Technical Commission on Ententes, functioning within the Ministry of Economy and Finances, has the authority to proceed against anticompetitive practices of cartels under an *ordonnance* with standards derived from Article 85 of the Rome treaty. It has been moderately active, having issued eighty-six findings between its inception in 1953 and June 1971.[54]

But a meticulous examination of its decisions through June 1971 shows not only that the Commission on Ententes has all too frequently excused restrictive practices because they could be viewed as promoting technical improvements; but also that in most instances its adverse decisions have had no effect because the Minister of Economy and Finances has failed to take action against the offending cartel. Moreover, the commission must certainly have permitted many pricing agreements to escape scrutiny. "The small number of its [the commission's] employees responsible for [regulation] of competition will not allow investigations of all the agreements of which there is knowledge, or of detection of secret agreements, or control in a satisfactory way of the behavior of those agreements examined."[55]

In April 1971, for example, a report of the Commission on Ententes disclosed that sugar refiners were operating a pool to dispose of surplus refined sugar by denaturing it. The Director of price control served notice on the eleven firms concerned that he would not tolerate the continuance of such practices. The Minister of Economy and Finances did not, however, refer the report to the courts for possible criminal action. Nor again in 1973, when it was disclosed that the major oil companies had conspired to share markets, including sales to government authorities, and to put independent distributors out of business, did the government take the case to court. [56]

Strengthening the Law

Both the scope of the statutes and regulations protecting competition and the enforcement of the law leave much to be desired. A report of the Committee on Competition of the 6th Plan (1970) recommended that the powers of the Commission on Ententes be extended to permit it to move, not only to check against restrictive practices of trade associations, but also to take effective action against anticompetitive behavior of specific firms. The committee recognized that there were many areas of manufacturing, commerce, and services which were only lightly touched by the forces of competition. [57]

The committee report acknowledged that no French statute controls mergers, forbids monopolies, or checks the concentration of economic power. And yet, even though the committee recognized this policy gap, it did not propose that the Commission on Ententes be given the statutory power to move directly against *structural* concentration. It proposed, instead, another study of the problem.

The view that French industry prefers to be noncompetitive, if left to itself, finds ministerial expression in a disposition to view imports as the most important, if not the only, disturbing influence in the market. The econometric model of the French economy, known as *Fifi*, used in forecasting the effects of the 6th Plan, assumes that those industries that do not extensively export or which are not faced by imports can, in effect, set their prices without regulation. They are characterized as "sheltered," in contrast with the "exposed" sectors which face foreign competition. [58]

Unfortunately, the French have not developed pricing data which would permit a comparison of the behavior of the more highly cartelized or collusive sectors of their economy with the more competitive sectors. [59] Even so, the summary report of the Commissarist du Plan on the general economy and financing draws certain broad conclusions about the influence of market control on prices.

> The cost inflation that can be seen is fed not only in the so-called sheltered section but also in certain branches of industry which have a sufficient

control of their prices to be able to reflect increases in their costs. Besides, the distinction between activities subject to international competition and protected activities encounters great difficulties, and only serves awkwardly as a criterion for action since the two types are closely interlocked. Even for some products subject to international competition, the procedure of price formation can escape the free play of market forces, because of dominant positions or concerted practices.[60]

It is significant that even after calling attention to the widespread imperfections of the market, including the serious weaknesses of the Commission on Ententes, the Committee on Competition of the 6th Plan rejected the establishment of an independent agency that would be charged with enforcement of competition. This would have represented too sharp a break with prevailing attitudes. The "policy of competition must be considered as an instrument of general economic policy, and the enforcement agency will have a *consultative* function, the final decision always being left to the authority responsible for choices of economic policy." A critic of the current feeble policy has, with some justification, concluded that "the idea of competition is . . . new in a society which for centuries defined itself by the preservation and conservation of social and economic equilibrium, by organizations, and by controls."[62]

PRICE CONTROLS

Early Years

The French techniques of price control have evolved in response to the changing character of the inflation. A general freeze or *blocage* has been used primarily to cope with a rapid and substantial price rise resulting from excess demand or from devaluation.

Thus, the *ordonnance* of June 20, 1945 froze all prices at the September 1, 1939 level, or at any higher level they might have reached subsequently as a result of offical decisions. All subsequent forms of price control take their authority from this 1945 administrative *ordonnance* which has never been submitted as a bill to the Parlement. To implement the *ordonnance* of 1945, some 26,000 *arrêtés*, or regulations, were issued through September 1971, and as long as these remain in effect, the freeze is legally the rule, while pricing freedom is the exception.[63] Each *blocage* is succeeded, after a few months, by *dérogations*, or exceptions, allowing increases under various pretexts so that the price level continues to move up. In recent years, the Price Control Office has not availed itself of the technique of a general freeze; indeed, the procedure has been disavowed by the Minister of Economy and Finances.

Prior to 1965, some five major categories of price control techniques could be distinguished, in descending order of severity, between freeze and complete liberty: (1) Direct price fixing, sometimes on the basis of an examination of the accounts of key firms. Prices of services of nationalized firms, such as railways, electric and gas distribution, and some agricultural products, including milk, sugar, and flour, have been fixed by decree. (2) Structured prices (*cadre de prix*) under which firms can set prices, but only by following strict rules. Prices for products made to order, for instance, have to follow precise directives. (3) Setting distribution profit margins in percentages or in absolute amounts. The prices of butter, potatoes, sugar, and rice, for example, have carried absolute margins, while to the invoice costs of chocolate and pharmaceutical specialties, percentage margins have been applied. (4) Controlled pricing freedom, under which the producer must file a proposed increase with the Director General of prices who has the option, within a time limit (usually a month), of refusing to let the increase go into effect, pending justification. A great many industrial products have fallen into this category. (5) Supervised pricing freedom, when price information has to be made available to the Director General who can, if he finds the freedom abused, impose some other form of control. In 1964, the prices of bread, margarine, aluminum, tires, and organic chemicals were included in this category.[64]

The Contrats de Programme

In 1966, price control procedures and the implementation of the 5th Plan were linked by the *Contrats de Programme,* a novel institution which in revised form has replaced most of the earlier mechanisms. Originating in the *Contrats de Stabilité* which were introduced in 1965 to provide some relief from the general freeze of 1963, these *Contrats de Programme* are negotiated between the Ministry of Economy and Finances and the trade associations. With a few exceptions, individual firms have participated only by subscribing to the agreement. As a reward, businesses are relieved of direct supervision by the Price Control Office and enjoy a *liberté contractuelle.*[65]

In their original form, the *Contrats de Programme* obligated the trade associations and their members to contribute to the realization of the 5th Plan and subsequent plans. Their commitment was to the broad objectives set for output, foreign trade, research, and productivity.

Under the agreements (details of which have never been made public), there were apparently no formal commitments to any particular level or schedule of prices. The firms' behavior was, however, reviewed from time to time.

> In the past the procedure provided for one or two meetings a year between the representatives of the government and those of the industries. These meetings were confined to a simple exchange of information along lines such as: 'How are things going in your sector? — We have to raise our wages by X percent, which obviously has led to a price increase of Y percent. In the future we don't foresee anything abnormal.' Things would be left there with those lines that were subject to international competition.
>
> With other industries, those composed of superannuated firms, without dynanism, or not subject to competition, the contrats de programme amounted to a half-freeze . . . . [66]

The liberty won by adherence to the *contracts* was short-lived. After the general strike of May 1968 and the wage concessions which directly followed (known as the Grenelle settlement), the government set a 3% limit on price increases for the second half of 1968. In November 1968, the Director General for prices tightened the rules of the 3% limit. At the same time, however, he extended to the commercial and service sectors an option similar to the *Contrats de Programme* in the form of so-called *conventions*. But in August 1969, as a result of devaluation, the government froze all prices at the level of August 8. The freeze lasted until September when, in still another step which *Le Monde* called "eight years of a hesitation-waltz between liberty and control," the government ordered all firms to return to the practice of filing new prices with the administration. In this "controlled pricing freedom," exceptions were allowed for increases in raw materials costs. The rule of prefiling was again relaxed in February 1970 and was supposed to be abolished by September 1971.[67] The business community, however, was not completely happy with the procedures developed under the prefiling requirements. Publishers, for example, have found it unprofitable to reprint books because prices cannot be raised to cover higher material and labor costs.

Increases in the costs of energy, transport, or local taxes were not automatically accepted as justification for higher prices. Instead, the Price Office tried to persuade industrialists that they could initiate increases in productivity to offset increased external costs.[68]

The Anti-Hausse Contracts

In any event, the promised freedom was again postponed in September 1971. Monthly increases in the consumers price index in Paris had exceeded 7% (annual rate) in February, April, May, September, and October of 1971. Reacting swiftly, the Minister of Economy and Finances, M. Giscard d'Estaing, wrote directly to the head of of the French Employers' Association and proposed, as a more agreeable procedure than a general freeze, that the association, its branches, and its individual members subscribe to *anti-hausse* (anti-price increase) contracts to remain in effect for six months. The signers were obliged to restrict their price increases to an average of no more than 1.5% in order to achieve an annual rate of increase limited to 3%. Within a month, four hundred meetings took place, and by the 30th of October, seventy-three amendments to existing *Contrats de Programme* had been signed; and thirty more were being negotiated. Almost all of the then existing 110 *Contrats de Programme* were adjusted with minor differences. The chemical industry agreement, for instance, provided for less than a 1.5% upward average adjustment.[69]

In its turn, the government agreed not to raise any of the prices of public services during the six-month period. In addition, profit margins on the distribution of manufactured products were not to be changed, and retail food prices were frozen in November 1971.

At the expiration of the amendments in March 1972, the Ministry removed all price controls for producers with less than 20 employees. Prices of luxury products, moreover, such as TV sets, records, and liquors were left to free market forces. In a striking innovation, the Minister declared that industries which were subject to effective competition would also be relieved of price controls. To illustrate his approach, some fifty-four industries were arranged according to the importance of their exports or competitive imports. To qualify, both exports and imports had to reach at least 25% of domestic production. The Commission on Ententes was to remain on the alert to review the selling behavior and competitive status of exempted industries. The balance of the firms were asked to subscribe and remained governed by a new set of agreements.[70] Under these rules, for instance, on June 15, 1972, " . . . after 27 years of *blocage* and *programmation . . . ,*" organic chemicals and machinery (except for some metal fabricated products) were given pricing freedom.[71]

The agreements which the trade associations again dutifully signed were to expire on April 1, 1973. They combined features of both the *Contrats de Programme* and the *anti-hausse* contracts. That is, the firms were free to set prices as they pleased (whereas if they failed to participate they were required to file all price increases which would then be subject to possible disapproval), with the proviso that the average increases were not to exceed 3% on an annual basis. In reviewing the price changes, the government intended to press for a relative price reduction on the part of those industries that realized more than the average gain in productivity, while those industries that were not so advantaged would be allowed a slightly higher average price increase.

In June 1972, the Finance Minister expressed satisfaction with the performance of the economy under the *anti-hausse* contracts as well as confidence that inflation would be checked under the agreements.[72] Over two hundred such agreements had been approved by the middle of October 1972, and penalties for violations had begun to be publicized.

Sharp price increases in the fall of 1972, however, approaching 7% on an annual basis, threatened to upset the timetable for greater realization of controls. Loath to give up his long-range plan, Giscard d'Estaing, in December 1972, launched a package of fiscal devices which included borrowing from individuals on a bond tied to the value of gold and a reduction in the "value added tax" paid by consumers of beef and *patisserie*. The Minister also pleaded with manufacturers to take no more than a 4% increase in prices in 1973 and appealed to workers to press for no more than a 7% wage increase.

In 1973, price increases of public services were held to a 4.4% average, and the *anti-hausse* contracts continued in force. The Finance Minister announced in November they would be applied with "increased rigor." But this was not sufficient to cope with the accelerated rate of inflation in the last half of the year. Absolute profit margins were therefore established for meat and vegetables. Prices of various breads not previously controlled were fixed to prevent bakers from shifting their product mix away from that price-controlled favorite, the *baguette*. Noting that competition in international markets had evaporated, the Minister announced that all industrial products were once again to be subject to *anti-hausse* contracts, except for those firms with less than twenty employees.[73]

Inflationary Bias of Price Controls

One almost despairs of reducing the complexities of the French price control system to an orderly outline. In summarizing the price control systems of the members of the European Economic Community as of June 1966, an official research report devoted nineteen pages to France, more than was needed for the five other countries combined.[74] By 1971, French price controls had been operative for twenty-seven years with only seven months of freedom.[75]

And as an illustration of the administrative jungle, it suffices to look at the retail price regulation adopted in November 1973. Consisting of three closely printed pages plus appendices, and requiring the integration of wholesale prices, transport cost, value added taxes, and retail margins developed by a weighted average and broken down into quality groups, its computation and enforcement must surely present difficult problems at the retail level.

Even under the *Contrats de Programme,* most industrialists have been required to justify price increases by cost changes under fairly close administrative supervision. It seems fair to conclude that French industry has come to associate cost increases with perhaps delayed, but nevertheless inevitable, price increases. Moreover, in spite of the efforts of the Director of Price Control, the system of price control downgrades the entrepreneurial role of increasing productivity or introducing innovations to offset costs.[76] The price control office reviews product costs, which means those of the least efficient firms, to avoid being accused of "killing" a marginal enterprise. The price control mechanism works in one direction only: those factors that might decrease unit cost and justify a reduction are not revealed to the price control office. The existence of a *blocage,* even though it limits maximum prices, is infused with an aura and establishes a price level that makes it more difficult for consumers to bargain for lower prices.

In still another way, pervasive and prolonged price controls are likely to introduce rigidities or upward biases into the price structure. On the whole, the *Contrats de Programme* have been shaped through agreements with trade associations in an atmosphere where discussion of price policy and cost behavior among competitors is the order of the day. The procedure has been characterized as follows:

> The heads of businesses have acquired an inflationary mentality, and are uncomfortable when placed in a situation where they are responsible for new prices . . . . Many of them explain 'We manufacturers of a given product get together, under the aegis of our trade association, and decide on what order of magnitude we want for an increase. Then we file individual requests plus a collective file for the association. The individual requests have materials that the firms don't want their competitors to see.[77]

In the cogent summary of one French economist, "Historically, there has never been complete pricing freedom in France, in a country where prices are fixed by discussion between the administration [government] and the business firms."[78]

Through more than two decades of bureaucratic control, the price control apparatus has accustomed manufactures to avoid price reductions and induced retailers, on the other hand, to translate invoice and wage cost changes into more than equivalent margin increases. Prolonged price controls tend not only to rigidify pricing structures and practices, but to give them an upward thrust. The pricing distortion has been alleged to have encouraged investment in service industries which can more easily translate rising costs into rising prices at the expense of manufacturing and other basic industries, thus limiting the possibility of increased productivity.[79]

WAGE BEHAVIOR

There is no question that when average wage increases exceed average productivity gains, prices must advance if other claims (by stockholders, creditors, etc.) are to be met. In France, particularly since 1967, these conditions have prevailed. There is, in fact, some evidence to show that prices have risen less rapidly in industries where productivity has shown the greatest improvement.[80] But the method by which the potentially inflationary wage advance takes place has not been fully explored. In assessing the relative influence of unions, of labor market tensions, of wage policy, and of governmental influence on wage behavior, the approach has to be qualitative. Econometric studies demonstrating that wage changes do indeed

Chart IV-I

REAL AND MONEY WAGES IN FRANCE

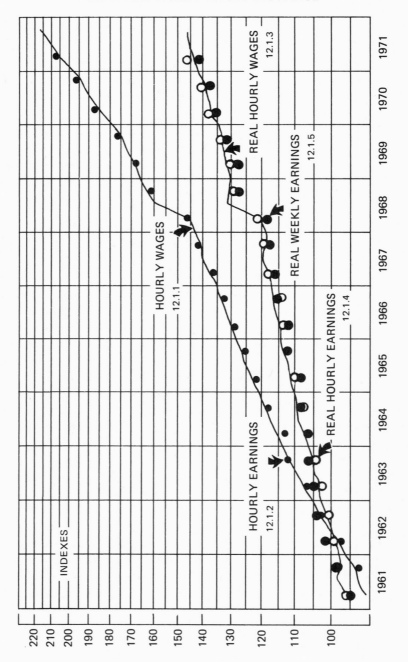

affect prices, and that price changes, while lagging, influence wages seem to restate the obvious in more or less complicated ways.[81] They do little to help us understand how the changing standards for cost-of-living adjustments in contracts involving nationalized industries influence wages in the private sector, or the degree to which upward movement of the official minimum wage is reflected in changes in pay scales and bonuses, or what determines the relative earnings of production workers and supervisors.

The actual wages are not easily available in terms of rates for particular jobs or industries. Wage scales appear in the scores of *conventions* (agreements) signed by the Ministry of Labor, industry, and unions. The lowest contractual wages are usually set forth as a percentage of the minimum guaranteed wage which is itself subject to periodic revision. Yet the scales are only a base; the rates received includes *primes*, or supplements, that are not published in the contract. Professor Helmut Arndt has found in Germany that business recession or a slackening of demand in certain industries can lead to a decline in wage rates; but this observer has been unable to find any instance of such a reduction of *primes* occurring in any French industry. And French economists do not believe such reductions take place. Chart I shows that changes in basic hourly wage rates and hourly earnings have followed almost perfectly in step. Only a slight deviation in 1964 suggests that the primes may have been cut.

There can be little disagreement with the "many academic and foreign observers" who assign a very minor role to French union bargaining pressure in producing wage increases.[82] On the other hand, the government, because of its position as the single most important employer, strongly influences wage movements. But political pressures count much more than conventional bargaining — pressures ranging from the month-long general strike in 1968 to the endemic work stoppages, marches, and meetings at *La Mutualité*.

Whatever the cause, French wage rates have risen rapidly in the past five years, first with government support at the time of the Grenelle settlement, and subsequently, in spite of the government's opposition. The average increases of hourly wage rates of more than 10% have been well in excess of the annual increase in productivity, which is approximately 5.5% as indicated by Table IV.

Direct government influence on wages has been manifested in four ways: the state can first of all intervene in a serious emergency to

Table IV-IV

ANNUAL PERCENTAGE CHANGE IN WAGE RATES AND PRODUCTIVITY
IN FRANCE, 1965-1973

Year	Wage Rates (1)	Productivity (2)
1965	6.0	4.4
1966	6.0	5.0
1967	5.8	4.6
1968	11.8	7.5
1969	10.5	3.6
1970	10.6	5.0
1971	10.7	6.1
1972	12.2	6.3
1973	15.9	5.1

*Defined as gross value added, divided by number of hours worked.
Source: Col. (1): Conseil Economique et Social, *Conjoncture Economique au deuxième semèstre, 1971*, p. 102; I.N.S.E.E., *Tendances de la Conjoncture*, March 15, 1972, p. 96; June 15, 1973, p. 96; March 15, 1974, p. 96.
Col. (2): I.N.S.E.E., *Rapports sur les Comptes de la Nation, 1969, Part 2*, 1970, p. 51; *Rapports sur les Comptes de la Nation, 1973, Part 2*, 1974, p. 59.

impose broad policy decisions on private parties. In 1958, for example, to check a serious price rise, cost-of-living adjustments were
stricken from all wage contracts. And following the general strike
and rebellion of 1968, the government participated in the Grenelle
settlement under which hourly rates rose by an average of 15.3%
between March 1968 and March 1969. Secondly, the government
sets the wages of its *fonctionnaires* (government employees, including teachers). Their wages usually lag behind those of employees
of private industry since the government tries to impose a kind of
tacit, but unofficial, incomes policy in that sector where it has direct
control. Thirdly, in nationalized industries such as the railways or the
automobile manufacturer, Renault, labor contracts can embody policies regarded as desirable and which the government hopes will be
adopted generally. It is indicative of the relative success of government policy that gross wage and salary payments in all nationalized

enterprises, including the post office, telephone and telegraph, increased only 9.9% in 1969 compared with 16.0% in private industry. The wage agreements negotiated in January and February 1971 with workers of the French National Railways, electrical and gas workers, coal miners, and the Renault autoworkers all incorporated a form of cost-of-living adjustment — thus reversing the position adopted in 1958 — based on a belief that such a clause would moderate demands for immediate wage increases. Finally, the government determines the magnitude of changes in the minimum wage which, directly, affects 700,000 workers, and, indirectly, several million more whose pay is linked to changes in the official minimum.

In an effort to improve productivity and the atmosphere of labor-management relations, the government has taken the lead in negotiating *Contrats de Progrès* in state-controlled enterprises. These provide not only for increases in real wages over the life of the contract, but also incentives to raise productivity. But the future of these agreements is cloudy. Up until now, such contracts have not been wholly successful in preventing strikes to obtain added concessions. The cost-of-living adjustments apparently have not sufficiently protected workers in times of rapid inflation.

Wage structure and income distribution in France have continued to provoke widespread and deep-rooted resentment. French production workers have been paid substantially less, and their wages have tended to rise less rapidly than the salaries of foremen, technicians, and supervisory employees. Studies have shown that while the semi-skilled or unskilled French factory worker is paid lower wages than his German counterpart, the French upper echelons have been paid more in absolute terms. While official statistics show average hourly earnings of production workers rising somewhat more rapidly than monthly salaries of higher level employees in the years 1968—1970, grave inequalities still exist. According to one estimate, the average management employee in France is paid 5.5 times as much as the semiskilled or unskilled production worker compared with a ratio of 2.4 in the United States.[83] One must, of course, take into account the government "family allowances" (based upon the number of children in a household), but these have declined as a proportion of net wage and salary income, from 10% in 1959 to 8% in 1971.[84]

About 20% of French households have been classified as poor, meaning that, with allowances, their incomes are at best no more

than enough to cover bare necessities of food, lodging, and clothing
(less than 4,000 francs —$800— annually in 1962).[85] Given the wage
inequities, the hundreds of thousands of workers receiving only the
minimum wage (about 44¢ an hour in January 1965) and the millions of households close to the poverty line, the psychological foundation was created for the 1968 rebellion. Since this upheaval, as
both private and public employers have become more responsive to
demands for higher wages, the annual rate of wage increase has approximately doubled.

Nevertheless, the wage earners' share in national income had not
moved above the 1965 level of 62.5% by 1971. This presents an
interesting contrast with the United States where, as the inflation
took hold in 1965-1971, corporate profits dropped by 4.0% as a
share (percentage) of national income, and the share of wages and
salaries rose by 3.9%.

Wages and Inflation

But it would be myopic to attribute the post-1968 inflation exclusively, or even predominantly, to wage behavior. "Responsibility"
for a cost-push, or more precisely, a "constant shares" inflation must
rest with all segments of the economic community. Only if those
with above-average incomes accept a permanent downward shift
in relative income (and a relatively decreased standard of living)
would it be possible to improve the lot of the poorest while maintaining price stability. But nothing in the data available up to now
shows that such a redistribution has been achieved in France, either
among workers or between workers and other classes of claimants on
national income. To fully explain the inflationary process, one must
therefore take into account the generation of all types of income (as
well as payments to the state), since changes that leave certain groups
worse off than before will result in political or economic efforts by
those groups affected to regain their relative shares of income.
In a complex society where strategic decisions, particularly price
decisions, can be made only subject to the application of certain
bureaucratic restraints — such as price controls — the mechanism
does not respond instantaneously. In his analysis, Professor J.P.
Mockers has shown how the nonwage variables, including taxes, have
been as powerful as wages in creating inflation.[86] That the improvement in real earnings which has taken place since the Grenelle settle-

ment has been no more than roughly equivalent to the increase in real output demonstrates the underlying correctness of his thesis.

Unemployment

In attempting to check inflation, the French authorities have become troubled by the slowly rising total unemployment in the years 1970-1973. An economist for the Economic and Social Council put the problem succinctly in a report published in September 1972: "On the one hand it is necessary to slow down the price push, on the other hand, it would be desirable to reach the rate of growth of the 6th Plan in order to balance employment; but then wouldn't industrial prices resume their forward march in spite of [the] current controls?"[87]

Unfortunately, reliable data on unemployment are available only after the I.N.S.E.E. processes a yearly area sample. In between the I.N.S.E.E. surveys, one must make do with incomplete data — monthly totals of registered unemployed, lists of job offers, and the number of persons receiving unemployment compensation. The first two series of statistics are influenced by the availability of national employment agencies which are increasing in number, but which are still not sufficiently numerous to serve all persons looking for work. Hence, inferences from the trends in registered unemployed and job offers filled necessarily remain speculative.

The level of registered, unsatisfied demands for employment, corrected for seasonal variation, was 70% higher in December 1971 than in January 1970, stabilized in 1972, and rose slightly in 1973. According to the best estimates, the number of unemployed (defined as those without jobs, but able and willing to work) stabilized in 1972 at about 450,000.[88]

An analysis of the character of unemployment has led French economists to conclude that much is traceable to structural causes. Geographical immobility has been partially responsible. But with perhaps 1.5 to 2 million foreign workers in the labor force,[89] a high rate of unemployment among women and young persons could be taken as evidence of their unsuitability for, or unwillingness to accept, employment lines customarily using foreign workers: construction, mining, domestic service, and other jobs which are considered unpleasant, boring, insecure, demeaning, or that require inconvenient working hours. In trades requiring a fairly rigorous apprenticeship, such as metal working, there have been many more job openings than available workers. These discrepancies led the I.N.S.E.E. to remark in August 1971 that " . . . one can speak of an increase of unemployment, and of overemployment [coincidentally] ."[90] There was one job offer for each skilled worker seeking work, but only one job offer for every two semiskilled workers, and only one job offer for every four unskilled workers registered for work. The development of the industrial complex at Fos (near Marseille), which had been thought to be an area of labor surplus when the location was chosen, has been seriously delayed because of a shortage of skilled construction workers.

A commonly-held thesis is that the presence of large numbers of foreign workers constitutes a cushion or buffer against unemployment. If unemployment rises to serious levels, it is argued, then foreign workers can always be sent home, thus providing jobs for French nationals. The French experience suggests, however, that the flows are not as easily manipulated as the thesis would suggest, partly because French and foreign workers are far from being close substitutes. The Algerian, Portuguese, Spanish, and Yugoslav immigrants could be replaced, perhaps, by unemployed French workers, but only in rather extraordinary circumstances.

This suggests that a more realistic estimate of unemployment might be derived by deducting, in the statistics, foreign workers from the total labor force. Then, the unemployment rate in 1971 might have been as high as 2.7%, compared with 2.2%. Or, using the U. S. Bureau of Labor Statistics definition, it would have risen from 2.7% to 3.2%. These rates are not high by American standards, but French expectations are different.

In fact, it is difficult to imagine the circumstances in which many foreigners would be completely replaced by French workers. Expelling the foreign workers would reduce output and raise costs. Yet, the longer they remain in France, the more likely it is that they will insist on wage levels equivalent to those of French nationals, producing, in turn, another potential inflationary pressure.

CONCLUSIONS

France has managed at one and the same time to suffer from a more than average rate of inflation and to enjoy almost uninterrupted economic growth. Both these trends have been maintained along with comprehensive price controls and a highly centralized economy. Yet, in other respects, the French inflation bears more than a superficial resemblance to the cost-push variety that has plagued other European countries and the United States in recent years. Wages have climbed faster than productivity, and until October 1973, service prices rose faster than the prices of manufactured goods. In effect, all sectors of the economy have tried to maintain their proportionate share of national income and have therefore contributed to an overall inflationary pressure.

If given the choice between growth and price stability, the French will clearly opt for growth. Only rarely, and in moderation, has the government used restrictive monetary and fiscal policies. In fact, the government, on occasion, attempts to reduce prices by cutting indirect taxes and hesitates to raise interest rates too far. While Minister of Economy and Finances, Giscard d'Estaing, voicing a position that would be supported also by much of the left opposition, argued that as long as housing, hospitals, and prisons require improvement, France should not be satisfied with zero growth as a counter-inflationary measure.[91] It is unfortunate, however, that a large part of the recent growth has been diverted from these worthy aims into expenditures on superhighways, seaside and alpine condominiums, and the *force de frappe*. While not purely wasteful, they are certainly of marginal benefit and have substantial external social costs.

Should one then conclude that, contrary to the customary teachings of economic analysis, the French have managed to outperform their rivals in expanding real output because of their legacy of protective centralism, their outmoded distribution system, and their proclivity for diverting governmental resources to prestigious and wasteful projects? To a degree, the paradox makes sense. It is just because the French economy, through the centuries, has come to harbor so many institutional inefficiencies that their elimination can contribute substantially to economic progress and still provide a surplus for the projects like the *Concorde*. One must give credit to the educational system and life style that have infused the French worker and businessman with a sufficient degree of independence and disposition to innovate to offset the suffocating pressures of the all-pervasive bureaucracy.

At the same time, Common Market competition has emerged to combat and, in some industries, eventually put an end to the "Malthusianism" that flourished as long as the French market was isolated. Inefficient small farms are disappearing, freeing young people for other occupations. The steel and, to a lesser extent, the textile industries have been renovated into modern, optimum-size plants. The railroads continue to improve their already outstanding technological performance. And total resource productivity cannot help but rise, as indeed it has.

Had it not been for the opportunity and the willingness to improve efficiency, a high growth rate couldn't have been achieved and would not have persisted. And this presents the danger that within the not too distant future, when French agriculture has been recast into a small number of large farms, the artisinal features of manufacturing have finally been suppressed, and retailing is no longer dominated by the single-family proprietorship, the growth rate must drop. In these circumstances, France will be able to move ahead no more rapidly than the United States or, perhaps, even Britain.

Would this alteration in structure likewise reduce domestic inflationary propensities? It seems unlikely. Instead, the reshaping of manufacturing industry to a pattern closer to that of the United States or West Germany, dominated by larger, more diversified firms, will probably lead to greater emphasis on advertising, product differentiation, and the application of more "scientific" methods of budgeting and pricing. Different justifications will be given for pricing structures which may not turn out to be any more flexible than those devised by family-owned firms. As the corporate chains come to dominate distribution, margins may initially decline; but the United States experience shows that, eventually, rising overheads will be reflected in higher unit costs and operating expenses of the giant supermarkets and shopping centers. Vigorous price cutters like Edouard Leclerc will find their policies to be popular neither with the business community nor with their stockholders. Nor will they be widely imitated. As long as substantial income disparities exist, workers will continue to demand wage increases in excess of average productivity gains.

In the process of transforming the economy to increase efficiency, much that is characteristic of the French countryside, cities, and government institutions will be relegated to the historical past. Whether one can count on substantially offsetting benefits in terms of a reduction in the rate of inflation or an increase in the continuing growth rate is far from certain.

V

THE GERMAN EXPERIENCE

INFLATION WITHOUT UNEMPLOYMENT: THE EFFECT OF COMPETITION

Helmut Arndt

The persistent rise in the exchange rate in the German Mark, the relatively low rate of inflation, the surplus in the German balance of payments, and the high rate of employment have been outstanding features of the economic situation in the Federal Republic of Germany during the last twenty years. In contrast to the economic development in other industrialized countries — like the United States, Great Britain, or France — West Germany has principally experienced inflation, but not stagflation. In the years between 1960 and 1970, the average annual rate of inflation was 3.0%, while the average annual rate of unemployment remained at a low 1%.

Prices in May 1973, for example, were about 7.8% higher than a year earlier, but unemployed numbered only 211,000, or 1% of the labor force, while some 653,000 job vacancies were registered. At the same time, some 2,400,000 "guest," or foreign, workers from Turkey, Yugoslavia, Italy, and other countries, amounting to more than 10% of the labor force, found employment in the FRG. In spite of the oil crisis, the number of unemployed in January 1974 was only 620,000, no more than 2.7% of the entire labor force including the foreign workers; and prices increased about 7.4%. Even during the "Erhard recession" in 1966-1967, unemployment rose briefly to

I wish to express gratitude to my colleagues Kenneth J. Arrow, Milton Friedman, Gottfried Haberler, Hendrik S. Houthakker, and Paul A. Samuelson for their remarks on some of the issues raised in this chapter. For any errors, I accept full responsibility.

Chart V-I

UNEMPLOYMENT RATE IN U.S. AND FEDERAL REPUBLIC OF GERMANY
LABOR MARKETS 1954-1973
GUEST WORKERS AND JOB VACANCIES IN F.R.G.

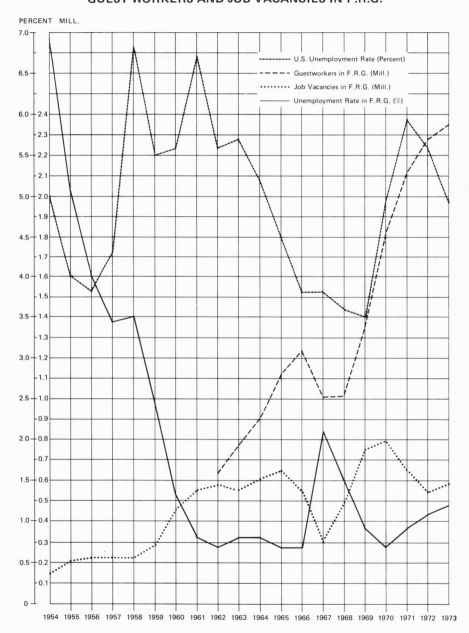

a peak of 700,000, or 3.2%, during one month (the annual unemployment rate did not rise above 2.1%), a rate lower than that achieved in the best postwar years in the United States (Chart I). And still, one million foreign workers accounted for about 5% of the labor force. Clearly, West Germany has experienced inflation, but simultaneously with *over*employment (*cf.* Tables I and II).

Table V-I

LABOR MARKET OF THE FEDERAL REPUBLIC OF GERMANY, 1954 TO 1973

Year	Employed (000's)	Guest workers (000's)	Unemployed (000's)	Percentage Rate	Vacancies (000's)
1954	16,599	—	1,228	6.9	140
1955	17,496	—	935	5.1	203
1956	18,384	—	767	4.0	222
1957	18,945	—	668	3.4	221
1958	19.175	—	689	3.5	220
1959	19,748	—	480	2.4	284
1960	20,257	—	271	1.3	465
1961	20,730	—	181	0.8	552
1962	21,032	629	155	0.7	574
1963	21,261	773	186	0.8	555
1964	21,484	903	169	0.8	609
1965	21,757	1,119	147	0.7	649
1966	21,765	1,244	161	0.7	540
1967	21,054	1,014	459	2.1	302
1968	21,183	1,019	323	1.5	488
1969	21,752	1,366	179	0.9	747
1970	22,246	1,807	149	0.7	795
1971	22,396	2,128	185	0.9	648
1972	22,340	2,284	246	1.1	546
1973	22,463	2,523	274	1.3	572

Source: *Monatsbericht der Deutschen Bundesbank,* 8 (1974).

The first part of this chapter will explore why West Germany has maintained — at least in the past — a high flexibility of prices and wages. The second will treat the question of why Germany has suffered from inflation, but not from stagflation, and why the value of the German Mark rose between 30% and 40% against the U.S. dollar. The last section will account for why recessions have been overcome in West Germany by increasing exports, while in some other countries — notably the United States — recessions have been reinforced by increasing imports. In this connection, the question will arise as to whether it may be the higher rate of economic competition, in itself, which explains why Germany has been more successful on the world market than most other nations.

Table V-II

LABOR MARKET OF THE UNITED STATES, 1954 TO 1973

Year	Employed (000's)	Unemployed (000's)	Percentage [1] Rate
1954	61,238	3,230	5.0
1955	63,193	2,654	4.0
1956	64,979	2,551	3.8
1957	65,611	2,936	4.3
1958	63,966	4,681	6.8
1959	65,581	3,813	5.5
1960	66,681	3,931	5.6
1961	66,796	4,806	6.7
1962	67,846	4,007	5.6
1963	68,809	4,166	5.7
1964	70,357	3,876	5.2
1965	71,088	3,366	4.5
1966	72,895	2,875	3.8
1967	74,372	2,975	3.8
1968	75,920	2,817	3.6
1969	77,902	2,831	3.5
1970	78,627	4,088	4.9
1971	79,120	4,993	5.9
1972	81,702	4,840	5.6
1973	84,409	4,304	4.9

Source: Federal Reserve Bulletin   1. Unemployed as a percentage of the civi-
        lian labor force.

THE FLEXIBILITY OF PRICES AND WAGES

First, economic conditions in West Germany differ from the conditions of countries like the United States in at least four points:
(1) a relatively high rate of competition in the markets for manufactured goods;

(2) a sufficiently high rate of competition in the labor market;
(3) a different kind of behavior by trade unions (at least in the past);
(4) a different type and rate of inflation.

High Rate of Enterprise Competition

The relatively high rate of competition among industrial and business enterprises in the Federal Republic of Germany is in large part a result of the economic organization of the European Common Market which has abolished the traditional trade barriers, at least for manufactured goods.[2] Goods produced in any member countries of the European Community can be imported without tariff protection and are, as a result, as fully competitive in the German market as domestic products. The French, Italian, or Dutch producers of automobiles — Citroen, Fiat or Daf — sell their products in Germany under the same conditions as the German enterprises Volkswagen, Daimler, Opel, or BMW. At least fifteen European car producers are still competing within the Common Market (Chart II and Table III).

Conventional concentration ratios for the German automobile market (Table III) are misleading for three reasons: (1) The German markets for industrial goods are only a part of a larger E.E.C. market. All auto producers, for example, of the European Community are free to sell their cars in the Federal Republic under the same conditions as the German producers. (2) A high percentage (nearly 60%) of cars produced in Germany is exported. And (3) producers in other European Community countries, selling most of their output in their home countries, are, in general, equally as large as German firms and are able to compete on the same scale as German producers. Fiat, for instance, is not much smaller than Volkswagen. The four biggest firms on the European market account for only 56.2% of auto production, compared with 85.4% of the four leading American producers in the U.S. market (Table IV).

Competition in many other product markets in the European Community is also relatively high for the same reason. This is true, not only for finished goods like shoes, textiles, and household appliances, but also for many goods required in the production process itself — machines, half-finished products, etc.

This relatively high rate of competition is one of the chief reasons why German firms cannot succeed in applying, in their home mar-

Chart V-II

MARKET SHARES OF CAR PRODUCERS IN THE FEDERAL REPUBLIC OF GERMANY IN 1972

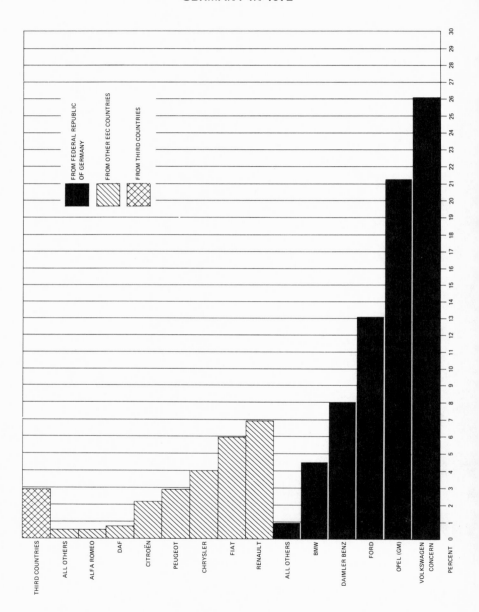

kets, the method of "target pricing" in either the short-term or long-run forms identified by Gardiner Means and John Blair [3] — at least so long as there are no European or international cartels and no market leaders. If firms had the power of target pricing, as they have in many markets in the United States, they could raise their prices when demand declined in an effort to maintain the same rate of profits. But fewer goods would be sold, with the result of a higher rate of unemployment. The result of such target pricing would have

Table V-III

THE MARKET SHARES[a] OF CAR PRODUCERS IN THE FEDERAL REPUBLIC OF GERMANY (in percent)

1. From FRG	1969	1970	1971	1972	1973 Jan.-Oct.
Volkswagen Concern[b]	32.8	31.8	29.0	26.1	28.1
Opel	19.0	19.2	18.7	21.3	20.8
Ford (Köln and Genk)	15.6	14.7	14.6	13.1	11.5
Daimler Benz	6.9	6.9	7.3	8.0	8.2
BMW	4.0	4.1	4.1	4.5	4.6
All others	1.3	0.7	1.0	0.9	0.4
Sub-total	79.6	77.5	74.8	73.8	73.6
II. From other EC Countries					
Fiat	6.7	6.1	6.5	5.9	5.2
Renault	6.1	7.0	7.1	6.9	7.0
Chrysler[c]	2.9	3.5	3.9	4.0	3.8
Peugeot	1.5	1.8	2.4	2.8	2.8
Citroën	1.2	1.5	1.8	2.2	2.2
British Leyland[d]	—	—	—	—	0.8
Daf	0.5	0.6	0.7	0.7	0.8
Alfa Romeo	0.5	0.4	0.5	0.5	0.9
All others	0.1	0.3	0.4	0.5	0.3
Sub-total	19.4	21.2	23.2	23.4	23.8
III. From third Countries	1.0	1.3	2.0	2.8	2.6
	100.0	100.0	100.0	100.0	100.0

[a] The figures are based on the number of cars registered.
[b] In 1969 Audi and NSU were merged with the Volkswagen AG as majority shareholder.
[c] Includes Chrysler, France and since 1973 Chrysler, England.
[d] Since 1973 Great Britain has been a member of the European Community. Before, the figures for Leyland and Ford England were included in figures of third countries.

an adverse impact on the ability of German firms to compete in foreign trade, and employment would be even worse if, as exports drop, imports rose. But if the rate of competition remains sufficient and prices remain flexible, as it has been the case since the abolishment of trade barriers within the European Community, a decline in domestic demand can be compensated for by foreign trade, where products can be sold outside the home markets.[4]

Table V-IV

THE MARKET SHARES OF CAR PRODUCERS IN THE COMMON MARKET AND UNITED STATES (in percent of produced cars)

I. Common Market	1969	1970	1971	1972
Fiat	23.1	21.1	21.5	20.6
Renault	11.4	12.3	12.0	12.9
VW-Audi/NSU	15.5	15.9	14.1	12.1
General Motors	10.6	10.5	10.0	10.6
Ford	9.7	9.7	9.5	8.4
Citroën	6.4	6.7	7.8	8.0
Peugeot	6.2	6.7	6.9	7.0
Chrysler	5.6	5.6	6.0	6.7
Daimler Benz	3.1	3.2	3.4	3.5
BMW	2.0	2.1	2.1	2.2
Alfa Romeo	1.7	1.6	1.7	1.8
Daf	1.1	1.1	1.1	1.1
All others	0.1	0.2	0.1	0.1
Sub-total	96.5	96.7	96.2	95.0
Imports	3.5	3.3	3.8	5.0
Grand-total	100	100	100	100
II. United States				
General Motors	46.8	39.8	45.2	44.4
Ford	24.3	26.4	23.5	24.4
Chrysler	15.1	16.1	13.7	13.8
American Motors	2.5	3.0	2.5	2.8
Sub-total	88.7	85.3	84.9	85.4
Imports	11.3	14.7	15.1	14.6
Grand-total	100	100	100	100

Competition on the Labor Market

In the collective bargaining process in the United States, periodic wage increases are usually specified so that even in the face of declining demand and growing unemployment, automatic wage increases occur. Excerpts from such a collective agreement between Chrysler's Kentucky Airtemp Plant and the UAW Local are shown in Table V. The following points should be noted in the agreement: (1) The difference between minimum and maximum wage rates is small; (2) the increases in wage rates provided for in this agreement are relatively large (33.3% within 27 months); and (3) the increases in wage rates do not depend upon supply and demand conditions in the labor market.

But in Germany — and this is a fundamental difference — wage rates established in a wage agreement are only minimum wages. Individual firms are not prevented, in actual practice, from offering above-minimum wage rates at one time and reducing such an offer at another, so long as wages offered remain equal to or above the established rates. In order to get better workers — or, at a time of full or overemployment, any workers at all — firms can and must compete on the labor market by paying higher wages than those specified in the wage agreements. The wages paid for regular work time excluding overtime payment (effective wages) are therefore higher in many factories than the wages set in the wage agreements (contract wages). An increase in wage rates in a collective agreement does not necessarily mean that effective wages increase at the same rates. If the demand for labor should decrease, it is possible that effective wage rates can actually decline. Automatic increases in wages do not exist in West Germany, thereby eliminating a built-in, cost-push inflationary pressure which exists in a good many other countries. Wages are relatively flexible. They not only increase, but also decrease.

During the Erhard recession, for example, effective wages had a tendency to decline as big enterprises such as Siemens reduced wage rates. Significant declines also occurred in the construction industry. Before the recessionary period, the wages of construction workers in West Berlin exceeded, at least in some cases, the contract wage by nearly 100%. During the recession, however, this excess was decreased by one-half, and the effective wage, at least for newly employed construction workers, dropped by about 25%. The average reduction of wages, generally, is considerably smaller.

Table V-V

SCHEDULED INCREASES IN WAGE RATES AT CHRYSLER'S AIRTEMP KENTUCKY PLANT, NOVEMBER 5, 1970 TO JANUARY 15, 1973 (in dollars)

Class No.	Classification Title	Present Rate			Increase Effective 11/9/70			Increase Effective 12/13/71			Increase Effective 1/15/73		
		Min.	Work	Max.	Min.	Work	Max.	Min.	Work	Max.	Min.	Work	Max.
0264	Assembler-Wiring	2.65	2.70	2.75	3.00	3.05	3.10	3.25	3.30	3.35	3.50	3.55	3.60
0243	Assembler-Major A/C	2.84	2.89	2.94	3.19	3.24	3.29	3.44	3.49	3.54	3.69	3.74	3.79
0252	Assembler-Minor A/C	2.55	2.60	2.65	2.90	2.95	3.00	3.15	3.20	3.25	3.40	3.45	3.50
1043	Truck Operator	2.65	2.70	2.75	3.00	3.05	3.10	3.25	3.30	3.35	3.50	3.55	3.60
1960	Inspector-General	2.84	2.89	2.94	3.19	3.24	3.29	3.44	3.49	3.54	3.69	3.74	3.79
7078	Welder-Pressure Vessel	3.00	3.05	3.10	3.35	3.40	3.45	3.60	3.65	3.70	3.85	3.90	3.95

Source: Wage Supplement to the Agreement between Chrysler Corporation for its Airtemp Kentucky Plant and the UAW Local 1644 of Nov. 5, 1970, *Production and Maintenance*, pp. 107-08.

From July 1966 to April 1967, the average effective wage per hour in the construction industry decreased from 101.4% to 99.1% (the average wage of 1967 being the base of 100), as shown in Table VI. In the construction materials industry, the wage index dropped from 100.5% to 97.9%, or slightly more than 2.5% between October 1966 and January 1967 (Table VII). In the chemical industry, the effective wage decreased between January and July 1966 from 97.0% to 94.5%, also slightly more than 2.5% (Table VIII). In the motor vehicle industry (including aircraft), the decrease was less because of increasing export business, but a reduction of more than 1.5% in the average effective wage also took place between July and October 1966 (Table IX). The wage drift of the hourly earnings in these industries is shown in Chart III.

Considering that this was a slight and short-lived recession, this rate of reduction was quite remarkable. This "recession" would have been, in the eyes of American economists, no recession at all: the annual average rate of unemployment rose to only 2.1% in 1967 and declined to 1.5% in 1968, with the slack period lasting little longer than a year.

The fact that wages in German industry not only rise but also decline has three important effects:

(1) Unemployment during a recession will be less. Lower effective wages reduce the pressure on firms to dismiss workers in sectors with decreasing sales and, at the same time, are a greater incentive to hire new workers in prospering sectors.

(2) Managers have less reason to increase prices, contradicting the laws of "supply and demand," if effective wages have a tendency to decline or remain relatively constant during a recession. In the absence of wage increases, neither government, consumers, nor trade unions understand or tolerate such price-inflating behavior.

(3) Unemployment is reduced by increasing exports and reducing imports, if prices and wages remain flexible.

Different Behavior of Labor Unions

The behavior of labor leaders in the Federal Republic is somewhat different than that of labor leaders in other industrialized countries. The concern that excessive increases in wages may be a cause of unemployment has been, at least in the past, greater among German labor leaders than among labor leaders elsewhere.

Table V-VI

INDEXES OF WAGE RATES: HOURLY EARNINGS AND WAGE DRIFT IN THE CONSTRUCTION INDUSTRY OF THE FEDERAL REPUBLIC OF GERMANY (monthly averages 1967 = 100)

	Actual Hourly[a] Earnings	Hourly Tariff Wage Rate	Wage Drift[b]
1966 January	97.2	93.9	3.5
April	101.0	98.6	2.4
July	101.4	98.6	2.8
October	101.2	98.6	2.6
1967 January	99.6	98.6	1.0
April	99.1	98.6	0.5
July	99.9	100.6	−0.7
October	101.4	102.1	−0.7

[a] Actual hourly earnings do not include overtime earnings.
[b] The wage drift is the difference between actual hourly wages and the established tariff wage rate or minimum.
Source: From data supplied by Wirtschaftswissenschaftliches Institut der Gewerkschaften (Economic Institute of the Trade Unions).

Table V-VII

INDEXES OF WAGE RATES: HOURLY EARNINGS AND WAGE DRIFT IN THE CONSTRUCTION MATERIALS INDUSTRY OF THE FEDERAL REPUBLIC OF GERMANY (monthly averages 1967 = 100)

	Actual Hourly[a] Earnings	Hourly Tariff Wage Rate	Wage Drift[b]
1966 January	93.1	93.7	−0.6
April	97.5	95.2	2.4
July	100.7	99.0	1.1
October	100.5	99.3	1.2
1967 January	97.9	99.5	−1.6
April	99.6	99.7	−0.1
July	100.8	99.8	1.0
October	101.6	101.1	0.5

[a] Actual hourly earnings do not include overtime earnings.
[b] The wage drift is the difference between actual hourly wages and the established tariff wage rate or minimum.
Source: From data supplied by Wirtschaftswissenschaftliches Institut der Gewerkschaften (Economic Institute of the Trade Unions).

Table V-VIII

INDEXES OF WAGE RATES: HOURLY EARNINGS AND WAGE DRIFT IN THE CHEMICAL INDUSTRY OF THE FEDERAL REPUBLIC OF GERMANY
(monthly averages 1967 = 100)

	Actual Hourly[a] Earnings	Hourly Tariff Wage Rate	Wage Drift[b]
1966 January	97.0	97.1	−0.1
April	96.2	93.7	2.7
July	94.5	93.6	1.0
October	94.8	93.6	1.3
1967 January	97.8	97.3	0.5
April	100.6	100.8	−0.2
July	101.2	100.9	0.3
October	100.3	100.9	−0.6

a   Actual hourly earnings do not include overtime earnings.
b   The wage drift is the difference between actual hourly wages and the established tariff wage rate or minimum.
Source: From data supplied by Wirtschaftswissenschaftliches Institut der Gewerkschaften (Economic Institute of the Trade Unions).

Table V-IX

INDEXES OF WAGE RATES: HOURLY EARNINGS AND WAGE DRIFT IN THE MOTOR VEHICLE INDUSTRY (including Aircraft) OF THE FEDERAL REPUBLIC OF GERMANY (monthly averages 1967 = 100)

	Actual Hourly[a] Earnings	Hourly Tariff Wage Rate	Wage Drift[b]
1966 January	92.0	94.8	−2.8
April	96.5	95.5	1.0
July	96.5	95.5	1.0
October	95.0	95.6	−0.6
1967 January	98.9	99.7	−0.8
April	99.6	99.9	−0.3
July	100.4	100.1	0.3
October	101.1	100.1	1.0

a   Actual hourly earnings do not include overtime earnings.
b   The wage drift is the difference between actual hourly wages and the established tariff wage rate or minimum.
Source: From data supplied by Wirtschaftswissenschaftliches Institut der Gewerkschaften (Economic Institute of the Trade Unions).

Chart V-III

WAGE DRIFT OF HOURLY EARNINGS IN CHOSEN INDUSTRIES OF THE FEDERAL REPUBLIC OF GERMANY (1966-1967)

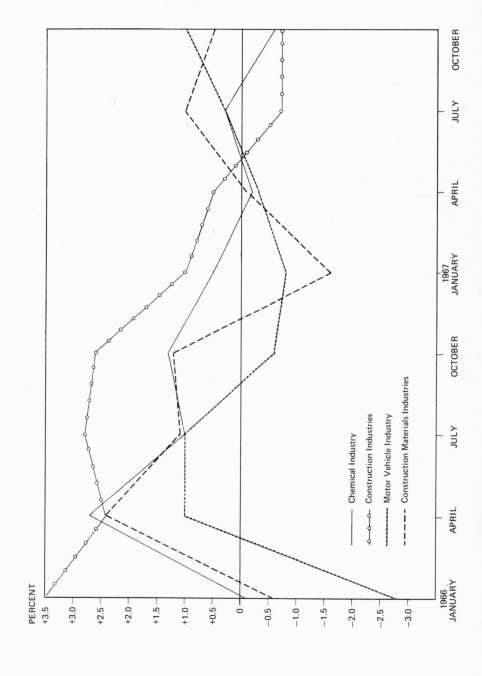

— Chemical Industry
—○— Construction Industries
········· Motor Vehicle Industry
– – – Construction Materials Industries

In order to prevent unemployment, union officials have been willing to accept lower wages or smaller increases in wages than might otherwise be achieved in the bargaining process. Such self-restraint could be noticed in the years following the 1948 currency reform, during the Korean war boom of 1951-1952, and especially during and after the Erhard recession of 1966-1967. In 1968, Herbert Giersch, the then leading economist of the German Board of Advisors, reproached the German trade unions because labor could have achieved a 4.2% increase in real wages in 1968 without any danger to full employment, but instead were content with an increase of between 2% and 2.5%.[5] Indeed, the leadership of the German trade unions was very cautious in pressing for higher wages during and after the Erhard recession in spite of the fact that the average unemployment rate was in no single month higher than 3.2%. It is true that there was a wage explosion in 1970 following the profit explosion of the year before, but again in 1971, 1972, and 1973, the trade unions were moderate in their demands. In the first half of 1973, the wage increases amounted from 9% to 10%, while the rate of inflation was nearly 8%. Taking the income tax progression into consideration, the real wage increase was just about zero. This and the growing pressure of the communist groups are the principal reasons why the trade unions demanded, in 1974, wage increases of some 15% and more despite the fact that their leaders are undoubtedly aware of the consequences for inflation and employment.

Several reasons account for the differing behavior of labor unions in the German Federal Republic and those in the United States:

As suggested above, German union leaders are fearful that increases in wages not justified by gains in productivity will cause unemployment. American union leaders usually believe that high wages are good for employment because they sustain consumer spending. This argument has advocates in Germany, but there is generally less faith in the effectiveness of Keynesian policies in combatting unemployment, at least under present conditions.

Past experiences, especially in the 1930's, have also been different. The German trade unions came into power immediately following World War I (1918-1919) and were expropriated and dissolved when the National Socialists came into power in 1933. Most of today's American labor unions, on the other hand, were nonexistent or ineffective until the world economic depression of the 1930's and ac-

quired their power during the Roosevelt era, especially through the
National Labor Relations Act (Wagner Act) of 1955. Both of these
changes were the consequence of the mass unemployment of the
period.

Such profoundly different backgrounds may be helpful in explaining the different behavior of labor unions in the two countries. The
German unions fear unemployment as a cause for renewed attacks on
the democratic system. Feeling threatened by the growing
radicalization of both the political right and the political left, they
have particularly strong reasons for an aversion to unemployment
and the potential thrust it could have for totalitarian government.

As long as German trade unions are convinced that increases in
wages not justified by increases in productivity will cause unemployment, wages usually will not increase beyond the level governed by
supply and demand. And in fact, wages are actually lower. Otherwise
the current level of overemployment could not exist — where 10% of
the labor force is composed of foreign workers, the level of job
vacancies in the summer of 1973 was still 4%, and the level of unemployment in January 1974 was only 2.8% — despite the disruptions
created by the energy crisis.

The flexibility of wages depends, therefore, not only upon objective conditions of competition, but upon subjective differences in
the behavior of union leaders as well. If in the past, trade unions in
West Germany had maximized wages in the same way as unions in
the United States or Great Britain, there would have been considerable unemployment, especially with the current level of foreign
workers.

RATE AND TYPE OF INFLATION

Differences in the Rate of Inflation

The rate and type of inflation in West Germany are also different
from those in Great Britain or United States, and the statistical figures are again misleading in this connection. The statistical rate of
inflation, of course, has not been significantly lower during the past
two decades in Germany than in the United States. Nevertheless,
these statistical figures are not relevant to our problem since the
statistical index contains prices which are of little or no importance
in the sphere of foreign trade, a particularly important area in sus-

taining German prosperity. Apartment rentals, for example, rose much more in Germany than in the United States because rents in Germany had been frozen for nearly half a century, from the end of World War I up to the 1960's. Within the last ten years, the average German apartment rental rose by about 200%, or 20% yearly on the average. Adjusting for this consideration, the German rate of inflation was 5.5% less, during the past decade, than in the United States.[6]

Another important consideration in Germany is that the statistical index generally measures the prices of goods which a household of four or five persons usually requires, and, while important to any internal indexes, these goods are not usually relevant with regard to competition in international trade. The German Federal Republic is not exporting housing or food but, instead, industrial commodities such as steel, pipes, machines, and other equipment; and the movement of these prices has been different.

Table V-X

WHOLESALE PRICE INDEXES OF MOTOR VEHICLES AND EQUIPMENT IN THE FEDERAL REPUBLIC OF GERMANY AND UNITED STATES, 1950-1973

Year	FRG	USA
1950	100[a]	100
1955	—	124.9
1958	103.1[a]	141.5
1960	102.6	143.1
1963	105.8	141.5
1964	105.8	142.3
1965	106.3	142.5
1966	108.2	142.7
1967	108.3	144.7
1968	99.8[b]	148.8
1969	100.6[b]	151.5
1970	107.8[b]	157.0
1971	115.2[b]	166.0
1972	119.6[b]	170.8
1973	123.8[b]	172.3

[a] Index of manufacturer's prices; wholesale prices are not available.
[b] Index calculated on basis of prices excluding sales tax (i.e. value added tax).
Sources: German figures: *Statistisches Jahrbuch für die Bundesrepublik Deutschland*
U.S. figures: Survey of Current Business.

Chart V-IV

TRENDS OF WHOLESALE PRICE INDEXES OF MOTOR VEHICLES AND EQUIPMENT IN THE FEDERAL REPUBLIC OF GERMANY AND THE UNITED STATES 1950-1973

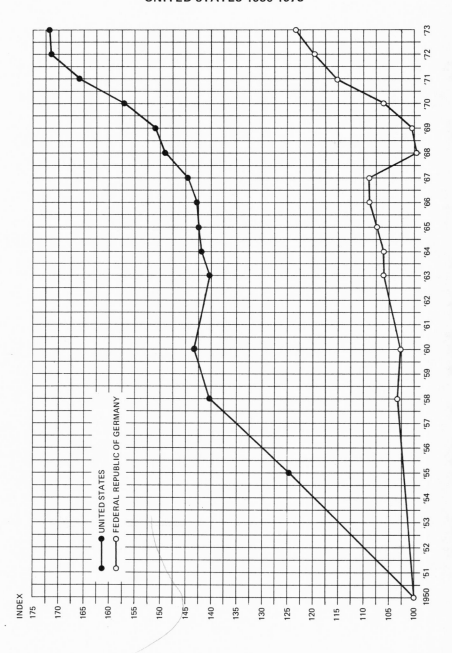

Between 1950 and 1967, the prices of motor vehicles and equipment, for instance, rose only 8% in Germany, while such prices increased by 45% in the United States (Table X). Only in the last four years has a reversal in this development, diminishing the competitive advantage of German producers, been observable. Nevertheless, prices for motor vehicles from 1950 to 1972 rose in Germany about 20%, compared with a rise of about 71% in the United States (see Chart IV).

"DOMESTIC" AND "IMPORTED" INFLATION

The different origins of inflation are also important. The inflation in the United States is principally a result of internal or domestic pressures, a result of deficit spending, target pricing, and so on. The inflation in the Federal Republic of Germany is due primarily to external or imported pressures resulting from the sustained surplus in the balance of payments — $12 billion in 1973 alone.

The "home made," or domestically-created, inflation, typical of many South and North American countries as well as Great Britain, Sweden, etc., hampers the development of a nation's foreign trade. If prices in a country rise *earlier* than those abroad, imports will be favored and exports depressed. In contrast, the "imported" inflation found in West Germany, Austria, the Netherlands, and Switzerland is the result of the growth of a nation's international trade. If inflation is imported, prices rise *after* exports increase and imports (at least relatively) decrease. In the first stage, a surplus in the balance of trade will result, and at the second stage, a rise of prices within the home country will be observed. Since exports of goods and services are greater than imports, foreign money flows in, which is then the cause for the increase of prices[7] — but with a time lag, and only after the increase of exports and the surplus in the balance of trade has been registered throughout the economy.

The impact of inflation resulting from such trade surpluses and inflows of currency can be diminished or moderated by national monetary policy. For the last decade, the German Bundesbank (the German Federal Reserve System) has, not without success, tried to neutralize the inflationary effects of inflowing foreign currency. Commercial banks are required to deposit the so-called "foreign money" with the Bundesbank. And since the Bundesbank does not

grant commercial credits, this money does not circulate within the
internal economy and, therefore, does not contribute to an increase
in prices, or only to a lesser degree.[8] Such a policy, however, cannot
be continued for long without a change of the currency rate due to
long-term increases in foreign currency holdings. When Germany
waited too long in 1973 to adjust its currency, the pressure of inflowing money became so strong that the Bundesbank could not
prevent an inflationary push. While the consequences of this phenomenon are not the focus here, it is the principal reason why the
FRG, like other European countries, let its currency float against the
rest of the world.

THE IMPACT OF FOREIGN TRADE ON EMPLOYMENT

The analysis would not be complete without a fuller understanding of the influences of foreign trade on the rate of employment. Two issues are particularly important in this connection: the
diverse effects which foreign trade may have on internal employment
and recession; and the influence of internal national employment
policy on other countries in a world of free trade and free exchange
of money.

Foreign Trade, Employment, and Recession

The influence of foreign trade on employment and recession again
can be seen clearly from the different experience in Germany and in
the United States. Since 1960, the yearly rate of unemployment in
the United States has in no year averaged less than 3.5%, while
during this same period, the average rate of unemployment in Germany never exceeded 2.1% and generally remained under 1.5%. If
foreign workers are taken into account, then the FRG remains in a
state of overemployment since the labor supply cannot satisfy the
need for workers.

The highest rate of unemployment occurred during the Erhard
recession which lasted from the end of 1966 until the spring of 1968.
Most German economists would agree that this recession was not
overcome by Keynesian employment policies since the loss of domestic demand for products was compensated for by an increase in
demand from abroad, not from an expansion of the money supply.
During the recession, the prices of export goods decreased, some

absolutely, and the rest relatively. In its annual report for 1968, the German Board of Advisors observed that "when West German export prices decreased after the middle of 1966, export prices of our most important partner countries increased by 7% on the average. The export prices of the Federal Republic in 1968 are scarcely higher than in 1964." [9]

In the face of decreasing demand, German firms have increased their efforts to sell on other markets, competing not only in price, but in quality as well. They have been eager to adjust their products, their conditions, their service, and their behavior to the needs of foreign buyers. Thus, not only by lower prices, but also by strong and sustained selling efforts, a country can gain a bigger share of foreign trade and keep workers, who otherwise would become jobless, employed by producing export goods. In this respect, German exports rose from 80.6 billion DM in 1966 to 87.0 billion DM in 1967 and increased further to 99.6 billion DM in 1968. This same behavior was equally apparent in 1974. While most other major trading nations experienced a decline in export sales, if price and currency exchanges are excluded, Germany benefited from an expansion of foreign trade.

When prices rise despite decreasing demand, as frequently occurs in United States, imports increase and exports decline for three clear reasons:

(1) The higher the rise in prices, the less a country can compete with other nations.

(2) The higher the prices in the home market, the less firms will be interested in entering foreign markets. Why should a firm expose itself, one must ask, to the difficulties involved in meeting competition abroad when it is much easier to attain a desired profit by "target pricing," when able, in its own country? And why should a firm be concerned about meeting special foreign requirements with regard to quality, design, size, service, reliability, etc., when it earns enough by selling its products on the home market? These factors will often be more influential than prices.

(3) If wages abroad are substantially lower, it is more profitable for companies to let subsidiaries in foreign countries produce goods and employ workers there, than to export goods produced at home. [10]

Experience with foreign trade during a recession in the United States again differs from the German experience. In 1958, for instance, when the U. S. rate of unemployment reached 6.8%, exports fell to $16.3 billion from $19.4 billion the preceeding year. In the following year, exports remained at the same level. With a time-lag, imports increased to $15.3 billion in 1959 from $13 billion in 1958. In other words, while the unemployment rates rose from 4.3% to 6.8%, exports decreased by about 19% and imports increased by about 18%. As a result, unemployment was intensified by the unfavorable balance in foreign trade.

Although the relationship in the United States has not always been the same in each recession, the phenomenon described is predominant. In 1949, unemployment reached a peak of 5.5%. Imports increased from $6.8 billion in 1949 to $9.0 billion in 1950, while in the same period, exports fell from $12.1 billion to $10.1 billion. But in 1954, the same phenomenon was not apparent. Then in 1961, the unemployment rate rose to 6.7%, while imports jumped from $14.5 billion in 1961 up to $16.2 billion in 1962. Exports increased only relatively slightly from $20.1 billion to $20.7 billion.

In the first half of 1971, both the U.S. balance of payments and the balance of trade became negative for the first time since 1893. During this same period, the rate of unemployment reached a peak of 7% in spite of — or because of — President Nixon's attempt to revive the American economy by Keynesian methods.

National Employment Policy and International Competition

John Maynard Keynes neither knew, nor considered, the circumstances of "stagflation," a situation where unemployment is associated at the same time with rising prices. He believed that if unemployment exists and no bottlenecks are present, deficit spending for increased employment will not cause prices to rise. But what is more important, he analyzed the problems of employment based on a model of a closed economy.

In chapter 23 of his *General Theory of Employment, Interest and Money*,[11] Keynes did consider the influence of foreign trade, but only from a negative point of view. He asked only how additional duties or other impediments to imports would affect employment in a country protecting itself against imports. He did not ask how this would affect the rate of employment of other countries, nor did he ask how a reduction in world trade would affect employment in the world as a whole. Keynes did not ask, especially, the question which is relevant here: namely, how increases or decreases in foreign trade influence employment in a liberalized world, a world without trade barriers. Finally, he did not ask how, in a world of free trade and free competition, different rates or different sources of inflation (domestically created or imported) would affect employment.

The problems and the conditions of employment policy have changed significantly since Keynes wrote his *General Theory*. In the 1930's, nearly every nation had been a closed economy due to of trade barriers and currency restrictions. Today the world is again liberalized under the agreements of the Havana Conference and the Kennedy round of trade negotiations. The effects of national employment policy in the 1960's or 1970's are therefore not the same as they were in the more restricted world of the 1930's.

In a closed economy, deficit spending does increase national employment, as Keynes and his followers taught. This effect, as such, is independent of whether deficit spending does or does not affect prices. This does not, however, exclude the possibility that the employment effect is greater if prices are frozen, as was the case in many of the European countries which tried Keynesian employment policies in the 1930's. In this respect, Keynes was perfectly correct in his analysis of the problems of his time.

But in a world of liberal trade and therefore in an open economy, the result is different. It is true that under these conditions a Keynesian policy will increase employment in the world economy as a whole, but not necessarily in the country that used this kind of policy since the influence of foreign trade must be taken into account. A change in international price relations cannot be neglected by any single nation. Assuming, for example, that in a home economy "deficit spending" causes an increase in prices while the prices of all other countries remain constant, then, in the home country, imports will increase and exports decrease. In other countries with constant prices, the opposite effect will occur. This is particularly important because fewer exports mean lower employment for the country with a policy of deficit spending, while more imports mean a higher rate of employment in other countries where no increase in prices has occurred as a result of such a policy. In such circumstances, paradoxically, a Keynesian national employment policy becomes the cause for rising unemployment in the home economy.

This is also true when inflation is worldwide, but the rate of inflation is different in the various nations concerned. Under these conditions, the national rate of employment will be influenced in two ways: countries with less inflation will experience full or, as it is the case in the German Federal Republic, even overemployment; and countries with more rapidly rising prices will suffer more deeply from unemployment.

In this connection, it is worth remembering that the expansion of foreign trade since the Korean war has differed in the United States from that in West Germany (*cf.* Table XI). The export of goods in the German Federal Republic rose from 22.0 billion DM in 1954 to 125.3 billion DM in 1970 and 149 billion DM in 1972. The exports of the United States increased from $12.8 billion in 1954 to only $42.0 billion in 1970 and $48.8 billion in 1972.[12] That means that the export of goods by the United States only somewhat less than quad-

Table V-XI

IMPORT AND EXPORT GOODS OF THE FEDERAL REPUBLIC OF GERMANY AND THE UNITED STATES OF AMERICA

Year	FRG (in Mill.DM)		USA (in Mill.Dollar)	
	Import	Export	Import	Export
1954	19,337	22,035	10,327	12,760
1955	24,472	25,717	11,475	14,209
1956	27,964	30,861	12,763	17,281
1957	31,697	35,968	13,291	19,390
1958	31,133	36,998	12,951	16,263
1959	35,823	41,184	15,294	16,282
1960	42,723	47,946	14,744	19,650
1961	44,363	50,978	14,519	20,107
1962	49,498	52,975	16,218	20,779
1963	52,277	58,310	17,011	22,252
1964	58,839	64,920	18,647	25,478
1965	70,448	71,651	21,496	26,438
1966	72,670	80,628	25,463	29,287
1967	70,183	87,045	26,821	30,638
1968	81,179	99,551	32,964	33,576
1969	97,972	113,557	35,796	36,417
1970	109,606	125,276	39,952	42,659
1971	120,119	136,011	45,563	43,549
1972	128,744	149,022	55,555	49,208
1973	145,417	178,396	69,121	70,799

Source: Federal Reserve Bulletin, Statistisches Bundesamt (Federal Bureau of Statistics) of the Federal Republic of Germany, *Monatsbericht der Deutschen Bundesbank,* 8 (1974).

Chart V-V

IMPORTS AND EXPORTS OF GOODS OF THE UNITED STATES AND THE FEDERAL REPUBLIC OF GERMANY

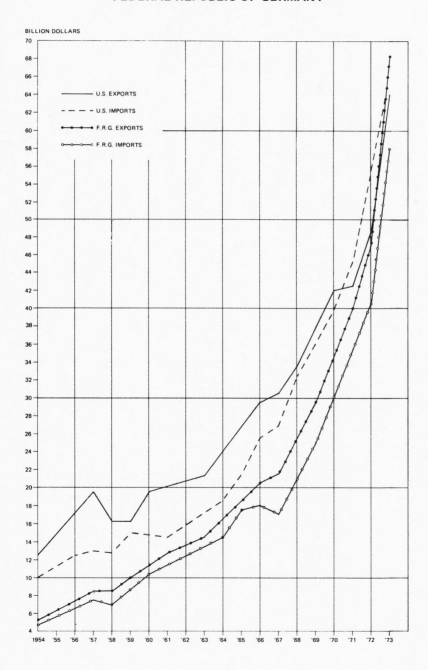

rupled during this period, while German industrial exports increased nearly sevenfold. This comparison is illustrated by Chart V.

The difference is still greater when the export of services is taken into account. Between 1954 and 1971, exports of goods and services together increased by 651% in Germany, but only by 356% in the United States. Between 1954 and 1972, exports and imports together rose by 915% in Germany, but only by 454% in the United States.

The kinds of goods exported have differed as well. While raw materials and agricultural goods still make up a relatively large share of American exports, German exports consist almost exclusively of finished industrial products. In other words, the export trade of West Germany has created, *in general,* more employment.

It is also interesting to note that this expansion of German foreign trade has not ceased. In spite of the fact that the Mark has been revaluated upward about 40% against the U.S. dollar, German exports have still increased. During the first seven months of 1973, exports were some 20% higher than in the same period in 1972, while orders from abroad in the last three quarters rose more than 30%. Imports rose, too, but only by about 15% on the average. The oil crisis did not substantially change the situation.

More recent figures once again confirm that the country with the lowest rate of inflation is in a better position with regard to foreign competition and national full employment. In 1973 and the first half of 1974, West Germany maintained the lowest rate of inflation of all industrial nations as her share of world trade continued to expand. The real volume of foreign trade of the major industrial nations dropped by more than $20 billion in 1973, but German foreign trade increased by nearly $13 billion. And while, in the first six months of 1974, the international trade of the leading industrial nations again declined, when the rate of inflation and currency changes are excluded, the German export — as well as the German import — trade still continued to grow,[13] as indicated by Table XII.

If Germany were unable to exploit her competitive position in the international market, the German unemployment rate would rise to considerably higher levels. In August 1974, the rate did rise somewhat, to 2.3%, although the rate was only 1.2% if those who are only capable of, or available for, part time work (housewives, those living on annuities, disabled persons, etc.) are excluded from the statistics. The real danger, then, for Germany is not inflation, as many may believe, but unemployment resulting from a potential decline of international trade. The future of the German economy depends heavily, as it has since World War II, upon this continued expansion of trade; and if competition becomes hampered by state barriers, as it was in the 1930's, German foreign trade will begin to decline. Then Germany will suffer considerably — from an increasingly high rate of unemployment.

Table V-XII

DEVELOPMENT OF THE BALANCES OF TRADE IN MILL. U.S. DOLLARS (PRICE AND CURRENCY CHANGES EXCLUDED)

Country	Year	1973		1974	
		1.Quarter	2.Quarter	1.Quarter	2.Quarter
Industrial Nations total	−20777	−5480	−5298	−14490	−18000[a]
Fed. Rep. Ger.	+12950	+2033	+2612	+4986	+4838
Denmark	−1434	−328	−430	−637	−541
Finland	−493	−139	−140	−239	−278
France	−1069	−296	−54	−1610	−2009
Great Britain	−8312	−1796	−1644	−3935	−4355
Canada	+1280	+217	+439	−108	−95
Ireland	−601	−162	−163	−278	−414
Italy	−5572	−1136	−1494	−2975	−3100
Japan	−1365	+274	−756	−3594	−3034
Netherlands	−664	+27	+60	−326	
Norway	−1876	−324	−293	−521	−608
Austria	−1832	−480	−436	−532	−456
Sweden	+1559	+306	+678	+269	−30[b]
Switzerland	−2137	−549	−487	−1440	−680
Spain	−4139	−819	−1152	−1602	−1584[b]
USA	−1885	−1256	−749	+112	−2395

* Source: W. Jensen, *Welthandel und Rohstoffmärkte,* (World trade and the raw material markets), Weltkonjunkturdienst (HWWA), 1974 No. 3.
a Partially estimated
b April/May

CONCLUSIONS

Since West Germany has been a member of the European Common Market, competition has been sufficiently effective to maintain enough price flexibility so that a relapse in demand on the home market has been offset by an expansion of foreign trade. If German firms are not members of international, or a least of Common Market cartels, they do not have the power to raise prices when demand weakens. They are unable to exploit the power of "target pricing." Competition and wage flexibility still exist in the labor market — or have until now — despite the negotiation of wage agreements by large centralized labor unions. The flexibility of prices and wages resulting from the relatively high rate of competition is the principle reason for Germany's relatively high share in world trade. It is also the reason why, until now, a recession could be offset by additional exports. Only her success in foreign trade can explain the continuing level of overemployment and prosperity. West Germany has experienced inflation, but without unemployment, because of the still existing price and wage flexibility, an outgrowth of a still sufficient rate of competition.

VI

INDUSTRIAL STRUCTURE AND THE PRICE PROBLEM

EXPERIENCE WITHIN THE EUROPEAN ECONOMIC COMMUNITY

H. W. de Jong

Comparative Employment Characteristics

Total population in the European Economic Community, excluding Great Britain which joined in 1973, but consisting of West Germany, France, Italy, the Netherlands, Belgium and Luxemburg, was 188 million persons in 1969, some 16 million more than in 1960 and 27 million more than in 1955. Of this population, 75.1 million were gainfully employed, a proportion of 40%, comparable to that of the United States, but much lower than in Great Britain (45.4%). More striking, however, are the differences between the E.E.C. countries and the United States and Great Britain with regard to the proportion of *salaried* employment. Table I gives the shares for the years 1955, 1960, and 1969.

The percentages indicate, of course, the higher rate of unemployment which prevailed in the Community during the mid-1950's in comparison with the two Anglo-Saxon countries. The main influence on the wide, though narrowing, discrepancies in salaried employment was due to the lower degree of industrialization in the E.E.C. Both the share of agricultural employment and of employment in the building and distributive trades were and are still higher in the E.E.C. than in the Anglo-Saxon countries. In 1964, for example, the E.E.C. countries had a proportion of agricultural employment (within the total civilian employment) which was twice as large as that of the

United States (17% versus 8%) and more than four times the share in Great Britain (4%).

Table VI—I

SHARE OF NON-SELF-EMPLOYED IN TOTAL GAINFULLY EMPLOYED; E.E.C., U.K. AND U.S.

	1955	1960	1969
E.E.C.	66.5	70.7	77.2
U.K.	92.6	92.9	92.8
U.S.	89.2	90.0	95.5

Source: E.E.C. National Accounts 1959 — 1969

Likewise, employment in the retail trades was relatively much lower, and productivity was correspondingly much higher in both Great Britain and the United States. Though wide differences have prevailed inside the Community (Belgian agricultural employment was 6%, the Italian 25%, of the total civilian employment in 1964), the importance of this fact can hardly be overrated. Since the agricultural and the distributive sectors of employment have been the ultimate sources of an elastic labor supply for industrial expansion (on top of the more regular and long-term growth of the employable population), the upward pressure on wages in a full employment economy was at least reduced by such an elastic pool of labor in comparison with the Anglo-Saxon countries.

Perhaps the percentages do not reveal the magnitude involved so much as do the crude figures. By 1969, the Italian agriculturally employed population was still 400,000 more than that of the United States, and the German and French labor reserves in this same sector were each four to six times as high as those of Great Britain! If the Common Market agricultural employment were on the same relative level as that of the United States, it would still have had a reserve capacity in agriculture of some seven million persons in 1969. Of course the comparison is misleading, for the E.E.C. can probably never hope to match the U.S. output ratios in agriculture because of inherent differences. Still, the comparison indicates a much higher long-run elasticity of supply for one of the most important factors of production. The ample supply of labor — sustained during the 1950's and early 1960's by the migration of East German workers to West Germany and the immigration of former nationals from colonial territories into the mother countries of France and the Netherlands — has at least facilitated industrial growth.[1]

Growth and Cyclical Characteristics

Rates of growth of the gross national product of the various European countries have been on a high level. For the Community at large, the expansion of output at constant prices has been rapid, having surpassed both Britain and America in this respect. Table II below distinguishes periods of more rapid and of slower growth, as well as the cyclical influence.

Table VI—II

AVERAGE RATES OF GROWTH 1950-1974,[a] GROSS NATIONAL PRODUCT

	1950-'56	1956-'59	1959-'65	1965-'70	1970-'74
E.E.C.	9.1	5.4	5.7	5.3	4.6
U.K.	3.4	2.0	3.6	2.1	3.7
U.S.	4.7	1.8	4.4	3.3	4.2

[a] Geometric average of the annual rates of growth at constant prices.
    1974 estimates by OECD.
Sources: E.E.C. National Accounts, p. 5.
    OECD — Main Economic Indicators.
    OECD — *Economic Outlook,* December 1973.

The cyclical variations, however, have been much more pronounced in both the Anglo-Saxon countries than in the case of the E.E.C., indicating a possible connection between structural growth and a sensitivity to cyclical variations. If the rate of structural growth is high, a downturn in the business cycle will probably exert a smaller effect on industrial output than in a relatively more stagnating economy. Also, the stagnation level of a rapidly growing economy in recession will probably be of shorter duration.

And indeed, cyclical intensity has been more pronounced in Great Britain and, a fortiori, in the United States than in continental Europe. If we take as an index of cyclical intensity the square aver-

age of relative deviations from a five-year moving average and use the
E.E.C. figure as a base of 100, Britain comes out at 122, and the
U.S. at 152 in the period from 1950 to 1968. It follows that cyclical
variations in output have been more in evidence in the United States
than in Europe, and more in Britain than on the the continent.

The explanation of this phenomenon is not wholly clear. As already indicated, relative differences in economic growth may lie at
the basis of the disparative cyclical behavior. Faster economic growth
may be expected to reduce the intensity and duration of the downswing.

On the other hand, the varying structural composition of the economies concerned might have an important influence. If the investment goods industries, or industry in general, account for a larger
share of the gross national product in one economy than in another,
we might expect larger fluctuations in the more industrialized economies. Curiously enough, the higher intensity of cyclical activity in
the United States cannot be explained on this account, for the share
of industry and construction is about as high as in the E.E.C. in a
sectoral distribution of the gross domestic product (Table III). Also,
the share of private consumption is higher, and the share of investment in both fixed assets and stocks of goods is lower (Table IV).

Thus the proportion of the highly volatile components of the
gross domestic product — gross fixed investment and stocks — was
highest for the E.E.C., not only in the years shown, but for most of
the postwar years as well. A finer division of total industrial production or investments would not show a greater relative U.S. share of
heavy investment goods or cyclically sensitive branches of industry.
The magnitudes do not differ importantly or in one direction. The
share of chemical and metalworking industries in 1963, for example,
was 18% of the GDP in the United States and 19% in the E.E.C. The
shares of construction and building were respectively 5% and 8%.

Besides the differing rates of growth, there may be another, perhaps more important, explanation for the differences in cyclical sensitivity: the existence of the E.E.C. itself as an institutional structure
comprising five different national economies with divergent economic policies. Whereas the United States and Great Britain are both
self-contained economic units pursuing a uniform and overall economic policy, the E.E.C. has five separate components which as yet
have not fully given up their autonomous economic policies. The

Table VI—III

GROSS ADDED VALUE AT FACTOR COST FOR LARGE SECTORS OF THE ECONOMY IN 1968: PERCENTAGE DIVISION.

	Agriculture, Fisheries, etc.	Industry & Construction	Services & Government
W. Germany	4.5	50.8	44.6
France	7.8	43.7	48.5
Italy	11.2	38.6	50.2
Netherlands	7.0	41.9	51.1
Belgium	5.2	40.7	54.1
Luxemburg	5.3	52.0	42.6
E.E.C.	7.0	44.8	48.2
U.S.A.	2.9	46.1	50.0
U.K.	3.1	36.2	50.8

Table VI—IV

EXPENDITURE ON THE G.D.P. (1969)

	Household consumption	Consumption of government	Gross Fixed Investments	Stocks (var.)	Current Foreign balance
E.E.C.	59.1	14.0	23.9	2.0	1.0
U.S.A.	61.5	18.1	17.5	0.7	0.5
U.K.	63.2	21.0	16.8	1.0	-0.2

Source: OECD — Main Economic Indicators.

consequence of this difference in institutional structure is that fluctuations in the main economic areas of the United States have run practically parallel during the postwar period, whereas the E.E.C. countries have shown divergences in both their cyclical peaks and troughs (Chart I). In other words, the U.S. business cycle has had a synchronous development in each of the main economic areas, whereas the European cyclical fluctuations have shown different timings for the different countries. In the E.E.C. as a whole, this has had a dampening effect which clearly shows itself in the graph proceeding from the middle 1950's.

Chart VI—I

CYCLICAL DEVELOPMENTS INSIDE THE E.E.C.
AND THE U.S.

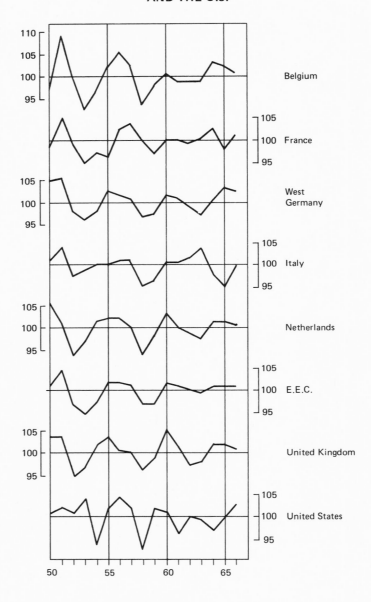

Deviations of the trend of growth in manufacturing industry. (Measured as percentages of
a 5 year moving average of the production index). Source: Dutch Central Economic Planning
Bureau, The Hague.

Asynchronous Cyclical Movements

This asynchronous movement has probably also contributed to the growing interpenetration of trade and services which has been one of the most outstanding features of postwar Europe. But the reverse relationship also applies: the growth of internal E.E.C. trade has affected both the competitive structure of the Common Market and its cyclical stability. Member countries have become much more sensitive to the fluctuations in economic activity of partner countries, and commercial and industrial penetration have exerted a double discipline:

(1) Individual firms and sectors of industry have had to reckon with a rather prompt and meaningful competition from their counterparts elsewhere in the E.E.C. if they went too far out of line in their pricing policies and price-cost relationships.

(2) National economic authorities have had to watch the growing dependency of their national economies on business fluctuations elsewhere.

The growing interdependence has meant that if one national economy were in a state of underemployment and underutilization of capacities, it could, at least to some extent, take part in the satisfactory economic development of partner countries by way of increased exports of goods and services.

Helmut Arndt shows in his contribution on the West German economy that this mechanism has functioned with remarkable effects. The same mechanism has operated as well in the Benelux countries and Italy. Tables V, VI, and VII give some evidence for this phenomenon during the 1960's.

From 1962 to the second half of 1964, Italy's economy boomed. The unemployment level declined, and the price level, both as far as wholesale and consumer goods prices are concerned, rose 8% to 13%. Both Benelux and West German exports were attracted, although the magnitudes involved were not large (Table VI). During the next two years, when the Italian economy began to stagnate under the influence of a strong anti-inflationary monetary policy, Benelux and German exports rose much less or even declined temporarily, as in the case of West Germany. The rises indicated for the whole of 1966 are nearly wholly due to the improvement of economic conditions during the latter part of that year. The quarterly figures would show this quite neatly.

Table VI—V

BENELUX AND ITALIAN EXPORTS TO FEDERAL REPUBLIC OF GERMANY 1962-1972

	1962	1963	1964	1965	1966	1967	1968	1969	1970	1971	1972
Fed. Rep. Ger.											
unemployment %	0.6	0.7	0.6	0.5	0.6	2.1	1.5	0.8	0.6	0.7	1.0
price index											
industrial prices	99.5	100.0	101.1	103.5	105.3	104.4	98.8	101.0	107.0	111.9	115.7
agricultural prices	98.4	100.0	102.7	106.3	113.2	108.4	99.0	102.6	98.8	96.8	109.8
consumer prices	98.5	100.0	102.3	105.8	109.5	111.1	112.7	115.8	120.1	126.6	135.5
Benelux exports to F.R.G.[a]	1742	2040	2413	3059	3117	3171	3899	5188	6450	7529	
Italian exports to F.R.G.[a]	935	927	1117	1641	1670	1609	2017	2415	3048	3404	

[a] in million $

Sources: trade = E.E.C. Statistics: unemployment = E.E.C. Social statistics: prices = I.M.F. Financial Statistics 1963 = 100

Table VI—VI

BENELUX AND FEDERAL REPUBLIC OF GERMANY EXPORTS TO ITALY 1962-1972

	1962	1963	1964	1965	1966	1967	1968	1969	1970	1971	1972
Italy											
unemployment %	3.0	2.5	2.7	3.6	3.9	3.5	3.5	3.4	3.2	3.2	3.3
price index											
wholesale prices	95.1	100.0	103.4	105.0	106.6	106.4	106.8	111.0	119.1	123.1	128.2
consumer prices	93.0	100.0	105.9	110.6	113.3	117.4	119.0	122.2	128.2	134.4	142.7
Benelux exports to Italy[a]	329	463	472	493	550	655	721	937	1124	1226	
F.R.G. exports to Italy[a]	1024	1278	1179	1090	1371	1697	2837	1335	2949	3127	

[a] in million $

Sources: trade = E.E.C. Statistics: unemployment = E.E.C. Social statistics: prices = I.M.F. Financial Statistics 1963 = 100

Table VI–VII

BENELUX IMPORTS FROM FEDERAL REPUBLIC OF GERMANY AND ITALY 1962-1972

	1962	1963	1964	1965	1966	1967	1968	1969	1970	1971	1972
Netherlands											
unemployment %	0.7	0.7	0.7	0.8	1.0	1.9	1.7	1.3	1.1	1.5	2.4
price index											
home & import goods	98.0	100.0	106.0	110.0	115.0	115.0	116.0	117.0	124.0	125.0	130.0
consumer prices	96.3	100.0	105.5	109.7	116.1	120.1	124.5	133.8	139.7	148.9	164.4
Belgium											
unemployment %	1.4	0.9	0.7	0.9	1.0	3.7	4.5	3.6	3.2	1.9	2.3
price index											
wholesale prices	97.5	100.0	104.6	105.8	108.2	107.0	107.3	112.6	118.0	117.8	123.4
consumer prices	97.9	100.0	104.2	108.4	112.9	116.2	119.4	123.8	128.7	132.1	143.8
F.R.G. exports to Benelux[a]	2085	2433	2884	3029	3546	3638	4183	5243	6692	7143	
Italian exports to Benelux[a]	281	351	448	551	629	682	787	900	1183	1285	

[a] in million $

Sources: trade = E.E.C. Statistics: unemployment = E.E.C. Social statistics: prices = I.M.F. Financial Statistics 1963 = 100

However, with boom conditions prevailing in West Germany in 1965 and with an unemployment rate of 0.5% and sharply rising prices, the Italians could increase their exports by some $520 million in one year, and the Benelux countries, by some $630 million (Table V). The next year it was the turn of the Germans. When the German rate of unemployment went up to 2.1% in 1966-67 and prices were stabilized, German exports found an outlet in both the booming Benelux and Italian economies. Between 1965 and 1968, there was an increase of nearly $800 million of exports to Italy and of more than $1,100 million to the Benelux countries. In 1967-69, the Benelux economy experienced relative stagnation with rising unemployment, especially in Belgium. Prices increased only slowly. (The adoption of the T.V.A.—value-added—tax system explains a good deal of the rise of the consumer price index for 1968-1969 in the Netherlands and for 1969-70 in Belgium.) However, Belgian firms soon found an outlet for their exports in the booming Italian and West German economies (Tables V and VI), with exports rising no less than $2,000 million to West Germany alone between 1967 and 1969.

Clearly then, the asynchronous development of the business cycle in the increasingly open economy of the Common Market has fostered an overall stabilization of the European economy. It has countered recessionary tendencies and dampened boom while promoting, at the same time, the interpenetration of mutual trade. Only in the beginning of the 1970's did this mechanism no longer seem to function. Beginning in 1971, all the countries mentioned above moved into a boom stage of the cycle, and this may well explain why prices in the Common Market economies increased simultaneously and more rapidly than before. As yet, it is too early to determine whether this represents a definite change towards more synchronous economic development or merely marks an intermediate stage in the economic structure of the E.E.C. The first kind of development towards permanent change would seem to be the more probable, now that a high degree of interpenetration has been achieved.

The phenomenon, moreover, is not only confined to Western Europe. The striking new development of the upswing of 1972-73 was the simultaneous expansion of the major industrial world economies — the E.E.C., the United States, and Japan. "Over the past fifteen years," according to the OECD's July 1973 *Economic Outlook,* "cyclical movements in [these] three main areas have been roughly coincident only at the time of the 1958 and 1971 recessions. In both the mid-1960's and the late 1960's booms, some major country or other had always been out of step with the world's business cycle. . . . On the present occasion, by contrast, almost all O.E.C.D. countries are expected to witness growth rates in excess of potential in 1973 and in the first half of 1974. . . . This in combination with shortages of many primary commodities helps to explain the unexpectedly fast inflation." [2] Had the oil crisis not intervened, this projected boom cycle would probably have continued unabated.

While we will not discuss the implications of this important phenomenon for worldwide inflation here, one would want to note that a boom, "the strongest witnessed . . . since the early 1950's" [3] and generalized throughout the industrial world, obviously would have its repercussions on materials and energy input prices because of the supply inelasticities. The profits of companies supplying these goods have indeed risen sharply after having been depressed for a number of years. All of a sudden, a unique chance has been presented to mid-Western American farmers, multinational oil and gas companies, socialist British mineworkers, Arab feudal rulers, and the like, to exploit worldwide scarcities. And the same experience occurred earlier with other suppliers of end products and factor inputs.

It shows once again that when conditions permit, groups of suppliers not only follow market demand changes with price variations, but also try, and often succeed, to alter in their favor the structural relationships.

This also clearly indicates that the present competitive process is a power struggle between organized groups. Each round of change creates a new constellation of data on which some other group is going to act and which it will try to change to its own advantage. Governments are, as a rule, both too slow and too weak to influence this power game more than marginally. In particular, the classical monetary and fiscal measures are inadequate to deal with these phenomena, as some monetary theorists have now come to recognize. The commitment of the responsible authorities to "save the appearances" — no high unemployment, continuance of orderly trade and production, avoidance of prolonged strikes, etc. — leaves them only one way out: inflation.

As the following sections indicate, the countries originally composing the European Economic Community have been able, up to 1970-71, to escape the stagflation problem resulting from the power battle. In a final section, it will be pointed out that economic conditions are changing in this area too, now that the process of economic integration and rapid interpenetration of trade is slowing down.

ECONOMIC PENETRATION AND CHANGES
IN INDUSTRY STRUCTURE

One of the most important results of the formation of the E.E.C. has been the relative growth of intra-E.E.C. trade in comparison with the gross national product. Chart II shows that the elasticity of intra-E.E.C. trade in comparison with domestic expenditure was some 2.5-3.0,* which was nearly double the elasticity of world trade for the periods 1953-57 and 1960-64. The share of intra-E.E.C. trade

Chart VI–II

ELASTICITY OF E.E.C. INTRA-TRADE

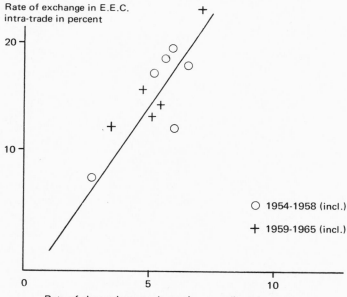

Rate of exchange in E.E.C.
intra-trade in percent

○ 1954-1958 (incl.)

+ 1959-1965 (incl.)

Rate of change in gross domestic expenditure in percent

Source: Dutch Central Economic Plan 1967.
Note: Expenditure weighted on the basis of shares of countries in intra-trade· intra-trade
leads with half a year; volume changes in percentage.

*i.e., a rise in domestic expenditure of member states was accompanied by an increase of 2.5% to 3% of intra-E.E.C. trade.

has therefore risen from some 30% in 1957 to 43.5% in 1965 and to 50.0% in 1971, and thus has doubled in comparison with the early 1950's. This growing interpenetration of the E.E.C. economies has probably been a more important long-run influence on the behavior of the individual economies and the private partners — employers and trade unions — than the equalization of business fluctuations. Specifically, it has exerted a sharp downward pressure on the degree of business concentration in the continental European markets.

Whereas economic concentration seems to have risen in both the United States and Great Britain, the European economy underwent a massive and prolonged deconcentration process during the 1950's and 1960's. And as will be seen, important consequences were bound to follow from this central phenomenon. We will first outline the theoretical process, deduce the consequences, and see how far these can be verified from the available evidence. Then we will examine the reactions of the business community and governments concerned.

Given a closed economy and working under the often stated classical assumptions (of an absence of change over time and of nonexistent or negligeable transport and distribution costs), structural concentration in a particular sector of industry can be defined as the relationship between the optimal size of a firm and the size of the market to be considered. This concept of structural concentration refers to the proportion or share of a given market taken up by firms of optimal size, without interference from government, institutional, or private entrepreneurial measures which would tend to influence concentration beyond or below the degree required for the operation of lowest average cost firms in that particular market. Dropping both assumptions leads us, first, towards the concept of the potential market awaiting exploitation by existing entrepreneurs in the field and by possible new entrants. The potential market will be appreciated subjectively by the entrepreneurs concerned even though they will have a larger or smaller number of objective reference points (number of customers, per capita spending power, etc.) depending on the circumstances.

If the particular sector of industry is still young and has a bright future, the potential market will be estimated to be large in relation to actual sales. Consequently, entrepreneurs will try to enlarge their sales by building up new capacities for production. They may do so, depending on the state of industrial techniques, either by means of building larger plants and achieving more mechanized output, or, in the event technological possibilities have already been exploited, by means of building more plants of a similar nature. Either way stimulates the growth of output as the race for more sales and/or a larger market share gets underway. New entrants will also join the already established firms, so that expansionary market growth will be accompanied by stable or declining horizontal concentration. This often refers to both absolute and relative concentration as well as to vertical integration. The latter will be reduced because more numerous suppliers can each achieve the higher level of optimum output made possible by the growth of the market.

However, no product has an indefinite future. The more the actual market is being enlarged, the more the potential markets will be reduced. The process may be interrupted by the discovery of new applications for an existing product at established prices, or the reduction of prices due to improved production processes, or both. But the expansion of demand will sooner or later be curbed. Limits may be of an absolute nature, as in the case of coal or steam-engines which are being replaced by substitutes that satisfy consumers better, so that output declines. Or the limits may be of a more relative nature, expressing themselves in a slower and declining rate of growth. The main difference here is a question of the time horizon considered, which does not currently interest us.

Both absolute and relative limits to the growth of demand will mean an increasing degree of market saturation the more the market develops. Thus, dropping the classical static assumptions leads us to the inevitable conclusion — save one proviso — that structural concentration will have to rise as the market for a product or group of products progresses and matures. The proviso is, of course, that the optimal firm size in that particular sector of industry does not decline. That would be a highly unrealistic assumption. Not only does industrial history teach us that the most efficient scales of production of automobiles, steel, cotton, and other goods have increased through the years, it has taught us also that a maturing industrial sector produces a larger quantitative output requiring more mechanization and an altered organizational structure (if only for logistic reasons).

It would at the same time be wrong to conclude that structural concentration in the economy as a whole, or in the manufacturing sector in general, would have to rise as well since this would depend on the relative weights of output of the various industry sectors or markets with different structural tendencies. We see here, at the same time, the principal error of Marx and the Marxists: being impressed by the rise in optimal firm size of the nineteenth-century textile or steel mills, they erroneously inferred that concentration will necessarily have to rise in capitalist society as a whole; whereas in reality, every new industry that is being created imparts a deconcentrating impulse, and it may be — depending on the time and circumstances — that these forces balance or outweigh one another. In any case, structural concentration in a closed but developing economy will vary for a particular sector of industry with the trend in optimum firm size and the degree of market saturation. And optimum firm size is dependent on:

(a) Economies of scale in plants which have a habit of rising over time when more elaborate and refined machinery or production processes are introduced to cope with a larger stream of goods demanded. Mechanization and standardization are intertwined.

(b) Economies of scale in organization or marketing which also rise because new principles of division of labor, whether manual or brain, are applied, often interacting with those mentioned under (a) above.

(c) Economies of scale arising out of vertical integration, especially when standardized output of components and parts is introduced.

It is certainly not maintained that these factors separately or taken together will make for high concentration. Indeed, in the majority of industry sectors, they may not. But they will, however, account for (1) a reduced influx of new firms in the later stages of market development and (2) a decline in the number of existing competitors since some firms are less qualified or less rapid in adopting new processes. Both factors will cause a decline in the number of firms operating efficiently and increase the relative size differences between efficiently producing firms and the others.

If demand growth slows down due to increasing market saturation, the two forces of scale and saturation will interact and produce rising absolute and/or relative concentration because the less efficient — or less financially strong — firms cannot sustain the ensuing price battle. This very often occurs because capacities, built to accomodate a rapidly expanding market demand based on past rates of growth, become underutilized when saturation sets in. So when firms drop out of the race, "spontaneous" concentration will emerge. On top of this, reduced rates of profits or direct losses prompt mergers or cartellization. The process is sometimes repeated once or several times as entrepreneurs go through a "learning process," teaching them that market conditions have fundamentally changed. As an industry matures, market relationships may become more stabilized, and whatever cost rises occur will be reflected sooner and more fully in the prices of end products than was the case when the industry first expanded. Also, the firms of such an industry will try to restore the reduced profit margins by means of price increases, a policy which is at least facilitated by the more concentrated structures.

The argument outlined above assumes that an industry in question is not monopolized in its early stages, as has happened often in the United States. Successful consolidation of firms into a merger, creating a monopoly or the monopolization of a sector of industry right from the start or before expansion begins, as occurred in the American canning, computer, aluminum, and oil industries typifies another pattern less representative of European developments.[4] In any case, this latter pattern does not apply to our analysis since effective deconcentration was the initial question.

What happens, one must ask, when the closed economy opens its frontiers to foreign producers newly residing in an integrated system of economies? That is, what will be the effect on the market process of national economies opening their frontiers to established or potential new producers abroad?[5] This establishes the crucial question of the effect of market integration on market power.

Obviously, we would have to suppress our earlier assumption that transport and distribution costs for sales in foreign markets exert no influence on the attainment of optimal firm size. For whereas such an assumption could be entertained, at least for the smaller economies, the larger economic unit, the E.E.C., resulting from the integration of several larger or smaller economies might have considerable transport and distribution costs. Since market integration abolishes custom tariffs, import licences, and other obstacles to intra-community trade, this becomes a central question.

Lumping such cost factors and others such as insurance premiums, packaging costs, etc., together under the heading of external costs, E per unit of output, as against the pure fabrication costs or internal cost, I per unit of output, enables us to introduce the concept of the sales determinant α. This determinant denotes the reach or range of the sales of the firms in an integrated system of economies and depends on the relationship of both internal and external costs.

Supposing that the development of the absolute levels of input prices for the firms in the integrating economies shows no disparate behavior—otherwise the lowest cost producers would encroach upon the markets of the others — the effects of integration can be approached stepwise:

(1) The potential market for firms in an industry rises with the purchasing power of consumers or buyers in the enlarged, integrated market, inducing an impulse towards a decrease of concentration. In principle, this is a similar effect to an increase in population, or an increase in per capita income, or both, in a closed national market. But the rise in the potential market by means of economic integration will come about more suddenly, impress dynamic entrepreneurs, and prompt them to make substantial investments in order to reap the fruits of an enticing potential market. This is what happened after the foundation of a unified market in the German Zollverein (1834) and again in the German Empire (1870), twice followed by a "Gründerperiode" — an investment period of magnified proportions for both established and new firms. It also occurred in the North American economy after the Civil War (1860-65) and again in Europe after the second world war with the establishment of, first, the Coal and Steel Community (1953) and, later, the Common Market (1958).

(2) Such integration movements also initially induce a reduction of external costs so that the sales determinant α rises, imparting a downward impulse to structural concentration. Because the potential market expands and α rises in the initial stages of market integration, the urge to penetrate the other markets in the integrating system will be extended.

(3) Whereas formal, statistical concentration is reduced overnight with the integration of economies, structural or real concentration adapts itself only gradually to this reduced formal level as the interpenetration of trade proceeds. This is mainly a function of the aforementioned investment process, and it stimulates competition in the enlarged economic unit. The competition will become fiercer, the

more firms encroach upon each other's markets, now made possible by larger production capacities, the reduction of obstacles to trade, and the improvement of transport costs and marketing facilities.

Reconcentration

(4) This enhanced intensity of competition is not, however, a permanent phenomenon. Sooner or later a reversal will take place, depending on the operation of the following factors:

(a) Intensified competition eliminates the profits of the firms operating in enlarged markets or reduces them in such a way that a number of companies will stop competing altogether, reorganize, or merge with others. Assuming similar input price levels and entrepreneurial aptitudes between efficient firms of different integrating countries, the remaining firms will be spread more or less evenly over the participating countries. Assuming, also, different factor cost levels and/or different entrepreneurial attitudes, the firms of the lowest cost countries or those with the more dynamic entrepreneurs will

Table VI—VIII

INTERPENETRATION OF TRADE 1958-1970
(1970 LEVEL AS A MULTIPLE OF 1958, IN CURRENT DOLLARS)

to:	Fed. Rep. Ger.	Benelux	Italy	Total E.E.C.
From:				
Fed. Rep. Ger.	—	5.38	7.38	—
Benelux	6.95	—	7.70	—
Italy	7.54	9.00	—	—
Total E.E.C.	—	—	—	6.36

lead the way, and gains will not be evenly spread. The last assumption is more realistic and, in fact, Italian entrepreneurs in several branches of industry (durable consumer goods, shoes, bicycles, cars) penetrated relatively more in other countries for both reasons during the 1960's. Likewise, the low cost level of Dutch and Belgian firms (the latter ones to a lesser extent) has given them the edge in competition with West German firms, although not against Italian firms. Table VIII gives the results for the 1958-1970 period.

(b) As the most efficient or strongest companies grow at a relatively quicker pace, rationalization and specialization of firms proceed over a broad front, and several will be able to reap economies of scale. The larger market permits them to utilize production techniques adapted to the output of longer series, sometimes known before, but not economical due to the previously restricted size of the market. The increasing intensity of competition, moreover, forces these companies to hand over at least part of the gains to buyers. This is borne out by the behavior of wholesale prices up to 1968 when the price rises in the industrial goods sector and for imports in the E.E.C. were modest for most countries concerned.

Tables V-VII indicate the magnitudes: from zero to some 10-20% for the years between 1962 and 1968, a time when most of the price increases were due to agricultural price rises. The Netherlands is an exception for the period 1964-68 because of the "wage explosion" due mainly to a too successful wage restriction policy during the 1950's. Table IX shows the rise in export prices for the ten-year period 1955-66. With the exception of France which went through repeated devaluations of her currency, the Common Market countries have shown a better record than the Anglo-Saxon countries even though their overall price levels increased more.

This diverse behavior between the E.E.C. and the Anglo-Saxon economies points up a probable explanation of Common Market experience. Inflation in the latter has been of the demand-induced type, stimulated by the investment boom during the 1950's and a good deal of the 1960's. This continuing investment boom followed the classical pattern of building up enlarged facilities for production in an expanding market, a result of market integration and rising purchasing power. The introduction of improved production techniques, however, reduced unit production costs, while intensified competition ensured that export and wholesale prices rose only moderately, or not at all (Italy).

But the boom has also spread the rise of incomes to those sectors (services, construction, and government) where the economies of scale had no effect, and prices in those sectors were driven up disproportionately. Thus, the integration process explains why European export prices for industrial goods, with the exception of France, rose less than those of the Anglo-Saxon countries, whereas consumer prices rose more. The Dutch consumer price indices are typical in this respect: whereas food prices rose 27.3% between 1964 and 1970, rents increased 42.5%, and medicare prices, 96.1%! On the other hand, durable consumer goods and household energy prices rose only 15.0% and 16.1% respectively.

Other consumer prices fell in between, with prices of industrial goods rising proportionately less, with a few exceptions.

Table VI—IX

AVERAGE ANNUAL RISE OF THE PRICE LEVEL OF EXPORTS AND OF THE G.N.P. PERIODS 1955/66 AND 1968/70.

| | 1955-1966 | | 1968-1970* | |
	Exports	G.N.P.	Exports	G.N.P.
U.S.A.	1.3	2.1	3.4	4.8
U.K.	1.5	3.4	5.7	5.0
Fed. Rep. Ger.	1.3	3.2	0.4	4.0
France	3.2	5.1	5.2	5.7
Italy	−1.0	3.6	2.6	3.9
Belgium	1.0	2.7	3.1	3.5
Netherlands	0.5	4.2	1.9	5.0

*   in national currency
Source: Central Economic Plan, The Hague, 1971, p. 37.

(c) Market integration thus has had rather favorable consequences during the sixties. However, these were and could not be permanent. As interpenetration of trade and the elimination of the highest cost producers proceeded, the optimal scale of output increased, the saturation of markets rose at an increased rate, and external costs went up as well. With this last factor, the reduction in customs duties and the improvement of transport costs was a one-time reduction, spread out, in the case of the E.E.C., as a graduated decline over a ten-year period. With increasing interpenetration, sales and transport costs started to rise again since larger distances had to be covered and opposition to the intruding firms increased from established national firms. This, in turn, required additional advertising and sales promotion costs and higher outlays for penetrating the distribution channels in partner countries.

Because of these reasons, structural concentration is bound to be lifted upward, and mergers will sooner or later reflect the underlying tendency towards increased structural concentration in the integrating economies. The extent and timing of this reversal will vary in different branches of industry, and some will experience merger waves earlier than others. European motor car producers, for example, had most of their mergers in the 1965-68 period, whereas durable consumer goods producers (washing machines, refrigerators, cookers) started to integrate only after 1968-69. In this last case, market saturation became apparent towards the end of the 1960's. [6]

For individual countries and particular industries, there is clear evidence that the number of mergers and the amounts of capital involved increased spectacularly between the 1950's and 1960's. The number of Italian mergers varied between 15 and 50 in the years 1957-60, and the amounts of nominal capital involved were between 2 and 4 billion lires. The figures rose to 477 in 1966, 689 in 1967, and still further in 1968 and 1969. Nominal capital increased to 350 billion lires and more. Dutch mergers, which averaged sixteen annually in the years 1958-60, quadrupled in the period 1960-65, and experienced two other waves from 1966-1968 (135 per annum) and in 1969-71 (more than 320 in each of these years). The French mergers rose from 120-150 per year during the early 1960's to more than 200 during most of the years following 1965, with a 4.5-fold increase in the net assets involved. In West Germany, the number of large mergers, (i.e., those which had to be notified under article 23 of the cartel law) more than trebled between 1958-59 and 1965-67, with further quadrupling in later years up to 1971-72. Only Belgium was, to some extent, an exception, but mergers had already been promoted there on a large scale by means of two laws during the 1950's and one in 1962 which excluded mergers from taxes on hidden reserves in conjunction with the cessation of business activities or the sale of fixed assets. Moreover, Belgian financial holdings were consolidated long ago, and it is not always easy to trace the changes of ownership of companies belonging to these conglomerate groups.

This European-wide merger boom was predominantly of a horizontal nature. The share of Dutch horizontal mergers was 62.4% on average for the period 1958-1970, with an increasing share for the later years (69% in 1967-69) as intra-European competition rose in fierceness. This shift occurred simultaneously with the rise in the number of mergers. Similar tendencies prevailed in West Germany (about 70% horizontal mergers) and the other E.E.C. countries.

Another general characteristic of many merger activities was the clustering in industry sectors such as automobiles, chemicals, iron and steel, coal, oil and energy production, mechanical and electrical engineering. This, to some extent at least, casts doubt on a favorite explanation that the American and British multinational companies were mainly responsible for the merger wave. For there are no American coal or steel firms (carbon steel) operating in Europe, and European chemical firms increased their share of world markets all during the 1960's. It is true that transnational intra-E.E.C. mergers and participations remained substantially below those between E.E.C. companies and third-country firms (mainly of U.S. and U.K. origin). The shares were respectively 35.2% and 64.8% for the five-year period, 1966-70. These international mergers, however, were far outdistanced by the total of national E.E.C. mergers, even though we have no measure as to the relative assets or sales sizes of both groups.

Finally, an idea of the growth of large business is provided by the increase in the rate of overall concentration between 1960 and 1970. The measure is the proportion of the sales of the x-largest firms in the gross domestic products (Table X).[7]

Table VI—X

	SHARE OF X-LARGEST FIRMS			**INCREASE OF SHARES**		
	1960	1965	1970	1960-1965	1965-1970	1960-1970
4 largest	5.8	6.8	8.1	1.0	1.3	2.3
8 largest	10.4	11.8	14.6	1.4	2.8	4.2
20 largest	20.9	22.5	29.0	1.6	6.5	8.1
50 largest	35.1	35.1	45.7		10.6	10.6

Source: Calculations made by Institute des Sciences Economiques, University of Louvain, Belgium.

It will be readily seen that the fifty largest firms did not increase their share during the first half of the decade. The second half, on the contrary, saw a spectacular rise, no doubt mainly as a result of the merger wave. Moreover, the figures relating to the increase of shares show that it was the group of the twenty to fifty largest firms which grew fastest.

The general conclusion from the foregoing analysis is that, at the outset, economic integration decreases market concentration and intensifies the competitive process. Prices decline — at least relatively — for the goods which are internationally traded, and an investment boom will be stimulated as the more dynamic firms capture newly opened actual and potential markets. But the process is reversed after some time when optimal scale increases, markets get saturated, and penetration costs increase. Horizontal concentration — artificially, by means of merger, or spontaneously, by the dropping out of the firms from the race — will be stimulated. Likewise, the asymmetrical structure of industries will be promoted by the proportionately more intensive merger activity of larger firms.

THE DEVELOPMENT OF PRICES

Effects of Deconcentrated Industrial Structures on Prices.
     One of the main initial effects of economic integration has been a much fiercer price competition inside the Community. Because other partner countries are the main customers of Common Market member states, the producers of the member countries had to "internationalize" their price cuts to buyers. The result has often been a generally lower level of prices for export goods over the level of prices which have prevailed within a particular country. The battle for markets, necessitated by the investment process and generated by expansion into the larger E.E.C. market, required these competitive export prices. Many capital-intensive industries have sold additional outputs abroad at prices below the full-cost level.
     A first indication of the divergence between national and export prices is provided by E.E.C. statistics. For the period 1958-1967 inclusive, the absolute levels and annual average rates of increase for total consumer prices, total wholesale prices (with subdivisions), and average export values are given in Table XI.
     It will be seen that in all countries, consumer prices rose more than wholesale prices, and that wholesale prices (both for all goods and for the sub-classes, agricultural and industrial goods) rose more than average export values, except in the case of Western Germany. Inspection of the German series reveals that the rise of export prices of 0.8% on average for those nine years was due in large part to the monetary revaluation of 1961. Without this revaluation, the increase would have been confined to a mere 0.2% on average, or practically

Table VI—XI

CONSUMER, WHOLESALE AND EXPORT PRICE DEVELOPMENTS IN THE E.E.C. 1958-1967.

(1958 = 100)

	F.R.G.		France		Italy		Neth.		Belgium	
	a	b	a	b	a	b	a	b	a	b
Index of total consumer prices	123	2.3	140	3.8	137	3.6	137	3.6	123	2.3
Index of total wholesale prices	104	0.4	122	2.2	113	1.4	117	1.8	111	1.2
of which:										
agricultural products	106	0.7	122	2.2	119	2.0	128	2.8	122	2.2
industrial products	101	0.1	125	2.5	113	1.4	119	2.0	—	n.a.
energy products	105	0.5	115	1.6	102	0.2	102	0.2	96	−0.4
Index of average export values	107	0.8	105	0.5	93	−0.8	108	0.9	100	—

Note: a = index value 1967; b = average annual rise in percent; — = zero   Source: Bureau of Statistics E.E.C.

in line with the rise in industrial wholesale prices. Similarly, in the Dutch case, the rise in export values would have been halved without the revaluation. Another exception was Benelux energy prices which rose less than export values. Here the large expansion of oil refining activities and the discovery of natural gas in the Netherlands may have been the main influences. Further, it is noteworthy that export prices of the Community's main agricultural export countries, namely France and the Netherlands, rose more than those of the other countries.

It follows that industrial goods prices, both at the wholesale and export levels, have risen less than the prices of other goods. In view of the fast interpenetration of E.E.C. trade to levels varying between 40% and 65% of total imports of the countries concerned and the high proportion of industrial goods and energy in the composition of this trade (77.5% in 1958 and 81% in 1967), the conclusion seems unavoidable that such relative price stability was due to increased competition. The effective deconcentration and fiercer competition assured that the gains from large-scale operations, other productivity increases, and innovations were translated into stable or declining product prices.

(2) Likewise, the 1970 OECD report on inflation noted that

Until 1967, E.E.C. member countries as a rule experienced much lower price increases on exports (in dollar terms) than on domestic output of goods, with Italy as the most outstanding example. Since then, however, export prices of Italy and Benelux [countries] moved about in line with domestic prices. The same is true for German export prices. . . .[8]

In the United States and Canada, however, export prices rose faster than domestic prices during the same period, while the U.K. experience fell between that of the E.E.C. and North America with a roughly parallel rise of export and domestic prices until the late 1967 devaluation.

(3) A survey more on the individual business level was made by V. Terpstra in the mid-1960's.[9] Terpstra's survey of a sample of twenty-five large American firms (from Fortune's 500) which operated in the Common Market indicated that competition had greatly increased. Most of the interviews among the ten non-durable consumer goods firms, the ten industrial goods firms, and the five durable

consumer goods firms took place in 1964, with an additional gathering of data in 1966. "These 25 firms," Terpstra noted, "had a total of eighty-eight country production sources, i.e. the average firm was producing in more than three different member countries." The number of industrial plants was still higher as several firms had more than one plant in a particular country. About a third of the eighty-eight country production sources were added since the Rome treaty was signed (1958).

One of the general findings of the survey was that price competition increased in the E.E.C. after 1957. This was the experience of three-quarters of the respondent companies, especially of the manufacturers of consumer durable and industrial goods having greater opportunities for international sales. Among the reasons mentioned were excess capacity resulting from the expansion of production facilities, the breaking into new lines of production or markets, and the lower degree of profit consciousness of European firms due to the desire to maintain employment or exports.

Another notable finding was that the American companies have not generally been leaders in competition on a price basis in Europe and usually resented the price pressures from European competition. One automobile executive expressed such sentiments and said American competitors were "more sensible." A leading German industrialist also noted that "To date, the Americans have used no combative prices. They try to win the market most of all with intensive advertising campaigns." A packaging firm of American origin said there was excess capacity in the industry so that the firm was differentiating its products to avoid direct price competition. Another observation was that "American chemical companies let European competitors take over production of many staple items and then turned to special products where price competition was less."

Without going into the question of the rationality of this kind of behavior, we reiterate the two conclusions from this survey: first, that price competition increased notably in Europe during the 1960's, mainly because of economic integration; and second, that American companies were not the leaders in this process but tried to evade this kind of competition as far as possible.

We can make explanations of such phenomena as difficult as we like, but the most plausible conclusion is that deconcentration has made it necessary for most European firms to compete in price, while many American companies have transferred their American goals and behavior to the E.E.C.: "Some executives seem to feel that what is good for America is good for the rest of the world".[10]

A number of cases illustrate the impact of the sharpened E.E.C. cartel policy.[11]

(1) Since the middle of 1963, the photographic industry, Kodak in particular, has had general clauses for resellers regarding the (forbidden) resale of products in other Common Market countries and the fixing of prices. Both were adjusted after intervention by the competition authorities of the E.E.C.

(2) A Belgian sales syndicate for perfumes used collective price and distribution enforcements which were likewise adjusted.

(3) A joint sales office of French superphosphate producers for operations both inside and outside of the Common Market was adjusted after intervention in such a way that only joint sales outside the Common Market territory were approved.

(4) The Omega agreement for the sale of Swiss quality watches was approved only after two clauses were inserted: (1) that the exclusive national dealers encountered no restrictions on exports to other countries; and (2) that dealers were free to buy from every one of the five main national importers.

(5) The splitting up of markets according to nationalities was rather systematically rejected in accordance with the stipulations of article 85, paragraph 1. One prominent example was the noted Grundig/Consten case (1966) under which absolute territorial protection was defeated. "No other firm in France, apart from sole agent Consten, which intended to buy Grundig products could obtain such products outside France without getting into difficulties. Any such enterprise was solely dependent on Consten for its supplies . . . " and large price differences prevailed.[12]

(6) A similar case of market division was the Julien/van Katwijk case under which exports of paper tubes to Belgium and the Netherlands were restricted. This likewise received a negative decision.

(7) Comparable agreements in flat glass and window glass restricting sales between countries were abolished, and clauses such as the mutual adoption of sales conditions and the mutual delivery contract between manufacturers, excluding direct exports, were rejected.

Mr. Borschette, the E.E.C. commissioner for competition policy, stated in June 1971 that in 589 cases adaptations had been achieved, five agreements had been completely interdicted, and thirty-six agreements were voluntarily dissolved. He noted that "the written agreement, formerly classic among enterprises which restricted the competition and which foresaw conventional sanctions against those who did not respect the agreement, tends to disappear." Thus the classical cartel is on the way out on the E.E.C. level, both because of market interpenetration and because of antitrust policy. He did note, however, that "a much more refined form" of concerted practice — "difficult to detect" — was beginning to appear, probably reflecting the newly formed oligopolistic structures which resulted from the merger wave in recent years.

Concentration and the Acceleration of Inflation.

In recent years, the E.E.C. commission has sharpened its anticartel policy. The first sign of a more formal policy on competition appeared when some guidelines were laid down regarding mergers in the iron and steel industry early in 1970.[13] It was noted that internal expansion of iron and steel firms and mergers had led, since the establishment of the Coal and Steel Community, to larger enterprises and industrial groupings. Dominant positions had not yet arisen, however, according to the commission, and effective competition seemed assured on the basis of the investment projects made known for the period 1970-75. In 1968, there were 113 enterprises in the sector of iron and steel, producing 99 million tons. Of this total, the twelve largest accounted for 78.6%; the twenty-two largest for 91.7%. The situation at the end of the 1960's was such that there was considered to be no incompatibility between a policy aiming at effective competition within the Common Market and an industrial policy raising the competitive power of E.E.C. iron and steel firms in world markets.

Nevertheless, the commission outlined a "structural policy" for the concentration in the steel industry among E.E.C. enterprises because imports, amounting to some 5% of apparent consumption (or 4% of output), could not be expected to ensure a sufficient amount of competition. The commission indicated that the limiting rule would be a share of 90% of output of crude steel supplied by no less than ten firms. An oligopoly of such a number, of which the largest firm had at most 12% or 13% of the market, would be acceptable. But anything less than this number, or poolings of interests among firms by means of holding companies, or the mixing up of vertical sales lines and distribution channels would be viewed with suspicion.

It has been suggested that the rule would be undermined in case of British entry into the E.E.C., since the nationalized British Steel Corporation far surpasses the largest E.E.C. producers and would account for a share of about 20% in the enlarged Community. This might not be a continuing problem if B.S.C.'s share of the enlarged market were to drop within the next few years, as it has done as a percentage of world output in the postwar period. But B.S.C.'s massive investment program is meant to prevent this, and its high share might well act as an attraction for other companies to follow suit. The "parity level" was an argument frequently used in the 1950's as a rationale for fostering concentration among some smaller companies.

In other sectors, antitrust policy has also become more rigorous. Full-fledged, long-standing cartels such as the quinine cartel, the Belgian cement producers cartel, the Dutch cement traders cartel, the E.E.C. sugar cartel, and others have been forbidden and penalized. "Concerted agreements" were attacked in 1971 for the first time when the international dyestuffs producers were condemned for three concerted price increases during the 1960's. The case was won by the commission before the Court of Justice in 1972.

Other action with respect to dominant positions has also increased. Apart from the case of Continental Can, which provided the starting point for the Community's antimerger policy, two recent price discrimination cases intending to exploit market power by means of intra-Common Market sales prohibitions have been picked out by the commission. One concerned the U.S. subsidiary, Wea Filippachi Music in Paris, which was fined the highest penalty ever (1.5% of sales) because it prohibited distribution of records produced in France (where they cost $2.80) in West Germany (price $4.45). The other case concerned Pittsburgh Corning Europe which sold its products in the West German market at a price level up to 40% above that prevailing in the Benelux countries and which forbade its Dutch and Belgian distributors to equalize price levels by means of exports.

In one of the largest cases of European cartel policy, involving the synthetic fiber cartel, the commission refused to authorize a production and investment cartel among the five European producers controlling 90% of output even though there was, in 1971-72, a large amount of excess capacity in the industry. Likewise, the German Federal Cartel Office penalized producers in the same industry for price collusion in the German market.

These and similar national cases [14] indicate that competitive policies have been sharpened; but also there is now a widespread tendency among sellers to check their overt price behavior and to exploit their economic power positions in alternative ways. [15] New forms of price behavior are increasingly fortified by the ongoing concentration of power. The creation of oligopolistic structures in many European sectors of industry has increased the possibilities of coordinated price behavior. It has facilitated agreements, notwithstanding the increased attention from "Brussels," creating possibilities that did not exist, or did to a lesser extent, during the expansionary period of the 1960's when markets were still growing rapidly. Conditions have changed mainly for three reasons:

(1) The new products of the 1950's and the 1960's have run their course, and most of their markets have now matured sufficiently so that producers no longer gain by reducing or stabilizing their prices. If a large section of consumers is provided with a particular product and repeat sales become dominant, there is no longer an incentive to promote sales by means of price competition. To prevent "irresponsible" sellers from upsetting the balance, a cartel agreement or other concerted behavior is opportune. Still more effective is a takeover of price-cutters, especially where cartel agreements have been ruled out.

(2) The new potential markets of the Community which were opened as a result of the Rome treaty have, one after another, been conquered, and producers are more and more intruding into each others markets. Therefore, transnational competition killing mergers and informal agreement are a way out and may stabilize market relationships. The E.E.C. durable consumer goods industry (washing machines, refrigerators), the focus of fierce competition during the 1960's, is a case in point. Since 1969, mergers have crystallized the market structure to where now a handful of dominant suppliers have established networks throughout the whole E.E.C. territory.

(3) The increasing trend towards environmental consciousness has likewise been responsible for a slackening of growth in the more sensitive products (chemicals, plastics, oil burning), and concentration has been promoted because of the higher expenditures for pollution control. Unequal treatment of producers by various laws or institutions, as in the paper industry, has only added to the urgency.

The result of this increased concentration of output and sales is that prices in many sectors of manufacturing industry, which either declined or were held stable before 1968, have had a tendency to rise since then. This has meant that an important group of manufacturing and energy-producing industries — which had previously held back the rise of the general price level — no longer function as a brake on inflation. An example would be European automobile prices. The big industry mergers occurred in the 1965-1968 period. It was a reactionary movement following increased competition which had developed from the mid-1950's. Two main factors accounted for the nominal price stabilization (even price reductions) in the industry: increasing mass production methods which gave rise to cost savings, and the reduction of import tariffs on cars, which in 1960 amounted to 20% in the Benelux countries, but were higher in France and Italy. By the first of July 1968, these tariffs had disappeared altogether.

At about the same time, most small producers (Audi, N.S.U., and Glass in Germany, Saab in Sweden, Lancia in Italy, Jaguar and Rover in Britain, Panhard in France, and others) had either stopped production or were taken over, and several large scale mergers had occurred among the bigger car manufacturers. Since market growth slowed down from the hectic pace which had marked the industry in previous years, further gains from large scale economies were apparently exhausted.

After September 1969, the prices of automobiles started to rise. Volkswagen was the market leader, pushing prices upwards by 10%; and the other producers followed in the ensuing months. Though price increases have varied with the national origin of manufacturers, all have participated in the upward pattern (Table XII).

It should be noted that monetary influences (revaluations and devaluations) have had some influence on the pattern. Moreover, the price rises discount, in some cases, technical improvements such as more powerful engines and safer construction. The table records prices in the Dutch market which is fairly representative since more than 90% of cars sold there are imported, mainly from other E.E.C. countries. The price rises in the three years mentioned have at least paralleled the increases in wages and material costs.

Table VI—XII

COMPARISON OF AUTOMOBILE PRICES OF SOME POPULAR TYPES 1969-1972.

(prices in guilders)

	Jan. 1969	Jan. 1970	Febr. 1972	1969/72 +%
Austin/Morris Mini 1000	5,395	6,048	6,289	16.5
Citroen 2CV	4,350	4,795	5,195	19.4
Daf 55	6,595	7,575	7,895	19.7
Fiat 850	4,727	5,130	5,529	16.7
124	6,999	7,866	8,208	17.3
Ford Escort 1100	5,495	6,390	6,903	25.6
Opel Kadett (General Motors)	5,995	6,572	6,994	16.6
Peugeot 204	7,990	7,995	8,295	3.8
Renault 4	4,595	5,350	5,920	28.8
Simca 1000	5,195	5,495	5,695	9.6
1100	6,595	6,995	7,295	10.6
Vauxhall Viva	5,890	6,931	7,347	24.7
Toyota Corolla	6,475	7,399	7,999	23.5
VW 1200	4,795	5,580	5,928	23.6
1300	5,495	6,481	6,800	23.7
Rolls Royce Silver Shadow	88,000	106,875	107,320	21.9

Table XIII repeats the schema of Table XI for the years 1967-1972. It will be seen that the discrepancy between export prices and other prices, as well as between industrial wholesale and energy prices, on the one hand, and consumer prices, on the other, has largely disappeared. This new pattern does not permit more than a probable (negative) conclusion that the gains from integration, resulting out of economies of scale and fiercer competition, have by now been largely exhausted. It cannot be concluded that higher concentration is solely responsible for the domestic or export price increases. Other factors such as currency realignments and higher wages also play a role, although they may be but the reflection of the successful competitive performance achieved earlier by the E.E.C. firms.

Table VI—XIII

CONSUMER, WHOLESALE AND EXPORT PRICE DEVELOPMENT IN THE E.E.C. 1967-1972
(1967 = 100)

	F.R.G.		France		Italy		Nether.		Belgium	
	a	b	a	b	a	b	a	b	a	b
Index of total consumer prices	121	4.2	132	6.4	122	4.4	136	7.1	123	4.8
Index of total wholesale prices	111	2.2	130	6.0	121	4.2	112	2.4	114	2.7
of which: agricultural products	108	1.5	135	7.4	127	5.4	112	2.3	109	1.8
industrial products	111	2.1	126	5.2	120	4.0	112	2.2	115	2.3
energy products	122	4.4	137	7.3	121	4.2	115	2.9	114	2.8
Index of average export values	124	4.8	115	2.9	124	4.8	109	1.7	109	1.7

Note: a = index value 1972 (third quarter)   b = average annual rise in percent 1967-1972 (third quarter)
Sources: E.E.C. General Statistics   International Financial Statistics, December 1972

MARKET POWER IN SPECIAL AREAS

The general deconcentration movement within European industry and commerce, the intensified price competition, and the fiercer anticartel policy emanating from Brussels have not disrupted power positions in specialized sectors — the professions, government services, or local and regional industries. Generally, such sectors have experienced higher price increases than the internationalized sectors, and their isolation from the main currents of international competition has given them the protection to exploit their market power.

For our purposes, market power is the ability to have one's own way in market transactions. This can be a greater or lesser phenomenon and should therefore be represented as a continuous function of some variables. One of these is the market share m, the proportion of a particular market demand bought or sold during a specified period. But market power cannot be equated to market share, since the market share may be eroded quickly once it is exploited, or it may not be exploited at all. A monopolist, in the sense of the single seller, might raise the price of his goods, but at the same time, invite competition as a result — provided entry barriers are not high. Or a price rise might divert consumers to some other product or induce them to do without such goods altogether. In such cases, the monopoly would be considered to be weakly founded.

On the other hand, a firm with less than a 100% share of its market, but supplying a product deemed to be an essential in consumer expenditure, with no threat of potential competition, might well be able to exploit its market power better than a weak single seller. Thus market power reflects a double relationship: a relationship with consumers and a relationship with potential or actual alternative suppliers. These introduce the concepts of elasticity of demand and supply which can be viewed in a short-run and long-run sense. Both elasticities provide, as it were, a correction on the market share in order to arrive at an estimate of effective market power. Effective market power can therefore be either lower or higher than the statistically determined market share.

The market power positions examined here all have in common the fact that one or both kinds of elasticities are rather low due to the following considerations:

(1) Firms which are regionally or locally protected from competition because of high transport costs, administrative protection, the output of specialties considered necessary, or the command over a scarce resource. Examples would be beer brewing, building and construction, flour milling and bread baking, publishing and the press.

(2) The professions and related sectors, like medical people, dentists, and hospitals, lawyers, accountants and the like, who sell essential services. Competition within these groups is restricted and entry to the profession or sector is not free. Also, the long-run supply of the basic factors behind these services is very inelastic and often regulated.

(3) Government services such as the post office and the telephone and businesses where output depends on the granting of a license, as did the selling of alcoholic beverages in the Netherlands up until 1968.

In comparison with the industries discussed before, where the opening of the Common Market undermined the market power of firms because of economic integration and the increasing penetration of foreign trade, these economic units have been able to maintain or enlarge their market power. Economic integration has not fundamentally altered their positions. Prices in these protected sectors have risen relatively more than in the competitive sectors, and they have contributed a major share to the inflationary process of the past twenty-five years.

Regional or Local Economic Power

One study which clearly demonstrated the influence of regionally protected economic power on prices and profits was that of L. Buszmann.[16] The author studied the West German regional beer market and found a correlation coefficient between a degree of concentration and beer prices of 0.7136. Chart III shows the relationship; the regression line was characterized by the function Y (prices)= 1.157 + 0.0033 x (degree of concentration).

A rise in the degree of concentration of ten points increased the price by DM 0.033. Two regions — Nordrhein/Westfalen and Bremen/Niedersachen — were something of an exception. The latter was explained by the size of the region, comparable in surface to Bavaria, but it had only 46 breweries in 1961 as against 1536 for Bavaria. Transport costs therefore created dominant positions within the area.

Chart VI—III

PRICES AND CONCENTRATION IN WEST GERMAN
BREWING INDUSTRY (1961)

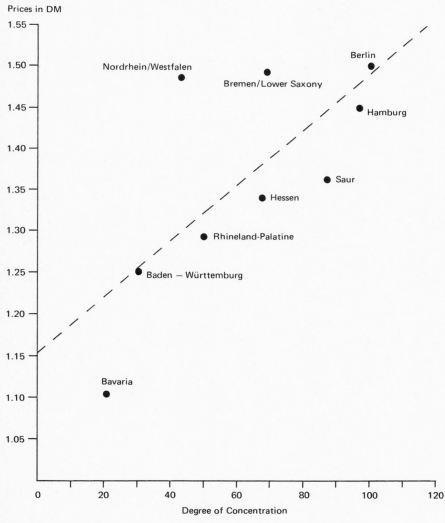

Source: L. Buszmann, o.c.

The first exception was more complicated and may have been due to high incomes and high beer consumption in an urbanized area. A similar but closer relationship was found for concentration and profits: r = 0.98. For every rise in the degree of concentration by 10 points, profits rose 0.095 points.

Another sector sheltered from international competition, often sheltered from even national or regional competition, is building and construction. The OECD report on inflation stated that "technological innovation has so far failed to prevent rises in construction costs from consistently exceeding, often by 50% to 100%, that for GDP as a whole."

How has this come about, and what has been the record? In the Netherlands, an index of construction costs computed by the Central Bureau of Statistics showed a rise of 250% between 1953 and 1970, while rents increased nearly threefold. The price record of the building and construction industries is mainly due to a combination of its costs structure, the product supplied, and the conditions under which this product is demanded.

As to the cost structure, building is an industry with a low relationship between constant and variable costs. As a result, the cost curve is rather flat over a long range of output (Chart IV). In addition, the product supplied varies greatly from large factories and office buildings to small houses and repair work, and price competition is weak. Other competitive parameters, such as quality, liaisons with buyers, delivery time, reputation, specific knowledge, etc., play a (larger) role, and, as a result, price can be manipulated. Both factors together determine a rather wide spectrum of sizes under which building firms can profitably operate.

As we noted before, market integration in Europe stimulated an investment boom. Investments impart a large impetus for work in the building and construction trades, so that this industry has been in a state of permanent, though not continuous, overexpansion since the war. On top of this, governments have stimulated housing and public building, especially during slack periods. Conditions therefore have been established for a major increase in building costs and prices and, consequently, rents. "The sharpest price increases were on average recorded in the building and service industries which in all countries accounted from 70% to as much as 90% of the total rise of the G.D.P. deflator."[17] The contribution to the total annual price rise by

Chart VI–IV

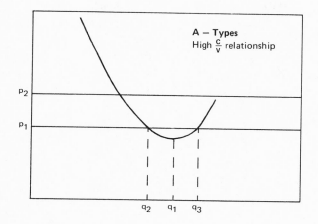

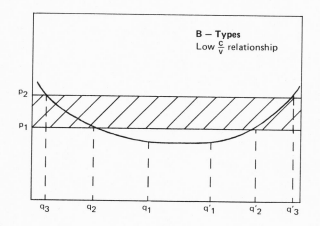

As a result of the high $\frac{c}{v}$ relationship in the A types of industry, optimal size q is (1) large, and (2) determined within narrow confines at competitive price levels (between q_2 and q_3). At higher price levels – e.g., due to cyclical conditions – this range will not increase markedly. Existing firms make good profits and will extend output and capacities to the utmost, thereby driving down the price again. But industries such as building will show many optimal sizes (q_1 and q'_1, q_2 and q'_2 at price level p_1). An expansion of demand, raising prices, will draw many additional firms into the field (optimal sizes q_3 and q'_3 at the price level p_2). Such firms can, moreover, due to the small relative importance of price in comparison with other aspects of the product gain a living more or less permanently. Prices are "made" by the firms within the shaded area of the chart, even in a normal market. Cartel agreements in the building trade are widespread, whether they are officially tolerated as in the Netherlands, or officially forbidden and operating underground as in West Germany building and construction was in many countries, except Britain, between 10%-15%.

A final example of a regionally sheltered market where national concentration has permitted higher prices is flour milling and bread baking. The Dutch market for flour is now dominated by two large companies which operate a cartel jointly with some smaller producers. Only the cooperative mill was an outsider, but this failed in 1973. Concentration has proceeded forward since 1958 with mergers and liquidations.

Table VI–XIV

MARKET STRUCTURE IN DUTCH FLOUR MILLING AND BAKERIES

| | Market Shares in Flour Milling | | Market Shares in Industrial Bakeries |
	1958	1970	1971
Meneba, Rotterdam	28	40	41
Sleutels, Leiden[a]	14		
Wessanen, Wormerveer	26	32	4
Noury-Lande, Deventer[b]	9	–	–
CO-OP, Rotterdam	9	11	20
smaller firms[c]	14	17	35

[a] taken over by Meneba in 1965
[b] closed in 1965
[c] the largest of the smaller ones was taken over by Wessanen in 1970
Source: *CO-OP Monthly*, Sept/October 1971.

The two largest groups have also integrated forward into the bakery sector. The number of bread factories declined from 12,000 in 1958 to 5,200 in 1971. The "industrial bread sector" (making continuous baking possible) doubled its share to 46% in 1971, and the integrated flour/bread groups now command two-thirds of the industrial bakeries. The largest group, Meneba, controls the largest bread companies, especially in the populous western sector of the country. Imports and exports of both flour and bread are insignificant, and bread prices have risen sharply during the concentration process. Overall consumer prices increased 42.1% between 1964 and the middle of 1971, but bread prices rose 49.3%, the fourth largest sectoral increase after medical care, rents and house repair, and shoes. It should, in addition, be added that until early 1971 the government "controlled" bread prices. From 1970 until the end of 1972, bread prices for a standard white load of 800 grams rose by 25%, again well over the general consumer price increase. The cases cited show that, for various reasons, the regionally sheltered industries have contributed disproportionately to inflationary tendencies, especially where firms have been able to increase their market shares.

Chart VI–V

PRICE OF BREAD: THE NETHERLANDS

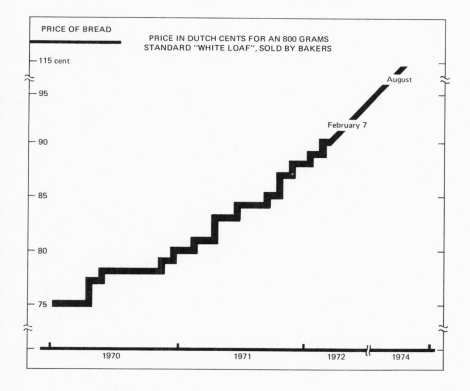

Professional Economic Power

There is no gainsaying that the professions have increased their market power since World War II. The development of technology and the increasing scale of organizations have given them a more pivotal position and, consequently, more power. This power is mainly derived and not original, in that it flows and follows from the development of large scale industry. Again, the interaction of demand and supply is crucial. In the case of most professions, demand for their services is highly income-elastic, but not price-elastic, and has risen rapidly and much more than supply. The short-term elasticity of supply is severely restricted, but even the long-run elasticity is rather low since the professions have fixed rules of admittance requiring special education and training. The educational capacity of the schools cannot be enlarged quickly in response to increased demand, which, it is said, has much to do with the rather traditional and coterie-like attitudes of the educators.

The contribution of these bottlenecks to the inflationary process has been significant. Take the medical profession and related activities — general practitioners, dentists, specialists, physicians in social medicine, nurses, hospitals and equipment. Table XV indicates that the price index for the general group of hygiene and medical care has risen by 90% since 1964 (1971 in comparison with the base year; the 1950's and early 1960's would not show a different record). But the medical care price index alone rose by 126.8%, notwithstanding the fact that during most of the period, there has been "price control" and price decisions by the government regarding doctors and dentists fees as well as specialist's salaries in the health system and hospital charges.

A long-run comparison would show that the number of inhabitants per general practitioner has about doubled during the past one hundred years, a clear, if rough, indication of failing supply. The number of specialists, on the other hand, has increased greatly, a development which is probably representative for all Western European countries. One may well question the economic sense of this far-fetched specialization. It may have led to a medical technology which has proved capable of many spectacular accomplishments, but which also may have increasingly lost contact with many real needs. F.J.A. Huygen noted a few years ago "that 80% to 90% of the medical demands of the population are met by the general practitioners who represent only one-third of all physicians and who have at their disposal only 10% to 25% of the total medical knowledge and techniques. Only 15% of these demands are met by specialists care and only 3% to 5% in hospitals."[18]

Table VI—XV

EDUCATION OF PHYSICIANS IN NETHERLANDS

	(a)	(b)	(c)	(d)	(e)
	Population	Number of general practitioners	Inhabitants per g.p.	Number of specialists	Number of specialists in soc. medicine
1850	3,000,000	2427	1260		
1870	3,600,000	2248	1590		
1900	5,000,000	2151	2370	136	
1940	8,900,000	3164	2820	1399	
1950	10,200,000	3482	2930	2194	
1960	11,600,000	4405	2624	3906	
1963	12,000,000	4587	2625	4503	55
1966	12,500,000	4477	2800	5076	932
1970	13,000,000	4470	2930	6740	1037

Source: C.B.S.
See F.J.A. Huygen, *Some prospects for the education of physicians in the Netherlands.*
Boerhaave Conference on Medical Education and methods, Dec. 1967, in: *Universiteit en Hogeschool,* vol. 14, no. 5.

The implication for the problem of inflation is that a somewhat different application of scarce medical capacities might well score better overall results at less cost. Like aircraft and space technology, medical technology seems to have lost contact with market demand and to have become a potential for inflationary impulses through the presentation of claims on society for more advanced equipment, buildings, education, and the like.

Institutional Economic Power

The economic power of institutions is a very broad area in which governmental and semi-governmental institutions play a preponderant role. We can do little more here than suggest that, again, the loss of contact with the "market" has promoted inflationary expenditure. As a result, the cost of such services has increased more than the average increase in prices, and people have had to pay since no alternatives are open.

Tobacco: — The French and Italian tobacco monopolies are prominent examples, as are the postal services in nearly all Common Market countries. The tobacco monopolies were condemned in article 37 of the E.E.C. treaty which stated that member nations are to effect a reorganization of their national monopolies to eliminate all discrimination between member states where supplies and outlets are concerned. But article 90 seemed to imply that "fiscal monopolies" may continue to exist, and the contradiction has enabled the tobacco monopolies to hang on for twelve years.

Until the treaty, only the tobacco monopoly was entitled to import cigarettes and to fix retail prices. When the treaty became operative, the Italian monopoly hurriedly reorganized itself, and a duty on tobacco and cigarettes was introduced and gradually abolished again. Foreign manufacturers were given a table listing possible supply prices along with the duty, tax, marketing charges, and the retail price. In addition, a deposit system was introduced under which a foreign manufacturer retained the ownership of the tobacco supplied as long as it was in the monopoly's depots. The foreign manufacturer could also indicate the quantities he wanted sent to each of the monopoly's twenty-two central depots.

But when tobacco supplies were transferred to the 630 wholesale subdepots, and from there to tobacco retail units, the tobacco was considered to have been sold to the monopoly. The subdepots and tobacco shops are operated by concessionnaires, and the monopoly claimed that the system did not discriminate between the monopolist's and foreign brands. Could not the tobacconists order their weekly wants? the monopoly argued. But the foreign supplies ordered were not forthcoming, often for weeks, and the excuse was always that central or subdepots had run out. While pretending not to, the monopoly was able to discourage the sale of imported brands by simply failing to supply the tobacconists. Not only have Italian tobacco prices been high and rising, but the system is inefficient. It ensures a priviledged status for several hundred thousand people involved in producing and handling tobacco. There are 16,000 employees of the monopoly itself and 59,000 more licensed tobacconists and their families as well as the subdepot licensees. Then there are the holders of leaf growing licenses who are not so much the farmers as the intermediaries between the monopoly and the real growers. They have a powerful parliamentary lobby.

Telephone and Telegraph: — A final example concerns the French telephone system, the inefficiency of which is legendary. No significant improvement in services has occurred over the years. Telephone density is low with seven lines per 100 inhabitants, half the average in Britain and one-seventh that in Sweden. In 1970, the waiting list was 500,000 households and businesses, with prospects of delays of between six months and a year from the time of application. Installation charges were high (Frs. 600, $125), and rates, likewise (Frs. 0.30 for a local call).

But the French telephone and telegraph services are highly profitable. In 1968 they made more than Frs. 1,000 million, equivalent to almost 20% of turnover, a profit which has increased in more recent years. The cash flow as well was excellent, equivalent to 40% of turnover. Profits have been used, as elsewhere, to subsidize the postal services where rates have also gone up rapidly. But the monopoly has been unable or unwilling to respond to expanding demand, and the technical standard of communications equipment has proved as inadequate as the installation facilities. It should be stressed that these are merely examples which can be generalized: in the Netherlands, the telephone system likewise has long waiting lists, prices and installation charges are soaring, and the system earns good profits.[19] But the state monopoly prevents alternative suppliers from stepping in and delivering competition. The profits earned by the system are fed into the state's exchequer from which it also has to draw the investment expenditure. Under such circumstances, it is obvious what the policy outcome will be.

CONCLUSIONS

In reviewing the Common Market economies during the past fifteen years, it may be noted that, at least up to 1968-69, inflationary tendencies were of the demand-induced type. Economic integration opened the partner economies to the firms willing to expand rapidly. The ensuing investment process had the effects of:

(1) lowering average cost prices per unit of product in manufacturing industry and energy production;

(2) encroachment of firms upon each other's markets, stimulating price competition and interpenetration of trade flows among partner economies much in excess of the growth in international trade;

(3) raising wage and salary levels in industry and trade which were reflected more in the service and building sectors where no unusual productivity gains were achieved;

(4) increasing the end product prices to varying degrees in nation-

ally or regionally sheltered industries.

From 1969 to 1970, certain aspects of these developments no longer held true. From the middle of the 1960's, a large and widening merger movement, mainly of a horizontal nature, increased concentration in many E.E.C. markets. Gains from increasing scale disappeared as markets matured (as in many durable consumer goods and industrial intermediate products), and cost increases have been passed on to consumers. Moreover, the asynchronous movement of the business cycle between countries which hampered and even countered the inflationary process during the 1950's and 1960's has given way to more simultaneous recessionary and expansionary movements which may well have an enduring character. Since late 1972, materials and energy prices, which at first responded to a business boom and then to the oil crisis, have risen on an unprecedented scale, giving an additional boost to inflation.

The reconcentration movement in European business has made possible a stronger defensive and collusive price policy by dominant firms, even though formal cartels are less in vogue than formerly. This follows the more aggressive policy against restrictive practices urged by both the Common Market authorities and some national authorities.

A causal connection between rising concentration and price increases cannot be proven apart from individual sectors. It may nevertheless exist. What is clear from the statistics is that the merger wave and higher concentration certainly have not contributed to declining or stable industrial and consumer prices as did the competitive process during the 1960's. There may thus be the suspicion that concentration has withdrawn the brake on the acceleration of inflation. European labor unions seem to share implicitly in this when they recently (1) started to organize themselves on a continental scale; (2) began to demand more price control measures from their national governments meant to contain profits; (3) have become more interested in the decision processes of large corporations, regarding both internal measures and mergers.

The 1970's may thus well see an increased power struggle between the main economic groups fought out against the background of a slower rate of expansion of real product and out of which more provisions for keeping life possible will have to be made. The first victim of such a battle is likely to be the value of money.

VII
INFLATION IN THE
SOCIALIST ECONOMIES

Norton T. Dodge

Inflation has been so much a part of capitalist development over past centuries, as well as in recent years, that it is difficult to avoid the conclusion that inflation is an intrinsic, inescapable feature of capitalism. The experience with inflation under socialism, on the other hand, has been much shorter and, as a consequence, judgments regarding its nature or persistence cannot be so well founded in experience. Nor can one be so certain as to whether inflation is inherent in the socialist system. Such a proposition would be an anathema, of course, to doctrinaire socialists who would view inflation solely as a capitalist phenomenon.

It would be helpful, therefore, to look objectively at the socialist experience over the past half century in order to gain some insight into the nature, sources, and probable persistence of socialist inflation. We shall also attempt to determine whether or not some of the same factors causing inflation under capitalism are also at work under socialism and, further, whether the mix of causal factors in the two systems differs in composition or in kind.

It will be impossible to cover here the entire inflationary experience of all socialist countries. Our principal emphasis will be on Soviet experience which is the most important and covers the longest period of time. But we will also consider other Bloc economies, particularly Yugoslavia which, as the sole example of "market socialism," provides a preview of what may be in store for other Bloc economies if the current reforms continue in that direction.

Focus

The other chapters in this book, dealing with the inflationary problem in a number of capitalist countries, recognize the obvious importance of demand-pull inflation at certain times, but they focus their attention and analysis on the persistent, yet neglected, cost-push and structural aspects of inflation. In this discussion of socialist inflation, the importance of demand-pull elements in the inflationary process is not denied. But, as in the other chapters, the focus will be on the contributions of cost-push elements and growing structural concentration in the inflationary process which have received little attention from Western analysts despite the increasing concern of some Eastern European economists.

Inflation, then, is typically characterized by the existence of excess demand, or the presence of rising prices, or some combination of the two. We choose this dual definition in contrast to that of Peter Wiles,[1] a leading British student of the Soviet Bloc economies, so that we can include under it: (1) the situation characteristic of many socialist countries where official prices are kept relatively stable but where product shortages are evident and liquid assest pile up in the hands of the public; and (2) the situation where, in the absence of excess demand, prices are pushed up by costs or by the efforts and ability of producers to increase profits principally by raising prices rather than increased efficiency in production. We are recognizing, therefore, cost-push as well as demand-pull inflation, although fully granting that price increases from the cost-push side must be accompanied by increased aggregate demand if the economy is to continue to grow in real terms. We will argue here that the cost-push causes of inflation are very real under socialism and not, as Wiles has suggested "extremely weak." [2]

The Anomoly of Socialist Inflation

Ia. A. Kronrod has been quoted as stating that " . . . inflation in socialist society has been eliminated."[3] This contention has long been the official position among socialist analysts who consider inflation the monopoly of the capitalist system. However, some public recognition of the existence of inflation in varying degrees or forms under socialism has begun to appear in the writings of Soviet scholars. Euphemisms such as "deferred demand," "unsatisfied demand," and "involuntary savings" are often used to describe it.[4] Eastern European socialists, on the other hand, have been quite open in recognizing the existence and problem of inflation.

But why should inflationary pressures be felt, one must ask, in the socialist countries in relatively normal times such as the 1960's and 1970's? In theory, a socialist economy should be subject neither to demand-pull nor cost-push inflation because control of all the crucial variables responsible for inflation — government expenditure and taxes, savings and investment, money supply and credit, wages and prices — are largely in the hands of the state. [5]

From Soviet experience and from the experience of the other socialist countries, however, it is evident that control of these key variables is not enough. An understanding of how to apply the controls effectively is also essential to avoid the problem of excess demand and to preserve the stability of prices. Soviet experience in this regard is instructive.

Effects of Inflation Under Socialism

Despite similarities between the causes of inflation in the capitalist and socialist systems, there are considerable differences in the effects. In the first place, the effects of inflation on the redistribution of wealth in socialist societies are rather limited since there are no significant amounts of private property holdings. During World War II, it is true, the Soviet peasantry and black marketeers acquired, in the government's view, a disturbingly large share of currency holdings as a result of wartime shortages that resulted in a high rate of inflation. However, with the currency reform of 1947, the value of cash holdings was largely destroyed so that wealth illicitly acquired by the speculators was wiped out. Peasants with accumulated currency stuffed in their mattresses had to return to the fields to acquire purchasing power instead of being able to draw on these hoards of cash when competing with industrial workers for scarce consumer goods.

While the tendency during inflationary periods of certain forms of income — pensions and some salaries and wages — to lag behind increases in the cost of living may cause severe hardship and injustice for some, the greatest concern to a socialist government is the possible adverse effect of inflation on the efficient operation of the economy. Inflation undermines the use of prices as guides to resource allocation by distorting the structure of production costs. It also leads managers of enterprises and administrators at lower levels to make decisions that are inconsistent with the broad decisions made by the highest authorities. In these and other ways, inflation makes it more difficult to administer a command economy.

Although Soviet-type economies are planned fundamentally in real terms, these economies employ money and prices to facilitate the planning process. If prices get out of line with costs that have been rising, an upward adjustment in prices is called for. The government prefers, of course, to keep prices stable, but periodic "once-and-for-all" price increases have typically been necessary. Prime examples were the changes in Soviet industrial prices made following the economic reforms of 1965 and the successive increases in agricultural prices made since 1953. The aim of these price changes was to relate prices more accurately to average costs and, particularly, in the case of agricultural prices, to provide proper production incentives.

However, Soviet planners as well as those in other socialist economies are concerned that such increases in wholesale or procurement prices not be passed on to retail prices since increases in consumer prices may have serious political repercussions. This was most dramatically illustrated by events in 1962 when Khrushchev passed on to the consumer part of the increase in the prices paid to farms for meat and dairy products. The reaction was negative, indeed, violent as shown by the riots and resulting casualties in Novocherkassk—an expression of citizen reaction unheard of since collectivization.[6] Khrushchev and the successive Soviet leaders learned a lesson from this experience, a lesson which the Polish leadership unwisely failed to heed in December 1970 when they raised the prices of meat and other foodstuffs. The Baltic port riots ensued, and Gomulka fell from power.

Thus, efforts are normally made to preserve the appearance of stability in retail prices by increasing subsidies, altering the turnover (sales) taxes, or by some similar measure. Consequently, the connection between cost-push pressures at the production level and retail price increases are normally more attenuated and less obvious in the Soviet or Bloc economies than in our own. This hidden inflation is illustrated in Table I where we compare the indexes of Soviet industrial prices for all industry with the indexes of basic industrial sectors, including and excluding the turnover tax. The indexes including the turnover tax show a much sharper decline between 1950 and 1955 than do those excluding the turnover tax. The difference is particularly dramatic for the food industry, both in this earlier period and in the 1955-1970 period (Chart I). From this table and figure,

Table VII—I

INDICES OF SOVIET INDUSTRIAL PRICES: SELECTED YEARS, 1950-1970. (1949 = 100)

Enterprise Wholesale Prices (excluding turnover tax)	1950	1952	1955	1958	1962	1966	1967	1970
All industrial production	83	72	68	67	71	71	77	77
Heavy industry	80	68	61	58	57	55	65	64
Light inudstry	91	83	80	80	81	84	84	85
Food industry	91	81	91	104	135	140	139	140
Industry Wholesale Prices (including turnover tax)								
All industrial production	80	69	61	60	61	59	64	65
Heavy industry	80	68	61	59	59	57	66	67
Light industry	88	88	70	70	70	67	67	68
Food industry	77	62	54	57	59	58	57	58

Source: Derived from Morris Bornstein, "Soviet Price Theory and Policy" in *The Soviet Economy: A Book of Readings,* Morris Bornstein and Daniel R. Fusfeld, ed., Homewood, 4th ed., 1974 pp. 89-90.

we see how the cushion of the turnover tax makes it possible to change enterprise wholesale prices without comparable changes in industry wholesale prices or in the retail prices based upon them.

THE SOCIALIST EXPERIENCE

It is difficult to measure the extent or degree of inflation in the socialist economies because there are no reliable or comprehensive published price indexes. For most socialist countries, official price indexes cover only retail prices which are largely controlled and inadequately reflect the actual extent of inflationary forces. Some countries, such as China and Rumania, do not currently publish any indexes, while Czechoslovakia does not publish a retail price index. Inflation must be assessed, therefore, primarily from indirect, non-statistical evidence such as the presence of long consumer lines at

Chart VII—I

**INDICES OF FOOD INDUSTRY PRICES INCLUDING AND
EXCLUDING TURNOVER TAX: SELECTED YEARS 1950—1970 (1949 = 100)**

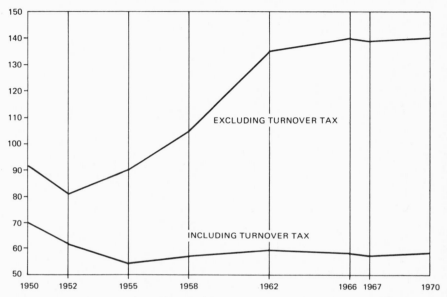

Source: Derived from Morris Bornstein, "Soviet Price Theory and Policy" in *The Soviet Economy: A Book of Readings*, Morris
Bornstein and Daniel R. Fusfeld, ed.,

retail stores, reductions in the quality of products, and large accumulations of cash in the hands of the public.

Runaway and Galloping Inflation

In times of chaos and economic stress brought on by war, revolution, or forced collectivization, socialist states have not escaped extreme or hyperinflation — inflation caused by much the same factors as in capitalist countries in comparable periods of stress. Runaway inflation existed in Russia during the period of War Communism and the early years of the NEP until it was brought under control in 1923. Again, during World War II, prices of consumer goods skyrocketed, particularly those on kolkhoz markets. In China, as the Red Army moved southward in 1949, prices spiraled upward at spectacular monthly rates. Severe inflation was also experienced in the Soviet satellite countries of Eastern Europe in the years immediately following World War II.

Galloping inflation, reflected in the rapid increase in private market prices, also existed in the Soviet Union during the period of collectivization and the first phase of forced industrialization. Between 1928 and mid-1932, the price of rye flour on the private market rose twenty-threefold, much of the rise coming between 1931 and mid-1932 when the price more than quadrupled. Widespread disorder and near warfare in agricultural regions were combined with adverse climatic conditions. The reduced agricultural output, shortages in manufactured consumer goods, and increasing sums of money in people's pockets were the major causes of this inflation.

Franklyn Holzman, in his classic article on Soviet inflation, has analyzed the way in which economic misconceptions of Soviet monetary managers in the 1930's made it impossible to contain prices.[7] He points out how, despite repeated deflationary budget surpluses, both the "real" and the "monetary" conditions necessary for inflation persisted in the form of overtaut or overfull employment planning and the creation of credit in excess of the budgetary surpluses. Enterprises under pressure to fulfill the plan would bid for additional labor at higher effective rates of pay with resulting overexpenditures of planned wage funds, expenditures which had to be covered by bank loans. These loans validated the above-plan outlays on labor and, on balance, added to the excess demand for available goods, the output of which often fell short of planned levels. We must infer that the higher rates of growth expected by the planners from the practice of overambitious planning were preferred to price stability, given that the connection between the two was understood.

In the period of the prewar, five-year plans, Holzman's figures show a slightly more than doubling of the prices of basic industrial goods, a fivefold increase in wages, a more than sevenfold increase in prices at state and cooperative stores, and a thirtyfold increase in collective farm market prices by 1932 — a period of agricultural failure and famine due to collectivization and poor weather. Collective farm market prices were brought down to seven times the 1928 level by 1936, but again rose dramatically during the war to more than 300 times the 1928 level. Industrial prices and wages rose moderately, but prices in state and cooperative stores increased to more than thirty times the 1928 level by 1946.

In the immediate postwar decade, Holzman found that Soviet authorities had acquired a better understanding of the inflationary effects of the net creation of credit in excess of budgetary surpluses as well as an awareness of the inflationary pressures created by over-taut planning.[8] Of particular note, in Holzman's view, was the relative stability of the wage level during this period, suggesting that the cost-push element of inflation was absent during the 1948-1954 peri-od when many retail prices were lowered each year. A better under-standing of how to control inflation, combined with improvements in the controls themselves, particularly those in the banking system, contributed to the postwar deflation and the relative stability which followed.

Our main concern here, however is with the much less well under-stood socialist counterpart of capitalism's cost-push inflation, name-ly, the repressed inflation which has persisted in the more normal periods of socialist economic development. Many of the forces re-sponsible for "stagflation" under "monopoly capitalism" have their counterparts under what may best be termed "monopoly socialism."

Creeping and Repressed Inflation

In the past two decades, most socialist economies have suffered from either a creeping inflation which has been generally recognized but often inadequately reflected in the retail price indexes of these countries; or, in some instances, from a somewhat more rapid infla-tion which has progressed at a slow trot rather than a full gallop.

If we look at the official retail price indexes of those Bloc coun-tries which publish them, we find the following record for the period 1950 to 1970:

Table VII–II

CHANGE IN RETAIL PRICE INDICES IN SIX BLOC COUNTRIES, BY FIVE-YEAR PERIODS, 1950-1970
(average annual rate of change in percent)

Period	USSR	GDR	Bulgaria	Hungary	Poland	Yugoslavia
1950-55	−6.2	−17.3	7.0	9.7	10.4	−5.1
1955-60	0.0	−1.9	0.1	0.2	2.3	2.4
1960-65	0.2	0.0	−1.7	0.5	1.3	11.3
1965-70	0.0	−0.2	−0.8	0.9	1.3	9.9

Sources: From the annual statistical handbooks of the respective countries.

Taken at face value, these statistics show little or no inflation in any of the six countries since 1955 except in Yugoslavia where the rate of inflation has been quite high since 1960. What these data suggest is that in the years following the postwar decade, inflation has been both better controlled and more effectively repressed in the first five countries than in Yugoslavia where inflation has been quite evident from the published retail price index. But it also can be argued that the Yugoslav index represents a more accurate picture of the general magnitude of the actual rates of inflation in the neighboring Bloc countries where inflationary pressures have been, in fact, poorly reflected in the official published indexes, a result often the intent of the responsible statistical agencies.

Nonetheless, repressed inflationary pressures have been present in these economies, as illustrated nonstatistically by the continuing shortages of goods, the queuing up of consumers when desirable goods appear in stores, the existence of long waiting lists for highly prized consumer durables such as automobiles, the continuing accumulation of personal savings, and so forth.

These problems and the inflationary pressures which they represent have become more, rather than less, noticeable as the Soviet economy has developed and become more affluent. With incomes increasing beyond subsistence levels, the structure of demand has changed substantially. In an article entitled "Tailoring Production to Fit Demand," the Soviet economist S. Partigul stressed that

> . . . even a relatively small increase in the incomes of the lower-paid groups of the working people sharply increases the population's demand for basic foodstuffs, fabrics, clothing, footwear and other goods. On the whole, in connection with the growing incomes of the population and changes in the income structure, demand is increasing for the most valuable foodstuffs and for industrial goods, especially cultural and everyday goods. Indicative in this respect are the changes in the structure of consumption (although consumption does not coincide with demand — as a rule, demand is broader than consumption). In an 18-year period (1951 through 1968) the consumption of baked goods declined by 13% and that of potatoes fell by as much as 45%, but on the other hand the consumption of meat and milk grew by 70% to 90%, that of eggs by 140% and that of sugar by more than 200%. The consumption of cotton fabrics increased during these years by 50%, and that of silk fabrics and knitwear by 300% to 500% and more. Sales of cultural and everyday goods grew by 830% in these years, as against a growth of 440% in sales of all nonfood items. . . . In this

connection, we should note another special feature of the structure of
demand. Demand for the more expensive types of goods is growing at a
faster rate.[9]

Thus, as the proportion of discretionary income has increased, Soviet
citizens have raised their sights as consumers. They are now much
more difficult to satisfy than in the time of Stalin. We see this
continuing phenomena of long queues for preferred items while, at
the same time, unwanted inventory of shoddy, poorly designed
goods—which no one wants at almost any price—continues to accumulate. Failure to accurately predict consumer wants and failure to
produce quality goods with attractive styling are problems the Soviets are struggling to solve, but without great success thus far.

One of the chief results of these failures is the overflow of spending into nonofficial channels which are as important in the eyes of
many consumers, according to former Soviet citizens, as the official
sources of supply. The principal areas which absorb much of the
excess purchasing power are collective farm markets, private housing,
special and secondhand stores, and the "grey" or "black" markets.

Although the government presently satisfies a higher proportion of
the demand for food products through official channels than previously, the state and cooperative trade system is frequently unable
to satisfy public demand for many products, particularly for perish-
ables in the off-season, with the result that people are forced to buy
such products elsewhere at the collective farm markets, frequently at
prices several times the quoted state prices.[10] Keith Bush cites several
examples to illustrate this point:

> It was reported from Cheliabinsk that "the buyer is forced either to stand
> in lengthy queues outside the shops . . . or to go to the kolkhoz market and
> pay his respects to enterprising private dealers who, thanks to their
> excellent business sense and the shortcomings of the state trading system,
> can name their own prices." According to another report from Kazan, "at
> markets in Kazan, for example, when there are no onions and potatoes in
> the cooperative trading shops, the prices immediately jump. And vice versa.
> It's like that everywhere. . . . " A correspondent reported from Saratov
> that the price of cucumbers was 1 ruble per kilogram at the kolkhoz
> market as compared with 14 kopeks in the stores, that of cabbage 40
> compared with 8 kopeks, that of carrots 70 compared with 14 kopeks.
> Prices at kolkhoz markets are dependent on the season. The prices quoted
> were from September when prices are at their lowers.[11]

Collective farm market prices increased at the substantial rate of almost 4% annually in the decade of the 1960's, as opposed to the stability in the official retail price index, as is shown by Chart II, reproduced from a Soviet source.

Had Chart II included data for 1972, a sharp increase in collective farm market prices would have been evident as a result of the agricultural failures in that year, although there has since been a decline.[12] The existence of inflation in agricultural prices and its negative impact on certain segments of the population is clearly acknowledged by the Soviet economist Yurii Yakovets:

> The raising of retail prices on meat, fats, potatoes, vegetables and various other goods, and the rise in collective farm market prices, has resulted in a slowing of the rate of growth of real income of certain groups in the population (especially individuals on fixed incomes). The buying power of the ruble has dropped somewhat, which was unavoidable in conditions of generally rising prices.[13]

Private funds also flow in substantial quantities into the construction of cooperative apartments with "extras" negotiated privately, *dachas* (second homes in the countryside), and even "extensions" to homes in resort areas which can be rented out at private profit. These privately owned properties may then change hands at inflated prices (sometimes with the payment of "key money"). The higher prices of these highly coveted properties are not reflected in any official price index.

Excess funds also flow into the special stores provided for certain of the elite and persons with foreign currency (gifts from relatives or earnings abroad), into secondhand stores, and into the "grey" and "black" markets. The latter may involve the resale at a higher price of items in short supply or with long-waiting periods (ranging from a set of Pushkin's writings to a Zhiguli automobile); the use of "blat," or "pull," to improperly or illegally obtain prized products through "connections" in retail trade organizations; and the purchase of repairs and services (ranging from plumbing to sewing). There is also an "unofficial" market for various handicrafts, recordings of Western music, modern art, and a variety of other exotic or foreign items in great demand. If one could measure the trend of prices in these unrecorded areas of economic activity, one would find, as in the

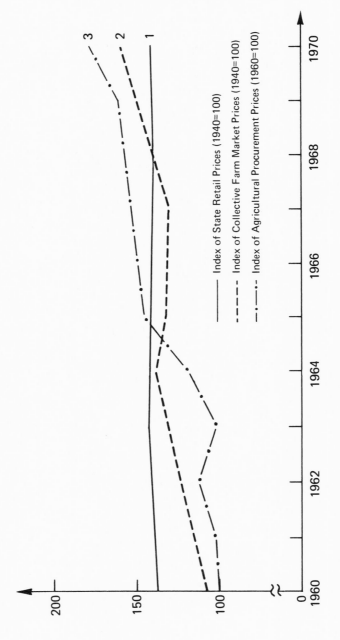

Chart VII—II

**DYNAMICS OF AGRICULTURAL PRICES
IN THE U.S.S.R., 1960-1970**

——— Index of State Retail Prices (1940=100)

– – – Index of Collective Farm Market Prices (1940=100)

–·—·– Index of Agricultural Procurement Prices (1960=100)

Source: Yurii V. Yakovets, *Tseny v Planovom Khoziaistve*, Moscow, 1974, p. 58.

index of collective farm market prices, the existence of inflationary trends not revealed by the official indexes.

Additional evidence of repressed inflationary pressures in recent years is provided by the dramatic increase in personal savings, a hidden or latent form of potential purchasing power. On this point, Bush observes:

> During the period 1966-70, for instance, savings deposits nearly trebled to 46.6 billion.... Undoubtedly, some of the roughly sixty billion rubles currently held in savings deposits does represent a voluntary withholding of current consumption for the projected purchase of a cooperative apartment, a motor car or some other future consumer good. But most of this appreciable volume of savings — the equivalent of four months' retail trade turnover — surely records an overhand of pent-up purchasing power attributable to the insufficiency of desirable consumer goods and services.[14]

THE SOURCES OF SOCIALIST INFLATION

While wholesale price increases are not normally passed on to the retail level if such a course can be avoided, increases both in wholesale and retail commodity prices and in wage rates are visible in two types of upward adjustments: (1) adjustments which have been made primarily at the initiative of the central government in response to the need to bring prices more into line with actual costs so that prices will aid in the effective operation of the economy; and (2) adjustments which have been pressed upon the government by enterprise managers or by forces felt at the enterprise level. These pressures from the economic grassroots may lead, of course, to the first type of adjustment, but the purpose in making the distinction between the two is to identify from where and from what causes price increases originate in a socialist economy.

Upward Wage Drift

Just as in capitalist economies, upward pressures on costs and prices in Soviet-type economies have come from wage increases which outpace productivity gains. Since labor unions have only minimal influence over wage decisions in the Soviet Union, the forces pushing the price of labor upward must lie elsewhere. Some of these forces are very general in character, taking the form of widespread dissatisfaction or feelings of injustice on the part of workers which are expressed in a lack of involvement in work and resulting low productivity. To this type of malaise, though it is expressed in no organized way, the government must respond, just as to union pressure in the West, by improvements in wages and working conditions if efficiency and some semblance of equity are to be maintained. More direct pressures for wage increases come, however, from management seeking to meet stringent production plans. Competition for labor to fulfill such production quotas leads to actual or disguised increases in wages.

Adjustments at the initiative of the government – An important factor leading to the persistence of excess demand in the Soviet Union in the post-Stalin years has been the upward leveling of wages, primarily by rises in minimum wages. Leveling-down has been quite limited, although some of the top academic, research, and other salaries over three hundred rubles per month were reduced slightly by Krushchev.

A minimum wage of 22 rubles a month was introduced in 1950 which was then increased to 27 rubles in rural areas and 30 rubles in urban areas in January 1957, raising the wages of the lowest paid workers by a third. The pay of some especially low paid groups, in primary and secondary education, the health service, retailing, and local government, was raised again in 1964. The minimum wage was further increased to 40 rubles in 1965, raising the minimum for urban workers by one-third and for rural workers, by about one-half. Service workers also received an increase with a new minimum wage of 60 rubles, introduced in 1968, which is again scheduled to be raised to 70 rubles.[15]

One positive effect of more than tripling the wages of the lowest paid workers over the past decade-and-a-half has been a substantial narrowing of differentials. But another less desirable result of this government-inspired form of cost-push wage inflation has been an increase in consumer purchasing power without a comparable increase in the output of consumer goods,[16] producing inflationary pressures of both a cost-push and a demand-pull nature.

Further government-induced inflationary pressures in the Soviet Union resulted from an expanded welfare program in the latter half of the 1960's. David Bronson and Barbara Severin have described this development quite fully:

In 1965, the new Brezhnev regime, making haste to identify itself with the Soviet war on poverty, ordered a speed up in carrying out Khrushchev's last announced welfare program. That program . . . boosted by more than one-third the minimum pensions of disabled workers and the minimum benefits of survivors; and . . . placed the 24 million to 30 million collective farmers and their families under a new statewide social insurance system similar to the existing one for wage and salary workers.[17]

In addition, pension and welfare grant payments have increased due to higher pay rates as well as the introduction of more liberal schedules of payments. Rural pensions paid from farm revenues are subsidized, although it was originally anticipated that no such subsidy would be required.[18]

It is evident then that government income policies have created both cost-push and demand-pull inflationary forces in recent years. Apart from the motives of reducing inequality and helping those in greatest need by raising wage minimums and increasing welfare payments, one suspects that the government is responding to the attractions of the money illusion as well. It is much easier to solve social and economic problems or, to put it more precisely, to *appear* to solve problems by means of greater money outlays than with increases in the output of real goods. When faced with hard choices, the government has preferred to suffer some inflationary pressure from increased wage and pension payments rather than impose more drastic controls on the money supply — a move which would be unpopular, cause hardships, and restrict output.

Adjustments at the Initiative of the Enterprise—Overtaut planning, characteristic of the Soviet Union and of most socialist countries, has resulted in the regular occurrence of sizable overexpenditures of wage funds. What was once considered a passing problem in the 1930's, easily rectified with better controls,[19] has proved to be a problem inherent in the priority system of the Soviet Union, a system which places the highest importance on achieving a high rate of economic growth. This has meant, in practical terms, that the fulfillment of the production plan has come before holding to the allocated outlays for wages.

Overexpenditure has continued to be a serious problem even in the more normal postwar years despite strict controls which permit extra wage expenditures only when the output plan is surpassed. But with production shortfalls occurring elsewhere in the economy, the net effect of these permissible increases can only be inflationary even if the controls are effective, which has not been the case. Robert Fearn, who has examined the problem in detail, explains that

> The existing practice of establishing special wage differentials at each skill level for the high priority raw material and producers' goods industries gives these enterprises a commanding competitive position in bidding for labor relative to the lower priority consumer goods enterprises. Further . . . the high priority enterprises, as a group, receive more lucrative allowances for additional wage funds in case of overfulfillment of output plans than do the low priority enterprises. Thus, the wage and financial system appears to be predisposed toward overspending of absolute wage funds in the very industries which do not produce consumer products upon which the additional funds may be spent.[20]

To prevent this kind of inflationary pressure, major changes in priorities as well as controls would be required.

As a result of the failure to control excess wage expenditures, the actual increase in wages has outrun the planned increase year after year. In 1962, for example, the wage creep was 0.7% (3.5% actual increase in wages against a 2.7% planned increase).[21] In other years, the creep has been higher. With regard to the future, Fearn concludes:

> Faced with the prospects of a 'wage creep' on the one hand or an adjustment of priorities on the other, the Soviet leadership may choose the traditional path of least resistance — a mild repressed inflation.[22]

In the socialist market economy of Yugoslavia, the upward pressure on wage payments which are paid out of gross profits takes a different form. There, the worker has as much personal interest in increasing profits (and the size of his share) by increasing prices as by reducing costs. Indeed, in the Yugoslav situation, where the opportunities to raise prices may be as great as the pressure to raise them, the interests of labor and management may often coincide in pressing for such price increases.

Upward Price Drift

Corresponding to the upward pressures on the price of labor are pressures which push and pull other prices upward. Some of the increases come at the behest of the government, but often these are a response to rising costs which have their origin elsewhere.

Government Adjustments in Commodity Prices — Examples of upward adjustment initiated by the government can be drawn from various sectors of the Soviet economy. Particularly dramatic were those made in agriculture following Stalin's death. Many agricultural procurement prices had not been raised since the 1930's, with the result that farm costs exceeded farm revenues for many products. Consequently, the more of a product produced, the greater the losses. To correct this situation, the prices paid for certain key agricultural products were successively raised in the post-Stalin era to provide an incentive, rather than a disincentive, to increase production. Major increases in the prices of grain and meat were first made in 1953 and then again in 1956, 1962, as well as in more recent years.

Over the entire ten-year period from 1960-69, the prices of food products distributed through Soviet state stores rose 5.5% according to the official index.[23] Bush has found, however, that for certain basic staple foods, the increase was much larger than that shown in the official index, averaging 35% over the same ten-year period. It is true that most of the upward adjustment came early in the period. Nonetheless, Bush's figures suggest that the official index understates the effective increases, quite apart from not reflecting the increases in prices at collective farm markets.

Soviet policies with respect to industrial prices have been similar to their policies for agriculture, although the need for upward adjustments in wholesale industrial prices has been less urgent than in agriculture. Nonetheless, upward adjustments of 58% on the average were made in industrial wholesale prices in 1949 to bring prices more closely in line with costs as defined by Soviet price setters.[24] In 1950, 1952, and 1955, heavy industry prices were reduced as a result of cost reductions. A more fundamental reform in industry prices was made in 1966-67 which, while altering the prices of many products, had little apparent effect on overall industrial price indexes.

The policy of avoiding increases in state retail prices (including the turnover tax), even if wholesale prices are increased, can be carried out rather easily with respect to manufactured goods, as has been shown in Table I. But a few clear increases at the retail level have occurred in recent years, although these were in the prices of non-essentials such as cognac and champagne.[25] Other price increases,

Table VII—III

OFFICIAL RETAIL PRICES OF FOOD PRODUCTS
IN STATE RETAIL STORES

	1960 (kopeks)	1969 (kopeks)	Approximate Price Increase/Decrease (percent)
Bread, rye (kg)	14	24	+70
Potatoes (kg)	12	10-20	−16/+25
Macaroni (kg)	45	58	+30
Rice (kg)	80	88	+10
Oil, vegetable (kg)	163	198	+21
Butter (kg)	273	360	+30
Cheese, cottage (kg)	85	88	+3.5
Cheese, other (kg)	240	270-300	+12.5-25
Eggs (ten)	79	90-130	+14-50
Meat and meat products (kg)	133	200	+50
Milk (liters)	22	32	+45
Tea (kg)	612	960	+55
Salt (kg)	3	10	+250

Source: *Radio Liberty Dispatch,* December 21, 1971.

however, have been disguised by the introduction of "new products" at higher prices, products which were essentially the same as the older products which they replaced. The classic example was the replacement of the old "Stolichnaia" and "Moskovskaia" brands of vodka with new brands bearing, as Bush has pointed out in a discussion of inflationary pressures, "a higher price tag, but with identical taste and after effects." [26] Also cited by Bush was the increase in the price of the GAZ-21 or Volga motor car from 5500 rubles to 9250 rubles for the GAZ-24, a so-called "improved version," [27] which in no way justified the 65% increase in price.

Adjustments at the Initiative of the Enterprise — For Soviet enterprises as well as for enterprises in other Bloc countries, the pressure to push up prices is considerable. In the post-reform period, with the new emphasis on profits as a success indicator, the pressure on Soviet managers to manipulate prices has significantly increased. The intent of using profit as a success indicator was, of course, to encourage improvements in the quality, and thereby the saleability, of products as well as to encourage reductions in costs. Clearly, the easiest way to increase profits and resulting bonuses, for capitalists and socialists alike, is to increase prices. The effort necessary to raise prices through an effective appeal to the State Price Committee often may be more rewarding than an equal effort made to reduce production costs and/or improve quality.[28] Recognition of this very real and persistent circumstance is crucial to explaining managerial behavior in the various market socialist economies which we are examining.

There have been many complaints in the Soviet Union and other Bloc countries about the efforts of management to secure improper price increases. We have already mentioned the introduction of so-called "new products." According to *Izvestiia,* Soviet investigators have uncovered many "completely intolerable instances in which individual enterprises are striving for higher profitability by means of overstating production costs."[29] A complaint about improper manipulation of prices was made by V. Sitnin, Chairman of the U.S.S.R. Council of Ministers' State Committee on Prices in the following terms:

> Recent check-ups have shown that certain enterprise heads consider it feasible to fulfill and overfulfill profit assignments by means of improper price manipulation. Thus, the Semipalatinsk Meat Combine, for example, unlawfully obtained profits of more than 100,000 rubles during the year just past and in January and February of this year as a result of direct markups in list prices for bone buttons. In 1969, the Ust-Kamenogorsk Reinforced Concrete Products Plant sold foundation blocks at prices that were more than 70% higher than the list prices. There have also been cases in which enterprises, instead of confirming their prices for new output, begin shipping the output at arbitrary prices. And in all cases these prices have turned out to be higher than they should have been . . . . The Ministry of Heavy Power and Transport Machine Building's Moscow Industrial Mechanization Association unlawfully obtained profits of more than 870,000 rubles last year by charging inflated wholesale prices for one-time orders. The director of the Moscow Metal Furniture Plant approved highly excessive wholesale prices on metal structures for 40 different kinds of furniture, and in 1969 the plant unlawfully made profits of 1,300,000 rubles.[30]

The Soviet economist, L. Maizenberg, summed up the situation well in an article in *Problems of Economics:*

> Profit is a universal index that ultimately reflects all aspects of the economic performance of enterprises. However, profit can also grow under

the influence of such factors as arbitrary price increases, violations of requirements for quality, and nonfulfillment of plan targets with respect to product-mix, i.e., factors that run counter to the plan . . . . Our experience points to the existence of a dangerous trend toward arbitrary price rises, which attests to the striving of the heads of some industrial enterprises to fulfill their sales and profits plans in the easiest way.[31]

Given our firsthand knowledge of the weakness of American regulatory agencies in controlling prices or rates and given the behavior of oligopolies in our economy, we should have considerable insight into the problem of the inexorable upward pressure on regulated prices in socialist countries. As we might expect, the problem of price increases becomes greater with the relaxation of central controls and as a result of any further movement, however small, toward market socialism where oligopolies or monopolies may have a freer rein in determining their own prices. On this point, P. Kuligin, writing about the problem of price formation after the Soviet economic reforms, states that

. . . there is the danger that . . . prices will constantly rise . . . . From time to time, such trends have arisen in the course of economic reforms carried out in the German Democratic Republic, the Polish People's Republic, and the Czechoslovak Socialist Republic where the various economic units, particularly enterprises, have striven to increase their income (profit, gross income) by the easiest avenue — by raising the sales prices on their outputs.[32]

Inflationary Consequences of Managerial Reorganization, Market Structure, and Industrial Concentration

In the first half dozen years immediately following the Kosygin reforms of 1965, many existing Soviet enterprises were joined into combines, associations, or "firms." This development reflected the lack of faith of many higher level administrators that the powers devolved upon the individual enterprise in 1965 would be intelligently and effectively used. The vantage point of the individual enterprise, it was felt, provided too limited a perspective. It was argued that only an administrative organ situated somewhere between the enterprise and the ministry could have sufficient perspective for long-range planning and development of new products and technology. Experimentation with organizations of various types was therefore undertaken. In many instances, intermediate administrative organs such as Chief Administrations (*glavki*), which normally served an administrative role between the ministry and a group of related enterprises, were converted into independent cost accounting (*khozraschet*) entities,[33] or in other cases related enterprises in an area were combined into single firms or combines. A "firm" was typically established by merging a leading (head) enterprise with several smaller and more backward enterprises.

When developments of this type occur in a capitalist economy, they are viewed as steps toward monopolization, cartelization, or, more euphemistically, rationalization. The Soviets themselves would, or course, use the latter term. Viewing their economy as one huge "firm," changes of this type could only have, in their view, administrative and not market structure implications. Nonetheless, one outcome of the changes in incentives introduced by the reforms of 1965 is that Soviet managers can be expected to act much as capitalist managers and to use all available means to expand their profit margins. However, the Soviets, as well as their Bloc neighbors who have traveled farther in the direction of market socialism, do not seem to be fully aware of the dangers of concentration. Officials at the ministerial level apparently view enhanced authority and decision-making power at an intermediate level as desirable. For them it is easier and more comfortable to deal with a small number of large combines than with many individual firms. For many enterprise managers, at least for those who emerge at the top, cartelization offers the prospect of greater power and autonomy. For those who are less able, merger into a larger firm may offer relief from the new and difficult problems of entrepreneurship for which Soviet managers are ill-equipped by experience, training, or ideology.

Despite the drawbacks mentioned, the general satisfaction of Soviet authorities with the shifting of significant decision-making powers to an intermediate level is shown by the decision made on April 2, 1973 to move ahead with a major reorganization of the administrative structure of industry drawing on the experience of the preceding half-dozen years. Under the new system, a middle level of management between the ministry and the enterprise will become standard. This new intermediate organization, called an association, differs little from those established earlier except that the new form will supersede those *glavki* or main administrations — the old administrative links between the ministry and the enterprise — which had not been converted to independent economic accountability (*khozras-chet*). That the new associations will coexist with and supplement the former in a two-level, three-level, and combined system seems apparent from the recent remarks of Professor G. Popov and N. Petrov in *Pravda:*

> The creation of all-Union industrial associations should in no way be accompanied by the "closing down" of economically accountable production associations. The 24th C.P.S.U. Congress pointed out that the course aimed at the creation of associations and combines must be pursued resolutely — in the long run they are to become the main economically accountable elements of social production. The newly created production associations can be subordinated directly to the ministries, forming with the ministries the simplest kind of two-level management structure.
>
> The combined system, in which part of the enterprise and production associations belong directly to the ministries (the two-level system) and part to the industrial associations (the three-level system), also has the right to existence in the branches.[34]

Broad territorial associations, made up of related enterprises situated in the same part of the country, are also being formed.

The enhanced powers which had been vested in the enterprise by the 1965 reform now belong to the associations.[35] The associations presumably will also perform some of the administrative functions previously performed by central ministries and will have a greater role than did the individual enterprises in drawing up their own plans. They are also expected to study consumer demand, a difficult task for the individual enterprise, and to perform research and development design functions.[36]

Of particular significance for our inquiry is that the creation of the new associations reinforces the pressures to increase prices which we have already noted in regard to the individual enterprises and the earlier combines and associations. With the increased powers and influence that these new associations possess, the capacity of the State Price Committee (SPC) to resist pleas and arguments for price increases will be diminished.

INFLATIONARY PRESSURE IN THE BLOC ECONOMIES

This problem of cost-push inflationary pressure originating from the enterprise or association under the system we have styled "mo-

nopoly socialism" is perhaps even better illustrated by the experience
of the Eastern European countries. These countries have such small
internal markets that, even without associations, oligopolies or monopolies can emerge because the efficient size of a firm in a number
of crucial industries is very large in comparison with the overall
market size. Furthermore, in these countries the enterprise or association is likely to have more freedom or influence in price determination than in the Soviet Union.

Hungary and Czechoslovakia are the only countries in Eastern
Europe, apart from Yugoslavia, which permit enterprises and associations to set prices for a significant proportion of the output of standardized production goods. John Montias stresses the importance of
price reforms which would more correctly reflect relative scarcities
and, in turn, function as a measure of efficiency. These more accurate prices equip "rationalizers" of production with a weapon that,
"while it might not be proof against political lobbying by threatened
interests, would permit them to offer a good deal more resistance
against arbitrary interference than in the recent past."[37] Yet in his
discussion of the objection to "monopolistic management," Montias
points out that, rather than more rational prices resulting from greater freedom in price setting, "a sales monopoly in a line of products
invites open price increases wherever prices are free to move and
covert increases where they are not."[38]

In an article examining the limitations of economic competition in
Hungary, Jeno Wilcsek demonstrates that Montias' concern is justified:

> ... Hungarian industry has a monopolistic organization character. This
> statement applies not only to state industry (although it applies here
> primarily) but also to cooperative industry. Leaving aside exceptions that
> undoubtedly exist, relatively few branches of industry have an organization
> which — presupposing an equilibrium — would promote competition.[39]

Although resolutions were passed in Hungary in an attempt to eliminate monopolistic elements, little progress has been made because
trusts and associations of the type now being developed in the Soviet
Union already play an important role. On their influence, Wilcsek
comments that

> There are examples of certain trusts and associations trying to perform a
> midmanagement organ's activity as before — deviating from our original

intent. This also reduced the possibility of developing real competition. The behavior of some ministries strengthened this trend because they hoped that ministerial direction would be made easier by the mid-level management character of associations and trusts.[40]

A similar lack of competition resulting in upward pressures on prices has been a problem in Czechoslovakia. George Feiwel reports that in 1967, Domestic Trade Minister, Jindrich Uher, complained of "a monopolization of industry which was not yet counteracted by sufficient import of consumer goods" and of "a proclivity to fix too high limited and free prices for newly introduced products."[41]

Although the Hungarian and Czechoslovakian experiences are instructive, Yugoslavia's market socialism provides the best insight into the problem of "monopolistic socialism," having progressed much further toward a free market economy than any other Bloc nation. Joel Dirlam has found that the narrow Yugoslav market and small number of firms has resulted in concentration ratios which are quite high. In 1963, in slightly more than half of the 103 market groups analyzed by Dirlam, 75% or more of the shipments were made by four or fewer firms. In three-quarters of the market groups, the percentage shipped by the largest four or fewer firms exceeded 50%.[42] In contrast, in the United States, only 27% of the more narrowly defined industries exceed concentration ratios of 50%. These Yugoslav firms are often linked together in business associations which allocate markets and production, and the process of concentration continues with further mergers and combinations.

Given the independence of Yugoslav firms, the high level of concentration, and the flexibility of price control, Dirlam believes that there is no reason to expect a Yugoslav firm to set prices in a significantly different manner from a capitalist firm. He persuasively stated this view in testimony before the U.S. Senate Subcommittee on Antitrust and Monopoly:

> In a market that is starved for goods, [a firm] will take advantage of inelastic demand to raise prices and increase net incomes — whether they are paid out or reinvested. If the firm has what amounts to a national monopoly, like JAT (the only scheduled airline), or a regional monopoly like Jugopetrol or INA (gasoline distribution), it clearly will have an incentive to restrict output so that the worker-participants enjoy larger incomes.[43]

To promote its policy of competition, Yugoslavia has a series of antitrust laws described by Dirlam:

> Article 30 of the Constitution prohibits mergers or associations aimed at preventing free commerce of goods and services for the purpose of material advantages not based on work, or promoting other relations of inequality in business. The basic Law on Commodity Trade, adopted in 1967, in Article 52 forbids agreements among business enterprises which achieve a monopoly or other discriminatory (favored) situation in the market.
>
> Prohibited agreements specifically include market sharing, price fixing on internal markets, production limitation or use of capacity, or other business activities resulting in limitation on prevention of free rivalry. Article 53 forbids speculation or activities resulting in shortages of goods on the market. Unfair ("*nelojalna*") competition is prohibited in Article 54. No precise definition of the term is given; it includes, generally, anything that damages other firms, consumers, or the economy. Deceptive labeling, packaging, or advertising practices are outlawed when they involve quality, quantity, or origin of a commodity or service.[44]

Enforcement of this antitrust legislation is the responsibility of regional economic courts and so-called "courts of honor" of the Economic Chambers. The latter determine whether an agreement represents a "good business practice" or tends to create a monopoly. But Dirlam has come across no instance of prosecution of monopoly practices under Section 52, although, in contrast, price cutting has been challenged.[45]

A further means of implementing competition in Yugoslavia has been import policy. However, the stimulus to competition from trade liberalization, particularly the tariff reductions of 1965, has been partly negated. John Blair has summarized this situation:

> In a move reminiscent of giant oil companies under capitalism, the worker-owned Yugoslav oil refinery urged that tariffs on petroleum products be increased. Going beyond the voluntary import quotas enjoyed by the U.S. steel industry, Yugoslav steel producers in 1968 secured higher steel tariffs, with differential rates depending on whether imports were in excess of a quota. In March, 1968, tariffs were increased on 20 groups of products, including typewriters, of which there were only 2 manufacturers: "Opinion," notes Dirlam, "was not unanimously favorable to the increase." Strong protectionist pressures have come also from other highly concentrated Yugoslav industries, notably automobiles, tires, tractors, railroad equipment, and electrical equipment. It would appear that, as in

capitalist countries, the absence of competition in the domestic market renders an industry ill-equipped to meet competition from abroad.[46]

In 1972 the system of price control in Yugoslavia was thoroughly revised with the aim of reducing price controls by relying more heavily on increased import competition. But as we have seen, domestic producers still demonstrate a strong capacity to maintain or increase protection. Similarly, many business associations, although precluded by law from limiting production, from excluding competitors, or from fixing prices on domestic markets, have a strong incentive to engage in monopolistic practices and to make a case for price increases. Dirlam points out that under the 1967 law it is possible for firms accounting for two-thirds of the production and consumption of a product to put into effect a price agreement approved by their Economic Chamber with the automatic approval of the Bureau of Price Control.[47] The large number of such agreements in force today are reported to have contributed to inflationary pressures.

In the absence of an active antitrust policy, the high degree of concentration fosters the development of "market power" which is further enhanced by any agreements on the part of business associations that limit competition. With the various possibilities for manipulating the price control process for the advantage of a firm or association, it is not surprising that the Yugoslav retail price index has recorded very substantial increases in recent years.

Yet the public is hardly aware of the problem of concentration since the relevant data are not made public. Furthermore, the demand-pull aspects of the inflation in Yugoslavia have tended to obscure the cost-push aspects and have contributed to the lack of official concern for the dangers of concentration. As Dirlam notes,

> As a substitute for setting up institutions to review pricing policies in concentrated firms, along the lines of regulatory commissions, or to prevent price agreements and mergers among competitors which do not lead to efficiency savings transmitted to the consumer, the Communist party appears to have concentrated its energies on devising a program of income limitation, seemingly in the belief that this will take care of both inflation and monopoly profits.[48]

If the Yugoslav experience is indicative, further difficulties with cost-push inflationary pressures are in store for the Soviet Union and other Bloc countries as their economies evolve further in the direction of increased concentration and/or more fully developed market socialism.

CONCLUSIONS

This examination of socialist experience with inflation, particularly in the Soviet Union, leads to a number of conclusions. Although the consequences of inflation may differ substantially between capitalist and socialist economies, the similarities of the inflationary problem under the two systems are notable, particularly with regard to causes and the difficulty of effecting cures. In times of stress — combined with inadequate or misguided countermeasures — extreme inflation has been as much a problem for socialist as for capitalist nations.

In more normal times, socialist economies have had a strong proclivity for overtaut planning. This approach has the advantage of avoiding slack, covering errors, keeping resources fully occupied, and promoting growth. But as a consequence, competition for labor and other inputs to meet production goals tends to push wage costs upward and to lead to overexpenditure of wage allocations. These overexpenditures in turn create excess purchasing power which exceed the production of goods on which the wages can be spent. Consequently, cash balances accumulate and a persistent state of moderate demand-pull inflation resulting from the pushing up of wages is the result.

Demand-pull inflationary pressures have been reinforced and encouraged by a number of the sources of cost-push inflation. The government itself has been responsible for adjusting upward the prices of many important goods and services which were considered abnormally low, especially agricultural products. For the most part, however, the government has tried to avoid or conceal obvious price increases at the retail level by adjustments in the turnover (sales) tax or, as a final resort, by providing subsidies.

In a similar fashion, minimum wages and the wages for certain occupations which were considered abnormally low have been raised. These increases have contributed to both cost-push and demand-pull inflation. Increased welfare provisions also have contributed to the latter type of inflation.

Greater enterprise autonomy and greater emphasis on profits as a success indicator — consequences of economic reforms in Eastern Europe and the 1965 economic reforms in the Soviet Union — in conjunction with increased concentration of industry resulting from the formation of combines and associations, have all led to upward pressures on prices. This type of cost-push inflationary pressure is directly analogous to similar pressures in the capitalist system, where regulated monopolies and oligopolies often use price increases as the easiest way to maintain planned rates of return. In both systems, validation by expansion in the effective money supply is required, but this validation has usually been forthcoming, although for somewhat different reasons in the two systems. Price controls in the face of excess demand are of little avail under either system. Resourceful enterprise managers can seek out and exploit numerous loopholes which are impossible, practically speaking, to close.

When price controls are more flexible or cover only major sectors in a socialist economy, as in Yugoslavia, inflation is more open and evident in the official retail price indexes. While antitrust legislation exists in Yugoslavia, real awareness of the problems and dangers of monopoly socialism appears to be only just awakening in Hungary and other Bloc economies. It is not unreasonable to expect that inflationary problems will become more pressing, the greater the extent of market socialism and the greater the degree of concentration of socialist industry in these countries.

Finally, we can find little comfort or guidance for solving our own problems from the socialist experience. Although the consequences of inflation are markedly different for the two systems, close examination of socialist experience has revealed perhaps as many similarities as differences in the sources of the inflationary problem and has revealed, likewise, no easy solutions for either system. Indeed, the problems of both systems seem to be deeply embedded in their "technostructures" and impossible to remove without drastic changes in both industrial organization and managerial motivations. Until these changes are made and the long-heralded appearance of the "new socialist man" occurs, we can expect the problem of inflation to continue to be as much a feature of "monopoly socialism" as our own world of "monopoly capitalism."

VIII
MARKET POWER INFLATION
A CONCEPTUAL OVERVIEW

Alfred E. Kahn

The last thirty-four years have been an age of inflation. We have had similar experiences in the past. Each of those times, no doubt, "informed observers" were persuaded that society had entered a new era; and each time they were wrong. We should be chary, therefore, of apocalyptic predictions. And yet, it is difficult to ignore the mounting evidence that this time is different — that we really have entered a new era of chronic, permanent inflation, at least so long as democracy and welfare-state capitalism survive.

There have also been wide fluctuations around the general inflationary trend of the last few decades, with corresponding reflections in the tenor of popular — and some not-so-popular — thinking about the nature of the problem. The greatest part of the total inflation in the period from 1940 to 1974, at least in the United States, took place during and shortly after the second world war and the Korean and Vietnamese conflicts. These experiences did not justify any inference that some fundamental change had occurred in the nature of the economy and its propensity to inflation: wars have always involved rapid expansions in aggregate spending and concurrent increases in prices. And so there was reason to see in the experiences of 1948-49 and 1953-54 — when comparatively mild setbacks of total spending, and increases in unemployment to comparatively moderate

I would like to acknowledge the helpful criticisms of Professors Erwin A. Blackstone and Joel B. Dirlam.

levels, by historical standards, sufficed weakly to reverse or moderate the upthrust of prices — the basis for the optimistic conclusion that the preceding inflations were nothing really different in kind, inevitability, or reversibility, from earlier ones from the eighteenth to the twentieth centuries. The comparative price stability that characterized the economic recovery of 1961-65 and the fact that it was, after all, largely the increased aggregate spending associated with the Vietnamese conflict that rekindled the inflationary process were, therefore, comparatively reassuring on this score.

The Possibility of Chronic Inflation

And yet concern has mounted. The realization that the modern economy contains inherent tendencies to chronic inflation has become increasingly convincing to growing numbers of economists. That it had become increasingly convincing to the American people at large was attested by the establishment — widely applauded at the time, and politically highly successful — of general wage and price controls in 1971, as well as by the widespread doubt that such controls should have been or can ever be completely dismantled. There are mounting reasons for that concern.

First, there is the sheer cumulative effect of thirty-four years of almost continuous inflationary experience and the anticipations of continuation that it generates — anticipations that can be self-fulfilling. These expectations can have enduring effects — negative ones — on the disposition of investors to make their savings available at accustomed rates of return, and — positive ones — on the attitude of both businesses and households towards going into debt. The consequence can be a cumulative, long-run tendency for interest rates and costs of equity capital to increase.[1] So, for example, we have become aware of the unexpected phenomenon of increases in the money supply, introduced to moderate tightening interest rates, giving rise, in turn, to such anticipations of accentuated inflation as to result in even higher interest rates rather than lower ones. With the disposition to save declining and the demand for loanable funds rising, the result of higher costs of capital is not necessarily a decline in consumer and business borrowing or a decline in installment buying and investment spending, but only higher business costs. And so the expectation of continued inflation proves self-justifying. This assumes, as we will explain further on, that business can translate those higher costs into higher prices generally, which assumes, in turn, an accommodating national monetary and fiscal policy.

Inflation cannot continue for long without dispelling the money illusion on the part of labor as well as lenders. It is the illusion that prices will remain stable that makes labor willing for a time to accept wage increases that seem satisfactory by historic standards, then only to see them eroded in real terms by rising costs of living. Sooner or later that experience is likely to sink in, producing a different concept of what constitutes a fair wage. Wage settlements will then get bigger, and the correspondingly increased unit costs of production will be translated into higher prices. Once again, this kind of inflation can feed on itself. [2]

Second, there is the fact that the recessions of 1949, 1954, 1958, 1960, and 1970 were shallow and short-lived by historical standards and, no doubt for this reason, did little more than slow down the rate of price increase while they lasted; and the 1969-70 recession did not do even that. Each was then succeeded by a recovery in which wages and prices essentially took off from their previous peaks. This experience reflected one undeniable long-run change in our susceptibility to inflation: the unwillingness of Western societies to tolerate the deep and sustained reductions in aggregate spending, production, and employment that could turn wages and prices downward and break the spiral of self-justifying inflationary expectations. It was precisely the preceding experience with (relatively mild) inflation and the fear of rekindling it that induced the abrupt shift to monetary and fiscal contraction in 1959, which in turn aborted the recovery of 1958-59. But while this reapplication of the monetary brakes may have contributed to the comparative price stability of the 1961-65 recovery, it also cost Richard Nixon the election of 1960. That lesson was not lost on him when, after a similar venture in 1969-70, he found himself with another presidential election some fifteen months away and with prices stubbornly rising in the presence of a 6% rate of unemployment. This time, he embarked on an entirely different kind of policy — monetary and fiscal expansion accompanied by wage and price controls.

The third reason for concern was the extraordinarily stubborn resistance of wages and prices to the deliberate contraction of demand in 1969 and 1970. In sharp contrast with earlier postwar recessions, average hourly compensation in the private nonfarm economy actually rose more rapidly during the 1969-70 recession than in the preceding year. Contrast that with the experience of the four preceding recessions (Table I).

Table VIII—I

ANNUAL RATES OF INCREASE OF HOURLY COMPENSATION, PRIVATE NONFARM ECONOMY SEASONALLY ADJUSTED

Cyclical turning points		Year before peak	Peak to trough
Peak	Trough	%	%
1948:IV	1949:IV	8.0	0.4
1953:II	1954:III	6.0	3.3
1957:III	1958:II	5.4	3.3
1960:II	1961:I	4.3	1.7
1969:IV	1970:IV	6.5	7.0

Source: *Economic Report of the President,* January 1972, p. 48.

These statistics suggest a possible long-run tendency for the traditional monetary and fiscal correctives to become diminishingly effective. If, on the one hand, it is going to take more and more restrictionism, recession, and unemployment to halt wage and price increases, while, on the other hand, society becomes less willing to pay the price of these traditional methods of containing them, we obviously do have a problem of increasing intensity.

All of the foregoing evidence, and much of what follows, is consistent with the hypothesis that the inflation that accompanied the recession of 1969-70 and the persistent 6% unemployment rate of 1970-71 were merely the temporary consequence of a carryover of inflationary trends and expectations from the years immediately preceding and could have been conquered by a more persistent and determined application of the monetary and fiscal brakes.[3] But even if this relatively optimistic interpretation were correct, it would still mean that we paid, and would have had to pay, a price measured in scores of billions of dollars of lost annual production and millions of lost jobs for the perversity and sluggishness of our wage- and price-determining institutions, and that the economy could, indeed, be facing an intensified threat of chronic inflation because of the unwillingness of the public to pay so high a price for its control. Not surprisingly, some economists are suggesting that our national "full employment" target be reduced from a 4% to a 5% unemployment rate, while others have suggested that even a 5% to 7% annual rate of inflation need not be as catastrophic as we used to think.

There probably has never been an inflation that some people did not blame on "profiteers." And since most prices rise not by levitation, but by human action — usually action by those who profit from the change — this popular view is seldom wholly incorrect. But the formulation of a serious thesis that inflation could be caused by the "perversity of our wage- and price-determining institutions" and that inflation is built into or inherent in our industrial structure is a recent development; and both its conception and validity are still the subject of intense dispute. The flavor of the debate is richly conveyed by the fact that one of its leading proponents characterized it as "a phenomenon in search of a theory," and one of its opponents, "a theory in search of a phenomenon."[4]

Most of the authors of this volume are persuaded that there is such a phenomenon, although they would also differ among themselves in defining it and assessing its importance. The purpose of this chapter is principally to outline a conceptual framework for relating the imperfect functioning of product and labor markets to the possibility of chronic inflation. While I make no attempt systematically to summarize or reconcile the differing viewpoints, the following synthesis does reflect an effort to put together a statement with whose broad outlines most economists would agree.

The Phenomenon Defined

The classic type of inflation is one in which an expansion of aggregate demand outruns the ability of the economy to produce and, therefore, to satisfy that level of demand at constant prices. The critical impulse and pressure comes from the demand side: inflation *is,* typically, "demand-pulled." This has surely been true of the major periods of general price increase since 1939.[5] To be sure, it takes real people to raise prices; but in such periods, prices and wages are typically bid up by buyers competing for scarce supplies. And prices would and do increase in these circumstances regardless of whether "profiteering" sellers have any monopoly power. Indeed, as we will see presently, it is precisely prices and wages in the most highly competitive product and labor markets that typically increase the fastest and most under general demand-pull.

The phenomenon with which we are concerned, in contrast, is attributable to imperfections in our economic institutions, the ones that determine individual wages and prices: specifically, to imperfections of competition and the presence of monopoly power. No matter, for the moment, whether the power responsible resides primarily in certain labor markets (in which event we think of the inflation as "cost-push" [6]), or primarily in certain product markets (the most familiar designation is "administered-price"), or in some combination of the two, some economists therefore preferring to use the term "sellers' inflation." In all the variants, the problem identified is the presence and exercise of market power.

In a sense, the concept is tautological. The phenomenon to be explained is a rise in the general price level at a time when aggregate demand is either declining or failing to increase as rapidly as production capacity — when, that is, inflation cannot be demand-pulled, by definition. If, then, the general price level is not being pulled up by excess demand, it must be that it is being "administered" on the supply side by sellers with the power to raise wages and prices in the face of stagnant demand. Hence, the newly coined, ugly term — and ugly phenomenon — "stagflation." [7]

When we refer here to "demand" or "aggregate demand," we are referring to the aggregate or "average" performance of the economy. In truth, demands and supply capacities in real markets do not move uniformly. In all periods of general inflation, some labor, goods, or services will be in ample supply relative to demand; and in all periods of recession, some will be in short supply, with all sorts of intermediate conditions prevailing as well. But the concept is that in the absence of market power, the prices of *most* products and kinds of labor would be rising during periods of inflation, while an exceptional few in excess supply would be declining. And the prices of most products would be declining in periods of recession, while the exceptional few products in short supply would be increasing. The conceptual problem of stagflation is one of explaining why most prices, or their "average," are increasing at a time when demand for most products is slackening or increasing less than production capacity. The answer is market power, by definition — or almost so.

But this does not mean that identifying the source of the problem is an empty exercise in definition. If market power is the source of inflationary pressure, continually or intermittently, this obviously has important implications concerning the appropriateness — or at least the *cost* — of using monetary and fiscal correctives. It also prompts a search for other economic solutions. So, then, the question of market power inflation is of substantial importance.

The most adamant opponents of the market power thesis have scoffed at the notion that inflation could ever be anything except demand-pulled. In its most naive form, the exclusive demand-pull thesis, too, is tautological: the "general price level" is a statistical reflection of the prices at which transactions actually take place, and transactions cannot be effected at increasing prices except if buyers actually make those purchases — that is, unless aggregate demand is sufficient. No one doubts that the increase in (average) prices must, if it is to take place, be validated by actual purchases. And no economist, to my knowledge, doubts either that the government could, indeed, through monetary and fiscal measures, sufficiently curtail aggregate demand to prevent or reverse an increase in the general price level if it were determined to do so.

But it could succeed in this purpose only by curtailing the total volume of expenditure, and this in turn would mean reduced sales and employment as well as prices. The stronger the tendency for wages and prices to rise when total spending is either "just right" (in terms of maintaining some desired level of employment) or when it is less than that, the greater will be the restriction on aggregate demand, sales, and employment required to hold them in check. The more resistant wages and prices are to the depressing effect of diminishing sales and employment, the deeper and longer sustained the recession or stagnation required to prevent inflation.

The essence of the market power hypothesis is not, then, that the exercise of that power can "cause" inflation without the help of an accommodating monetary-fiscal policy. It is that market power creates a dilemma for the makers of public policy: it forces them to choose between price stability and full employment. The expectation that market power does, in fact, give rise to chronic inflation is based on the recognition that governments have been unwilling or politically unable, in recent decades, to exact the price in recession necessary to avoid it. *In conjunction with* market power, the general political commitment to full employment seems to promise a monetary policy sufficiently expansionary to accommodate chronic inflation.

WAGE BEHAVIOR AND COST-PUSH

Most economists do not have serious trouble with the proposition that imperfections of competition in labor markets can create or accentuate this dilemma, or that they have in fact done so at times. What we do not understand very clearly is how the process operates. One source of confusion is the fact, already noted, that pure demand inflation pulls up wages and so presents employers with a cost-push that does not necessarily owe anything to the presence of market power. Of course, an employer knows when he has to pay much higher wages because he is avidly bidding for labor that is in scarce supply — a case of pure demand-pull — and when he finds himself forced by threat of a strike to pay higher wages even when labor is in ample supply — a clear case of pure cost-push. But the typical situation is far more difficult to characterize and explain.

There are several reasons for this difficulty. First, the most obvious source of monopoly power in labor markets is unionization. But only about one-fourth of the wage earners in the United States are organized in unions. It becomes very difficult, then, to attribute general, economy-wide wage-push inflation to market power on labor's side, especially since we have only an imperfect understanding of the relationship between the processes that determine wage increases under collective bargaining and in its absence. Second, even where workers are not organized, an employer will be influenced in his wage offers by the *threat* of unionization, immediate or remote. In this way, the power of unions to effect a cost-push extends beyond their actual membership, but in ways that are difficult to measure or observe statistically. Third, even apart from the possible danger of unionization, an employer must be concerned with the morale and loyalty of his labor force. The wage increases that he grants employees will therefore be influenced by considerations of fairness — which will be influenced, in turn, by the pattern of wage increases being achieved elsewhere, by any changes in the cost of living in the period immediately preceding, as well as by the kinds of increases his workers have become accustomed to expect from past experience. All of these, and not just union power, may dictate cost-inflating raises even when demand is comparatively depressed.

It does violence to the facts to try to classify all these considerations and forces exclusively under one heading ("demand-pull") or

another ("cost-push"). In all of them, one can see a possible role
both of market power and of pure demand considerations. No matter
what the temporary balance of supply and demand in labor markets,
employers are in competition with one another for labor in the
longer run, and that competition alone could dictate cost-inflating
raises to keep a work force content even in periods of temporarily
declining demand. Affecting all these decisions must be the employer's current or anticipated need for those workers as well as his
current or anticipated ability to pay, both of which will depend on
the state of *demand* for his products.

None of these considerations, it might be argued, would have any
effect in a world of *perfect* competition — in such a world no employer would have any wage policy at all — and in that sense, these
considerations all support the role of market imperfections as a possible source of inflation. But the point here is that in our imperfectly
competitive world, these factors contain as an important element
the state of demand, and any tendencies to inflation that they may
generate belong, at least partly, in the demand-pull category.

On the other hand, an employer's *ability* to pay may itself be
influenced by the extent to which he enjoys monopoly power in his
product markets. And his *willingness* to pay will be influenced, similarly, by how easily he anticipates he can pass higher costs on in
higher prices. And that, too, depends on the way product markets
are organized and prices set. We reserve fuller consideration of this
possible factor for our next section, pausing here only to note the
evidence that more concentrated industries do, indeed, pay typically
higher wages than less concentrated industries, even apart from the
extent to which they are unionized. [8]

As some of these considerations suggest, one major reason for the
difficulty of distinguishing cases of demand-pull from cost-push is
the pervasive influence of lags and anticipations in wage settlements.
Employers are sometimes willing to give cost-inflating wage increases
in periods of general unemployment because they feel their workers
will have alternative opportunities in the future when the economy
recovers, and it pays to secure their loyalty against that day. Long-
term contracts embodying cost-inflating increases may be signed in
periods when demand is strong and impart their cost-push effect
largely in subsequent years when product and labor markets have
turned soft. Again, employers may be particularly vulnerable to

threats of strikes in periods of recovering demand, just as orders are beginning to pour in, and so agree to large wage increases at those times even though labor supplies are still plentiful. Here the major impulse would be union push, although it is the anticipation of strong demand that helps determine what wage increases unions can achieve.

A final reason for the uncertainty among economists about the precise role of labor union power, as distinguished from demand factors, is that we do not have a satisfactory economic theory of union behavior. For all our uncertainties about the motivations of the business firm or its managers, we have been able to construct moderately successful theories of business behavior in different market contexts based on assumptions that they try to maximize something — profits, sales, growth, or some combination of these. But we have no clear conception of what it is, if anything, that unions try to maximize.

Whatever it is they try to maximize, what unions can get is obviously not independent of the demand for their services; in particular, they can not be indifferent to its elasticity — i.e., to the adverse effect of excessive wage levels or increases on the employment of their members. But for a large number of possible reasons that it would not be fruitful to try to summarize here, unions may choose to ignore that elasticity, or to assume it is small,[9] or to argue that it is the function of government to take care of any unemployment that might result from wage increases in excess of productivity, a tendency that they would in any event — except in obvious individual instances — typically deny.

It is clear that the considerations that motivate parties on both sides of the collective bargaining process are as much broadly political as economic in character.[10] Consider, for example, the effect of what are, in the first instance, clearly economic factors: the rate of productivity improvement and the state of prospective profits, which clearly help determine the wage increases that employers in particular industries are able to pay.

First of all, these would have no effect on wages in perfectly competitive labor markets. Labor of the same quality would command the same wage in all industries, regardless of their individual fortunes. But in a bargaining situation, these factors peculiar to the particular firm or industry almost certainly do exert an influence.

This means that unusually favorable wage bargains might be struck in industries experiencing above-average increases in productivity or profits and might, because of the productivity improvement, not even result in increases in unit costs or necessitate increases in price. But multi-year contracts negotiated in such circumstances have, at critical times in the past, imposed on those industries large annual wage increases in subsequent years, definitely contributing to cost-push.

Moreover, given the indeterminacy of wage bargains in purely economic terms, as well as such noneconomic considerations as fairness and employee morale, there is a strong pressure for uniformity of wage increases from one industry to another.[11] If above-average raises in industries with progressive technologies were consistently balanced by correspondingly below-average raises in industries with the opposite experience, the resulting price structure would be inefficient,[12] but the average would have no tendency to rise. But the opposite tendency — to uniformity — can be persistently inflationary when the widely publicized, pattern-setting contracts are negotiated at times and/or in industries of above-average productivity advance and profitability, with the cost-push showing up most clearly, not in the pattern-setting industries, but in their less progressive counterparts. It is here that the pattern wage increases, unmitigated by productivity advances, are translated directly into increases in unit costs and prices. There seems little doubt that this process has been operative in many of the service industries, which, though not particularly monopolistic and not as thoroughly unionized as manufacturing, led the advances in the consumer price index and GNP deflator in the 1950's and 1960's — until the outburst of demand-pull inflation in 1972-74.[13]

Here we see two examples of the ratchet-like behavior of wages in imperfectly competitive markets. There is a temporal ratchet effect: wage increases negotiated in times of rising demand and improving profits are not offset by corresponding decreases when demand and profits are falling, with the result that wages and unit costs are ready to take off from a new and higher plateau with the next recovery of sales and profits. And there is an inter-industry ratchet: wage increases negotiated in more progressive and profitable industries may set the example for corresponding increases — instead of being offset by lesser increases or decreases — in declining or less progressive industries, thereby producing an increase in unit costs in the economy at large. As a result, wages and unit labor costs move in only one direction — upward.

The common assumption that the demand for labor is not affected by the upward drift of wage costs involves an implicit assumption: that demand for final products is similarly unaffected by price increases reflecting those higher costs. The demand for the product of any one employer and, hence, of his workers might of course decline if his prices were raised alone while those of his competitors were unchanged. But this consideration is irrelevant if wage and price increases are typically more or less uniform for all firms in an industry. The microeconomist finds it difficult to accept a general hypothesis that industry demands are typically inelastic over some relevant range that shifts upward over time. But the fact that sales of the product of a particular industry will ordinarily decline if its price rises while all other prices and money incomes are held constant sheds little light on the motivations and results achieved by unions and employers in bargaining situations in which it is generally assumed that *all* wages and money incomes in the economy at large will go up more or less uniformly together.[14]

Conceivably, of course, increases in *general* wage levels, too, may produce increased unemployment, either autonomously (for some such reason as that higher wages cause employers to try harder to economize on labor or discourage investment, or that a rising general price level reduces the purchasing power of total cash balances), or by inducing the government to adopt restrictive monetary policies. But to the extent they recognize this connection at all, or are prepared to admit its existence, unions are likely to attribute any resulting increase in unemployment to causes other than their own wage policies and to seek remedies at the level of national economic policy.[15]

And so we return to our original statement of the dilemma posed by market power inflation: should government tolerate the high levels of unemployment required to dampen the inflationary spiral? Or accommodate to and validate the higher wage and price level by permitting expansion of aggregate demand sufficiently to take something like a full-employment gross national product off the market at these higher prices? Or try to escape the choice between unemployment and inflation by permitting a level of aggregate spending sufficient to absorb unemployment and by using direct wage and price controls to prevent inflation?

ADMINISTERED PRICE INFLATION:
THE ROLE OF PRODUCT MARKET MONOPOLY

Monopoly power permits a wider margin between price and cost than would prevail in its absence. But most economists cannot see how it could give rise to an *ever-increasing* gap between price and cost, unless the degree of monopoly power in the economy were itself to increase over time, in which event the profit margin could be expected to grow only as that process continued. This skepticism does not depend on any particular hypothesis about managerial or company motivations. Since we cannot conceive of monopoly power as unlimited, we cannot see how, whatever the motives of those exercising it, a seller can indefinitely increase the margin by which he exploits consumers.

For this reason, most hypotheses of chronic inflation in which market power plays a substantial role lay heavy emphasis on the role of wages; and most of those that attribute an important influence to monopoly in *product* markets are inclined to posit some complicated relationship over time between the exercise of *that* power and the determination of costs (primarily wages, but also, conceivably, managerial salaries and other perquisites), as a result of which, tendencies to inflation of the profit rate get transmuted and imbedded in chronically increasing unit *costs,* with realized profit margins relatively unchanging in percentage terms floating on top of that secularly increasing unit cost base. In support of this view, we have at least the general historical evidence that profit rates, as a percentage of either sales or investment, have not shown any long-term tendency to increase.

Cyclical Price Rigidity

There is a theory of the behavior of product prices over (shorter periods) of time in the presence of market power that antedates the concerns of the last thirty years and that must be considered if we are to understand the more recent controversies over the contribution that product market monopoly can make to inflation. In his "Industrial Prices and their Relative Inflexibility," published in

1935,[16] and then more fully in the National Resources Committee's *The Structure of the American Economy*,[17] Gardiner Means observed, first, that prices varied enormously in their short-term flexibility as measured by the frequency with which they changed from month to month. On the basis of this observation, he concluded that there are two kinds of prices, those that are "market-determined," hence highly flexible (frequently changing) under the influence of constant changes in supply and demand; and those that are "administered," or quoted by sellers, which tend to be more rigid. Upon subsequent discussion, it became clear that Means tended to think of the first group as competitively determined in the market place, and the second as embracing only those administered prices subject to a considerable degree of monopoly control.

He observed, next, that there was a definite and striking direct relation between the *frequency* with which prices changed and the *amplitude* of those changes over the business cycle. That is, the more clearly prices could be identified as market-determined on the basis of frequency of change, the further they dropped between 1929 and 1933 and the further they rose in the 1933-37 recovery. And the more prices could, on the basis of the frequency criterion, be identified as "administered," the more rigid they were over the cycle. He reproduces this very striking demonstration in his contribution to the present volume.

Means attempted, finally, to demonstrate that cyclical price behavior was functionally related to the presence or absence of "market power" by correlating industrial concentration ratios with indexes of cyclical price sensitivity. He did, indeed, find a substantial, though rough, inverse relationship between the two.

Means' work of the 1930's was subjected to intense criticism on both theoretical and empirical grounds. As for the former, there was no a priori reason, some economists asserted, for monopolistically determined prices to be more or less rigid than competitive prices. The proper measure of the effect of monopoly, they also asserted, would have to be the behavior, not of price, but of the margin between price and variable (more precisely, short-run marginal) costs.

As for the evidence, one powerful criticism of Means' proffered statistical verification was that prices quoted at wholesale, which he used, are an inaccurate reflection of the prices at which transactions actually take place. Specifically, actual transactions prices, reflecting the offer and withdrawal of more or less concealed discounts and premiums, will invariably change more often and fluctuate more than quoted prices. And, in fact, a detailed statistical study by Willard Thorp and Walter Crowder of the cyclical behavior of average unit realizations as reported by the Bureau of the Census (which would reflect actual receipts rather than quoted prices) failed to turn up any significant correlation with industry concentration ratios.[18] Richard Ruggles showed that unit realizations tended to move essentially in correspondance with average variable costs, without any obvious evidence of being affected by concentration;[19] and Alfred C. Neal showed that the statistical relationship between concentration and the behavior of mark-ups above direct costs in the period 1929-31 was weak, though nevertheless positive and statistically significant.[20] These were the main criticisms.

It would be impractical, and for our purposes unnecessary, to try to do full justice to those complex controversies, partly because to do so would require their virtually complete replication, partly because they have been ably summarized elsewhere,[21] and partly because some concensus has emerged, though far less than might have been hoped for from what purports to be an objective science.

The Exercise of Market Power

There are several reasons why one might indeed expect sellers to use such market power as they possess to stabilize their prices both absolutely and relative to the movement of direct costs over the cycle. Perhaps the most efficient way of explaining some of them is to begin with the opposite proposition. It can readily be demonstrated that under certain conditions a monopolist's theoretically profit-maximizing price will fluctuate as much as a price set under conditions of pure competition, with both of them moving up and down in correspondence with marginal cost — the price under pure competition being *at* marginal cost at all times, and the price under monopoly, at an unchanging percentage above that same marginal cost.[22] This means that there is no reason in these circumstances to expect prices to fluctuate less in the presence of market power than in its absence: the monopolist will charge a higher price than the seller subject to pure competition, but the ratio between the two will remain unchanging; and the two will therefore fluctuate over time with the same amplitude, in percentage terms. The intuitive explanation for this expectation is that the profit-maximizing margin above marginal cost and above the competitive price is determined by (specifically, varies inversely with) the elasticity of demand. (Obviously, the monopolist can raise his price more, the less the demand for his product is sensitive to the price he charges.) So in the absence of any reason, a priori, to expect the elasticity of the individual seller's demand to fluctuate systematically over the cycle in one direction or the other, there is no reason to expect any systematic tendency for the margin of monopoly exploitation, or the difference between the monopoly and the competitive price, to change one way or the other over time.

By the same reasoning, however, it can be demonstrated that if the marginal cost curve is relatively horizontal at lower levels of output and rises sharply at higher levels — that is, that competitive supply is elastic at lower levels of price and progressively less elastic at higher levels — the profit-maximizing monopolist's price will fluctuate less, conceivably very much less, than the competitive price in response to changes in demand. One can see the logic of this intuitively if one assumes that, at the extreme, rising demand encounters a marginal cost (a competitive supply) curve that is totally inelastic. At this point, the competitive and monopoly prices will be identical: the fixed supply will, in either case, be auctioned off to the highest bidders. But as demand drops, the competitive price falls rapidly along the steeply inclined marginal cost curve (because supply is totally inelastic), ceasing to fall only as it encounters its more elastic portion; whereas the monopoly price can, by curtailment of supply, be held as far above those lower levels of marginal cost as the inelasticity of demand dictates.

Surely we have here an explanation for the wide fluctuation of many market-determined prices in the absence of effective cartel or government controls — their steeply sloping marginal cost, hence inelastic supply, functions in response both to increases and to decreases of demand down to a very low floor at the point where supply finally becomes elastic. Within a wide range, the supply of natural rubber, or of crude oil under the law of capture, is extremely unresponsive to changes in demand. But if price gets low enough, there simply is no point in picking strawberries ripening in the field and bringing them to market.

Surely, also, this explains the logic of almost all cartels imposing production or sales quotas that vary with demand: they do so precisely in order to make supply elastic and thus stabilize prices that would otherwise fluctuate widely. It is not surprising that the market-determined prices that fluctuate so widely over the business cycle are the prices of primary products and scrap materials, whose marginal cost and supply functions, in the absence of cartel-like controls, seem to have this kind of shape. And that the prices of industrial commodities, whose variable costs are typically more nearly horizontal and supply more elastic within a wide range, tend, as Means observed, to be relatively rigid — almost without regard to the varying degree of competitiveness within the industrial sector. And that the introduction of effective market and production control of primary products has a dramatic stabilizing effect on price. Witness, for example, the wide fluctuations in petroleum prices when production was uncontrolled and their dramatic stabilization when it was subjected to "prorationing to market demand."

The other reasons why sellers would be expected to use market power to stabilize prices are more obvious and may be briefly summarized: (1) When prices are administered or quoted, it is often costly to change them frequently and more convenient to hold them stable until a substantial change is called for. (2) Customers are typically more upset by frequently changing, than by stable, prices. And sellers who are in a position to worry about customer good will and to act on the basis of that concern are likely to behave accordingly. (3) This behavior is even more likely when the sellers are not pure monopolists. Unless they are able to practice perfect collusion, oligopolists are typically subject to varying degrees of uncertainty about the prices they can charge, the prices their rivals are charging, and how those rivals will react to any changes they initiate. Frequent price changes are likely to be upsetting, to induce unpredictable patterns of response, emulation, or retaliation, and to interfere with the maintenance of the orderly recognition of mutual interdependence requisite for the maximization of joint profits. In these circumstances, prices are likely, therefore, to be altered only in discrete and substantial steps, when costs or market conditions have changed so substantially as to force one of the parties to act, or when a general consensus on the desirability of a change and a general understanding about its appropriate order of magnitude have been reached.

These considerations counsel firms with market power to take a longer view of price policy than firms lacking such power, since the latter have no choice but to follow the market from one moment to the next; and this longer view is likely to incline them toward cyclical stabilization. [23] Oligopolists will avoid price cuts in periods of declining demand, recognizing the likelihood of their detection and imitation by competitors, with a resulting loss of profits for all. They will do so also in order to avoid the necessity of offending their customers by recouping price cuts with quick subsequent increases as demand recovers. And in the absence of perfect collusion or its equivalent, they will hesitate about raising prices in periods of recovering demand, also, because they are uncertain whether or how they will be followed.

(4) Monopolists and oligopolists alike tend to have an influence, too, over the wage rates they pay, and they tend to exercise it in the direction of stabilization. They will try to avoid wage cuts in periods of declining demand as labor contracts expire, partly because they are typically under less pressure from competitors' price cuts to reduce costs correspondingly, partly in order to preserve the good will of their work forces, and partly because wage cuts contribute to uncertainty about the future of prices and may therefore undermine oligopolistic solidarity on the price front. Similarly, when demand is recovering and profits growing disproportionately even with unchanging prices — as they tend to do because some costs are fixed — firms with market power are likely to take into account the probability that the even better profits that "unnecessary" price increases would produce would expose them to demands for correspondingly larger wage increases.

Similar considerations may apply, at least on the downward side, to the prices of other purchased inputs. An additional one (5) counselling restraint in cutting input prices in periods of declining demand is the presence of vertical integration. When companies themselves produce a large part of their own raw material requirements, they are less likely when markets are soft to press for price reductions on the portion they buy from others. Any general undermining of those prices would tend to reduce the returns from their own integrated operations as well: to the extent you are vertically integrated, the raw material price you cut is your own. In the case of oil companies, there is the added motive that profits at the raw material production level are subject to more favorable federal tax treatment than profits earned in refining and marketing.

(6) One important additional consideration will tend to induce firms with market power to moderate the cyclical fluctuations in the *margins* they charge above direct costs, and that is the possibility of competitive entry. The hypothesis of cyclical rigidity of *prices,* when translated into a corresponding expectation of rigidity of *margins,* becomes, in its extreme form, an expectation that gross margins will actually vary *inversely* with the cycle in percentage terms. (If they are constant over the cycle, with prices therefore fluctuating along with and by the same percentages as direct costs, prices are in a sense not inflexible. Inflexibility would seem to require that prices fluctuate *less* than direct costs; and this means percentage markups decrease as direct costs rise and increase as they fall.)

Even this last expectation — which is more extreme than necessary [24] — is not an unreasonable one. The gross margin or markup covers fixed costs and profits. Because the first component *is* fixed, the latter component, profits alone, fluctuates sharply with the level of sales, even when the percentage markup above direct costs is unchanged.[25] This produces a strong inducement to entry of competitors (as well as to increased union wage demands) in time of recovery, and a weak one in time of recession. Consideration of this fact could well counsel restraint in pricing during recovery, and not just a preservation, but even an administered increase in gross markups during recession.

(7) Finally, there is the simple and undeniable fact that monopoly power expands the range of sellers' discretion (in the case of monopoly) and of uncertainty (in the case of oligopoly) over pricing behavior. Price-takers, in contrast, are inevitably profit-maximizers so far as their pricing policies are concerned. And pure competition tends to assure the results of profit-maximizing output and investment policy for their industries as a whole.[26] Price *makers,* instead, have at least the possibility of departing from maximization in both the short and long run; of striving for only "satisfactory" or "reasonable" profits, either year by year (as Blair now suggests) or over a period of years; of catering to managerial preferences for growth and/or a steady increase in other fringe benefits; of moving alternately, or with lags of varying length, closer and farther away from the industry profit-maximizing levels. We have already suggested

many reasons, fully consistent with firms attempting to maximize profits even in the short run, why the result of this discretion and uncertainty might well be a policy of stabilization over the cycle. Longer-run considerations of acceptable profit as well as of labor, customer, and public relations exert an influence in the same direction.

Verification and Refutation

What then of the attempts at statistical verification and refutation of the Means hypothesis? For reasons already given, I can offer little more than an impressionistic summary.

Unquestionably, the prices of most primary products, scrap, and secondary materials have shown extremely wide cyclical fluctuations, except where production or sales have been tightly controlled by a few sellers or a cartel. To the extent cartels have been effective, they have elasticized supply (producing more when there is more demand, and producing less when there is less demand) and thereby stabilized prices. Here the evidentiary support for Means is clear.

Unquestionably, too, the prices of most manufactured products move primarily with direct costs, as Alfred C. Neal first demonstrated thoroughly. The degree of monopoly as measured by one concentration ratio or another proves in all statistical tests to be a much less *consistent* and powerful determinant of prices than does direct costs.

The fact remains, first, that the two comprehensive and systematic investigations of the relation of market concentration to the behavior of (gross profit) *margins* above direct costs did indeed find that market concentration had a statistically significant and far from negligible influence in resisting compressions in prices in the post-1929 depression.[27]

Second, it is important always to keep in mind that concentration ratios are only a weak and imperfect measure of monopoly power for a large number of very familiar reasons. Particularly misleading would be the inference that because the ratios of concentration in the economy can be arranged to create a smooth and continuous array from almost zero to 100%, monopoly power alone (setting aside, for the moment, possible variations in the way in which that power is exercised) exhibits a similarly smooth progression. If one were to define market power, for example, as the ability to hold prices stable in the face of declines in demand or direct costs, the difference in this respect between industries with four-firm concentration ratios of, say, 25% and 75% may not be great. Nor would an industry with a 75% ratio necessarily have more power in this respect than one with 40%, or less than one with 85%.[28]

In these circumstances, it is not at all inappropriate to use, as an alternative measure of monopoly, some behavioral rather than structural characteristic of industries — such as the number of times their prices change per month or year, provided, of course, one has a measure of actual transactions, rather than merely formally quoted prices.[29]

Third, as we have already suggested, the behavior of wages and of the prices of other inputs is not independent of the presence of monopoly power in end markets. The causal connection does not run solely from direct costs, autonomously determined, to final product price. On the contrary, there are clear indications that the market power that is used to stabilize end markets also has the effect of stabilizing the prices of labor and materials, both automatically and as a matter of policy.[30] To the extent, also, that unionization is associated with concentration in product markets, the effectiveness of unions in preventing wage declines in periods of decreasing demand is not independent of product market monopoly. For all these reasons, statistical studies relating market concentration ratios to the behavior of *margins* will tend to understate the impact of market power on the behavior of *prices.*

A final consideration in assessing the relatively weak statistical findings about the relation of concentration to the rigidity of prices or margins, as we have already pointed out, is the fact that market power, by definition, permits its possessor to choose from a wider range of alternative pricing, investment, and output policies than are available to firms lacking such power. It does not assure that industry will consistently find it in its interest to hold prices up in periods of declining demand and declining unit costs. Market power merely permits industry to act in this way if and when managers believe this would be in their interest. It also permits them to define their interests in a greater variety of ways than firms subject to intense competition. The Means thesis is not rebutted by a showing that market power is not *consistently* accompanied by cyclical price rigidity. As we will explain more fully below, it requires only that cyclical price rigidity — or perverse price behavior — *when and if it occurs,* be consistently associated with market power.[31]

The Market Power Thesis Transformed: chronic upward creep

Even though controversy over the Means hypotheses of the 1930's continued during the 1950's,[32] it was widely remarked at the time that prices in many concentrated industries such as automobiles, and also union wages, had indeed lagged far behind competitive, market-determined prices (as black markets eloquently testified) during the rapid inflation immediately following World War II, just as Means had posited.

It was, therefore, with considerable surprise and skepticism that the world of economists reacted to Means' new suggestion of the 1950's, which Blair helped to develop and publicize through hearings and reports of the Kefauver committee, that administered prices were responsible for the "new kind of inflation" of that period. The whole point of his earlier argument was that administered prices tended to fall less than market-determined prices during recessions and to *rise less* during recoveries. It provided no basis for predicting that they would ever *rise faster* than market-determined prices, let alone lead competitive prices in a long-term increase. How could the Means hypothesis have been so transformed?

The posture of the economy and the focus of public concern had, of course, changed dramatically since the 1930's. At that time, the overwhelming reality was the Great Depression, and the overwhelming concern was the restoration of full employment. By the mid-1950's, however, there was the added concern about the possibility of chronic inflation. While economists could therefore regard the increase of most prices between 1933 and 1937 almost with equanimity, as part of a necessary process of recovery (although, as always, with the fear that what went up would sooner or later come down), they saw the much slighter rise of the general price level during the 1950's, a period of decelerated economic growth, as confirming the reality of this newly perceived danger. The commitment in the postwar world to full employment meant that the range within which governments could, with political impunity, use monetary and fiscal tools to hold inflation in check was narrow. And the effectiveness of such an effort depended, therefore, on the prompt response of wages and prices to deflationary policies. In these circumstances, the apparent unresponsivensss of administered prices to deflationary policies was once again the source of the problem.

In part, then, the phenomenon that Means purported to explain in the 1950's, and the explanation itself, were no different from those of the 1930's: it was the resistance of prices and wages to deflation in the presence of market power. The widespread interventions by governments to support market-determined prices that would otherwise have declined was another example of the same process — the exertion of market power to resist the impact of deflation on price. While unsupported, market-determined prices of competitive industries continued to fluctuate more widely in both directions, their downward movements at times and in markets characterized by inadequate or declining demand were seen to be progressively insufficient to do more than temporarily halt or slow down the continuous rise in general wage and price levels.

In part, the phenomenon had changed. For what was needed now was an explanation, not merely of the comparative *stability* of administered prices in recession, but of their perverse tendency to increase in periods of unsatisfactory economic expansion. But this required no great extension of Means' analysis — such perverse wage-price behavior, a fortiori, must have reflected the presence and exertion of market power.

So the administered price thesis was gradually transformed from an explanation and prediction of price stability into one of chronic upward price creep, first during the unhappy experience of the 1950's, then again in the late 1960's, when even sharper price increases were experienced during and following the deliberately invoked 1969-70 recession.

Market Concentration and Price Rises

The evidence concerning price behavior in the 1953-59 period was for a time sharply disputed. But enough of it is now in to demonstrate that Means was right. The increases in the general price level, not only during the 1954-56 recovery — which were influenced also by the simple pressures of demand in important sectors of the economy [33] — but during the 1953-54 and 1956-58 recessions as well were indeed heavily accounted for by the administered sector of industry. The relation between product market concentration and price changes was significant and positive, though modest.

It is important for our understanding of these controversies to note that the consistency and intensity of the statistical relationship between concentration and price increases was markedly greater when the price indexes were weighted by volume of sales than when they were unweighted. That is to say, both the coefficient of correlation (measuring the *consistency* of the relationship) and the coefficient of the concentration variable in the regression equation (measuring the *size* of the impact of concentration on price) show up fully twice as high when the various price indexes are weighted by the relative size of the industries as when they are all weighted equally.[34] Which is the appropriate measure depends on the hypothesis being tested.

If the attempt is to determine the consistency of the relationship between product market concentration and price increases as a general phenomenon, then the unweighted measures, which show a weaker relationship, are the appropriate ones. One observation of the relation between concentration and price behavior is just as important as another. If the tendency is real, it should show up as consistently in small industries as in large. If instead the question is the more specific one — how important was market power in explaining the increase in the *general price level that actually occurred* in the 1950's — and this was Means' question — obviously the larger an industry bulked in determining that price level, which is itself a weighted average, the larger the weight it must be given in testing the hypothesis.[35] It must be recognized, on the other hand, that the discovery of a strong positive relationship of the second kind affords a weaker basis than would a similar finding in support of the first hypothesis for predicting a recurrence of that experience.

As in the 1930's, changes in direct costs of labor, materials, and other inputs were a more important determinant of changes in the prices of manufactured products than was market concentration. But in the definitive study to date of this period which confirmed this fact, Leonard Weiss determined also that the relationship between product market concentration and *margins* between direct costs and price was likewise positive. Or to put it another way, the relatively greater increase of prices among concentrated industries was not explained away by a corresponding greater increase in their labor and material costs. It is true, however, that wages did increase more in concentrated than unconcentrated industries in this period — another factor explaining the relative increase in their prices.[36]

Product market concentration is never likely statistically to "explain" the major part of any increase in the general price level such as occurred in the 1950's or 1969-71. Apart from such technical reasons for this as the deficiencies of concentration ratios as a measure of the *power* to set prices perversely, there is the more fundamental reason that many factors other than market power determine which way prices move. Rises in concentrated industries may be partly or wholly "explained" by increases in cost, which may themselves be explained, either not at all, or only partially, by concentration itself. Again, prices in many *un*concentrated industries may move up at the same time under normal competitive market influences such as the pressure of increased demand on an upwardly sloping supply curve, decreases in supply (such as crop failures), or increases in cost. The Means' thesis is obviously not vitiated if some nonperverse price increases in unconcentrated markets occur simultaneously with perverse increases in concentrated markets.

The contribution of market concentration will be further obscured to the extent that price increases administered by concentrated industries directly raise the costs of inputs, hence the prices, in unconcentrated ones. Steel provided a striking illustration of this in the 1950's. The same will be true if wage settlements in the concentrated industries set the pattern for settlements in the unconcentrated industries.

Finally, as we have already suggested, prices in most concentrated industries may well behave "nonperversely." They need not always rise in time of stagflation. Most of them, indeed, may well decline at such times.

For all these reasons, a very weak statistical correlation between product market concentration and price increases can be entirely consistent with product market power being the *principal* explanation of such *perverse* price increases, or failures of prices to decrease, as occurred in these periods. And it is the *perverse* price behavior, in a situation in which most price changes may not be perverse at all, that is at the heart of the market-power explanation of upward price creep.

The controversies over the 1969-70 experience, as well as over the longer period of the 1950's and 1960's, have a familiar ring. The decisive evidence is not yet in. On the one hand, we have had the demonstrations by Means and Blair in this volume in support of the administered price thesis. Arguing to the contrary are statistical anal-

yses by J. Fred Weston, Steven Lustgarten, and Nanci Crottke.[37] I
make no attempt here to reconcile these conflicting findings or to
choose among them, but pause only to observe that the differences
between them in both statistical results and the conclusions drawn
from them seem to be explicable, at least in part, by many of the
considerations we introduced in analyzing the earlier controversies.

The Lag Thesis

Suppose that the ultimately decisive appraisal of the 1969-71 experience, like that of the 1950's, leaves intact the critical contention
of Blair and Means: namely, that monopoly power in product markets played an important role in causing or permitting the perverse
behavior of the general price level in that period. We would still have
to consider the possibility that the association was a temporary and
short-range phenomenon. We would, in other words, have to confront the fundamental uncertainty about any possible relationship
between such power and chronic inflation with which we began this
section; specifically, how could monopoly power cause a continual
increase in prices?

In point of fact, most of the studies of the 1950's did demonstrate
that the correlation between concentration and price, and concentration and wage increases ceased after 1958.[38] This finding tended to
reinforce certain earlier speculations that the phenomenon of the
mid-1950's, and especially during the recessions, was a merely
temporary one, reflecting a lag in the response of (some) monopolists
and oligopolists (and unions) to the opportunities for increased profit (and wages) offered by the demand-pull inflations of 1946-48 and
1950-53, when their prices (and wages) had fallen behind. John Galbraith has suggested that the relative stability of these prices in periods of increasing demand reflected a deferral in the full exploitation
of monopoly power, and that the stubborn tendency of these same
prices to rise in subsequent periods of less buoyant demand was
simply a fuller realization of those deferred monopoly gains — a gradual and lagged approach to the profit-maximizing point.[39]

In the same way, it seems highly likely that whatever positive
relationship there may have been between product market power and
perverse, upward price behavior during the 1969-70 recession represented a reversal of price trends during the preceding inflation and
was itself reversed in the increasingly pure demand inflation of

1971-74. And that here, again, the intervening stagflation, some might argue, represented, at most, the lagged adjustment of monopoly prices to the opportunities presented by the sharp increases of aggregate demand in the years immediately preceding.

In my opinion, the lag hypothesis has never been adequately rationalized so far as industrial pricing is concerned, although it makes a good deal more sense with respect to the behavior of wages. It is not clear why mere increases in demand, with no change in elasticity (at least none is typically posited), do increase the profit-maximizing price. The relationship of the profit-maximizing price to marginal cost depends only on the elasticity of demand, not the level of demand. Of course, increases in demand might be associated with increases in marginal cost, hence in the profit-maximizing price. But direct costs per unit tend, if anything, to decline as firms move from below to more nearly optimal levels of operation. Moreover, wage increases, when they occur, are typically translated quite promptly, even in the least effectively collusive oligopolies, into corresponding price increases.

Why, then, may not prices in concentrated industries move promptly to the new profit-maximizing level? I can think of only two possible explanations. First, as firms move to ever higher levels of operation, unit direct costs (hence, marginal costs) typically increase, even with wages and raw material prices constant. And oligopolists find it much more difficult to practice price leadership successfully and raise their prices uniformly in reaction to gradual cost increases of this kind than to newly negotiated wage rates. And, second, maintaining the accustomed percentage relationship of price to variable cost (and, a fortiori, of price to marginal cost, when the latter moves above average) would produce very sharp increases in profits, which might in turn attract entry or invite very large wage settlements. Either of these explanations suggests that the profit-maximizing price, considered in a perspective sufficiently long-run to take into account effects on wage settlements and entry, does *not* in fact move upward step by step with customer orders. And that the observed behavior of prices *is* therefore consistent with, say, intermediate-run, profit-maximization. If this reasoning is sound, it could be that the (intermediate-run) profit-maximizing price itself moves upward after demand has turned down!

But this rationalization still leaves us with only a lag phenomenon.

And that kind of pricing, like cyclical rigidity, cannot in itself explain or produce perpetual inflation. Presumably at some point, price *reaches* its profit-maximizing level, or the level itself stops increasing, however belatedly, and the inflationary potential of market power is exhausted — except, of course, as the power itself keeps growing.

Market Power and Chronic Inflation

And so we return to the fundamental dilemma confronting those of us who believe market power *is* a source of chronic inflation: our inability, consistent with traditional theory, to visualize how profit margins in industries with monopoly power can continue in the long run to widen relative to profit margins in other industries. Or how wage rates, in situations of market power (whether in labor or product markets), can diverge (upward) in the long run from wage rates in other markets.

The solution must, I think, be sought in a series of relationships that are typically ignored in that traditional, static theory. First, the structure of an industry — specifically, the degree and nature of competition in its product markets — influences the level of its own costs and their behavior over time. Second, when one industry produces inputs for others, its prices influence their costs. Third, and similarly, the wage bargains struck in one industry help determine the wages, hence the costs, of others. Fourth, and in a sense embracing the first three, the most important characteristic of the behavior of prices and wages in the economy at large is their interdependence: price determines wages, wages determine price. The price set by Firm A in one industry determines the price that will be set by Firm B in the same industry. The prices and wages set by A and B together will partially determine the prices and wages set in other industries—and conversely.

It is these interdependencies that make the lag thesis (the delayed exploitation of monopoly power) so inadequate an explanation of the role of monopoly in inflation. The problem is not simply that some industries with market power are laggards in exploiting that power and then, in time, simply achieve the same levels of price that they would have achieved sooner had they not been sluggish. Except in periods of clear and strong demand-pull, those industries surely play a role also, and perhaps primarily, of *pace setters* for the economy. By the prices and wages they set and refuse to reduce in time of recession, industries with market power alter the "equilibrium" levels for the economy at large. They set the floor from which the next round of increases begins.

Since it is difficult to conceive of product monopoly power or the degree to which it is exploited increasing unendingly, that power can be an agent of inflation only if the monopoly profits it makes possible are incorporated more or less continuously into an ever, though not necessarily smoothly, rising level of unit costs. These rising unit costs, in turn, provide the rising floor that establishes the basis for ever-increasing administered prices without ever-increasing profit margins. I do not suggest that we fully understand the process by which this occurs — doubtless because the pattern is neither simple nor unvarying over time.

One part of the process, as has persuasively been argued by P. J. Wiles, is the fact that the willingness of businessmen to pay higher wages depends, in important measure, on the ease with which they think they can pass them on in higher prices. And that depends, in turn, on the way in which the product markets are organized. Specifically, Wiles points out, there is no automatic mechanism for this process in industries whose prices are purely market-determined. Under pure competition, prices come to reflect increased marginal costs only as a result of a painful process of reduction in output and elimination of marginal producers. No wonder, he observes, such industries bitterly resist unionization.[40]

Perhaps another part is that the new price floor that firms with market power have succeeded in maintaining during recessions typically incorporates high *ex ante* profit margins, which turn into sharply increased *realized* profits as demand recovers. These rapidly recovering profits, in turn, set the stage for conspicuous and generous wage bargains. And these, in turn, heavily influence labor's expectations in the economy at large, regardless of the strength or weakness of other labor or product markets.

It is, in short, somewhere in the inter-relationship between product market power and the wage determination process — where wages themselves are strongly influenced, not only by current labor and product market conditions in particular markets, but also by considerations of what is "fair" and by rivalries among labor unions — that monopoly profits get transmuted into increasing unit costs, first in the concentrated sectors, then by spillover into the economy at large. The effect of such imitative wage increases on unit costs will, of course, be magnified in those sections of the economy where man-hour productivity increases are running below the national average.

Here is the probable connection between the market power thesis and the apparently inexorable rise in the prices of *services* that has figured so importantly in the surge of the cost of living in recent decades. Some services, no doubt, are sold under the influence of monopoly power. But others seem competitively determined, with long-term price increases reflecting the simple pressure of demand. The missing link would seem to be the impact of largely administered wage increases far outrunning the below-average growth of productivity in this increasingly important area of the economy.

CONCLUSIONS

Traditional microeconomic theory — the static models of competitive and monopolistic price-making — cannot, I believe, predict or explain a process of chronic inflation springing from defects in our price- and wage-making institutions.

But that does *not* mean that the process is a fantasy, or that the danger is nonexistent. All it may mean is that the economic theory that explains the achievement of static equilibria is incompetent to explain dynamic processes. The lag hypothesis springs from such a theory. It is grounded in the assumption that there is, for each market, some profit-maximizing price depending on the degree of market power present. And that for firms with market power, either that price itself lags behind the cyclical flow of demand, or monopolists lag in the rate at which they achieve it. And that at *some* point in the cyclical process — whether at the "beginning," before demand begins its recovery, or at the "end," some time after demand has turned downward — monopolists achieve that price. And that, hence, market power affects only the long-run equilibrium level of the price and the timing of its achievement, but not its trend.

Such a hypothesis is simply inadequate to explain the behavior of prices since 1945. Nor is a return to a pure demand-pull explanation a sufficient alternative. To explain the administered price inflation of 1953-58 as merely the delayed reaction to the demand-pull of 1945-48 and 1950-53 strikes this economist as implausible, excessively pat, and, indeed, almost metaphysical. There is no convincing reason *why* the "adjustment" should have taken so long. Moreover, such a hypothesis ignores the probable impact of the administered price and wage inflation of the middle 1950's *back* on the "equilibrium" level of wages, input costs, and, hence, output prices in the competitive sectors. To ignore the fact that even in the first half of the decade of the 1960's, a highly satisfactory period so far as price stability was concerned, prices *did* increase, although slightly, and apparently would have increased more but for the wage-price guidelines; to ignore the fact that wages, unit labor costs, and prices in both the concentrated sectors and in most of the economy have typically begun each new round of cyclical increase from a point close to, if not actually above, the previous peaks; and to attribute the continued, intractable inflation of 1971-72, in conjunction with a national unemployment rate at 5% or above, essentially to a changed structure of the labor market — all seems to be a refusal to face up to the underlying reality: the combination of labor and product market power and the governmental commitment to full employment are incompatible with long-run price stability.

The deficiency is not in the facts; it is in our theory. The apparatus of static, microeconomic theory, which can explain where wages and prices ought to settle if the determining conditions remain unchanged, is simply incompetent to explain a dynamic process, as much political in the broadest sense as economic, by which various groups in the economy fight over their shares in national income. An essential part of such a process is that when one segment of the economy reaches "its equilibrium," that fact itself changes the determining conditions, hence, the political and economic equilibrium for other segments and groups.

Once one recognizes the possibility that the deficiency may reside in the limitations of our static, partial-equilibrium models, a number of interesting possible bases for comprehending what has been happening or may happen open up. The relation of product market power to the wage determination process over time, in the context of a general expectation that "fairness" requires ever-increasing real wages, is only one.

A closely related one is the possibility that the behavior of costs under more and less effective competition may well diverge over time — in either direction. Joseph Schumpeter has supplied the rationale for expecting that technological innovation is more likely in the presence of substantial market power, thus leading to an expectation that prices in such markets would actually tend to *decline* in the long run, relative to more competitive prices. On the other hand, the notion is familiar to economists that the wages of monopoly are more an easy life than large nominal profits. We have already alluded to the possibility that monopoly "profits" may take the form of higher emoluments for the managers of companies that possess it, and there is no reason to believe that the zest for such improvements of managerial living standards stops once some "equilibrium" level is reached. And if monopoly permits a firm the luxury of paying less close attention to its costs, it may also produce a less favorable trend of costs *over time*.[41] The notion that market structure cannot be expected to have an effect on industry performance over time is inherently absurd.

Nor is the possibility that the profit-maximizing price may rise over time so inconceivable, once one asks what are the factors that determine its level. The preponderant determinant of the elasticity of demand for the services of an individual firm is, of course, the presence of competitors and the prices they charge. For a nation's industry, it is the prices charged by foreign suppliers and for substitutes. Obviously, then, what *one* cannot do, according to a partial equilibrium analysis, *all* can do. Chronic inflation has, in fact, occurred in all industries and in all countries. This is obviously not to suggest that its roots are to be found solely, or even primarily, in market power. It is to suggest, however, that the profit-maximizing price, whether for monopolists or firms in competitive industries, is not something static; its parameters move over time. And over recent decades, they have moved preponderantly in only one direction — upward.

Has market power played a role in this process? It surely has. It has shown its influence in intolerably slow reactions to monetary-fiscal contractions following periods of demand-pull as wages reflected past increases in the cost of living and sellers passed on increased unit costs. It has shown up in examples of perverse price setting as firms sought either to maintain or even increase target returns at fixed rates of capacity utilization when sales fell off. And it has shown up in the asymmetrical response of wages and prices to increases and decreases in demand — the ratchet effect that we previously described. This is behavior that could not have occurred in the absence of market power. It is intimately related to the process by which different organized groups try, each in turn, to maintain and to improve their shares of the national income pool, with the sum total of the dollar claims that they succeed in enforcing, always subject to an accommodating macroeconomic policy, simply exceeding the ability of the economy to supply at constant prices. As Gardner Ackley has put it, inflation occurs when labor's "markup" of wages over "cost" (the cost of living) and business' markup over its cost are inconsistent with general price stability; that is, add up to an attempt to take more than 100% of potential national output.[42]

None of this conclusion attempts to deny an important and possibly central role to government policy generally and aggregate demand specifically. Certainly the worst inflations have been principally pure demand-pull. Certainly, also, the inflations of 1966-69 and 1972-74 have resulted, in large measure, from failures of public policy — in particular, the failure to enact timely increases in taxes, to cut government spending, to moderate increases in the money supply. *But these government policies,* and their deficiencies, *are another reflection of the same process:* the inability of our administered economy, of which government is one agent, to so discipline the nominal after-tax income demands and receipts of all groups, including taxpayers and beneficiaries of government subsidy, protection, and outlays, that they add up to no more than full employment output at constant prices.

It remains true that there can be no inflation that is not validated by public policy. And that, consequently, it is faulty governmental policy that is, in a sense, "responsible" for all inflation. But if that statement is true, it is also vapid. The "government" is not a *deus ex machina,* "exogenous" to the economic process. It is part of the process, and its decisions are themselves molded by the private economic interests it is supposed to control. Every government expenditure, tax, and money transfer has, not only a macroeconomic, but a microeconomic consequence as well, and, even more important, an impact on the economic welfare of some group of private parties. The resistance of *aggregate* government taxes and expenditures to macroeconomic considerations, particularly to the requirements for controlling inflation, is explicable in precisely the same terms as the resistance of private price and wage policies. These individual governmental activities are part and parcel of the process by which income shares are determined. And when we attribute inflation to the actions by which private parties with economic power lay claim to the national product — in such a way that the sum total of those claims exceeds the capacity of the economy — we should obviously include among the methods for asserting those claims, not only the administration of wages and prices, but the exertion of influence over government outlays, taxes, tax preferences, and transfers. The government is not external to the process by which private power is exerted to produce inflation. It is part of that process.

The phenomenon of chronic inflation seems deeply rooted in the political and economic dynamics of a mature capitalistic society. It should not be surprising that it has gotten worse rather than better during 1973 and 1974, as the expansion of our aggregate productive capacity has begun to slow down. Peacetime inflation could become even more intractable than it has seemed to be so far if the expectations of perpetually rising standards of living now built into the American consciousness are doomed to progressive disappointment.

APPENDIX

APPENDIX
CONCENTRATION AND MARGINS
THE IMPLICATIONS FOR PRICE BEHAVIOR

Howard N. Ross

The failure of United States economic policy to arrest the forces of a long-term inflation appears at first glance to be a paralysis of political judgment. The recent summit conferences, the deterioration of the inflation into an inflationary recession, and a Presidential program suggesting nothing more than conventional monetary and fiscal policies have helped to sharpen the lines of debate so that the root of the crisis in policy seems far more a deep disagreement on the origins and processes of the inflation. If the proper diagnosis of the inflation is, as I think it is, shortages of agricultural goods, certain minerals and oil, compounded by monopoly behavior in important labor and product markets, the government should seek legitimate supplements to macroeconomic policies, if those policies are to live down the opprobrious label "old time religion." The neglect accorded to market imperfections as a source of bias and distortion in the price level dates back to the facile denunciations of Gardiner Means and his price studies of the Great Depression. In the years after World War II, recognition of the problem revived with the inflationary recessions of the 1950's, in the wage-price guidelines of the Kennedy years, and in the statutory price and wage controls of 1971-1973, but in each case, recognition was short-lived and did not

Because of its direct relevance to the subject matter of this volume, this analysis, given at the fall 1974 convention of the Southern Economic Association, is included herein.

permanently affect the strategy of economic policy.

Research on the relationship of monopoly to the price level has met with a fair number of obstacles, none of which should prove insurmountable. Data on unionization are partially available on a two digit industry level. B.L.S. prices may not be transactions prices, although the investigation by G. Stigler and J. Kindahl of buyers' prices has assured us that published prices are not a fiction.[1] Single equation regressions of prices on direct costs and concentration, a typical approach to estimating the residual power of concentration, result inevitably, and in some instances, tautologically, in the variance of prices being largely explained by the variance of direct costs, and raises questions about the sensitivity of such tests.[2] Suspected lags in the adjustment of prices to wages and raw material costs are confronted in several studies with unanimous results: prices adjust to changes in wages and raw material costs well within a year and thus obviate the need to dynamize price equations measured in annual data.[3]

If studies of relative prices have suffered in the past from a consistent weakness, it is the absence of analytical guidance. Why and when should we expect relative price behavior of concentrated industries to differ significantly from unconcentrated industries and what effect might this difference have on the direction of the price level and on output? The question embraces several analytical issues. However, the "why" and "when" will be primary concerns here. To rationalize the reaction of concentrated industries to cyclical shifts in demand and costs, I have found that a version of full-cost pricing amended to reflect a target rate of return to be particularly illuminating. The distinguishing aspect of this oligopoly model lies in the character of the margins between price and direct costs, i.e., overhead costs and profits. Full cost margins are predetermined at some standard output and are a determinant of the level of prices. The response of margins to fluctuations in demand and costs, and their effect on price, is the subject of elaboration for the succeeding section. In contrast to full cost margins, short-run margins in the theory of competition are residuals between price and direct costs and are determined by price. Predicted differences in the behavior of full cost and competitive margins and their implications for relative prices will be tested over a cross section of industries varying in concentration for the years 1952-1970.

FULL COST MARGINS AND PRICES

The development of the full cost principle has been character-istically empirical, grounded to a large extent on interview data and other statistical inquiries on the price policies of manufacturing enterprises, particularly large enterprises. The departure from short-run profit-maximizing behavior implied by these studies caused a minor furor in the so-called "marginalist controversy," a controversy which pales considerably in light of recent considerations of pricing constrained by uncertainty. In markets where a full cost price can be implemented, the rationality of such a price has been demonstrated in terms of a trade-off between expected profit maximization and the protection of margins. On the other hand, the rationality of equating marginal cost and marginal revenue under uncertainty in perfect competition or monopoly is restricted by extreme assumptions.[4] The overarching logic of full cost pricing as treated by many writers is that prices are unresponsive to fluctuations in demand; consequently, price changes are determined by changes in variable or direct costs, labor, and raw materials.[5] This follows from two ordinary assumptions posited in expositions of the full cost price: (1) at fixed factor prices, unit direct costs are uniform within the operational range of production, and (2) ex ante margins above direct costs are predetermined at some average experienced output or standard volume and are stable in the short run. Beyond these two assumptions, versions of the full cost price differ, and one fundamental difference is the estimation of the ex ante margin and its variability as the parameters of demand and costs change. I wish to circumvent the questions of whether the ex ante margin is computed as a mark-up on direct costs or as a fixed absolute amount on direct costs. My intention is to focus primarily on price movements in a full cost regime, and in this I am inspired by P. W. S. Andrews, who suggests that the stability of margins is diagnostic of full cost pricing.[6] Since Andrews, the work of A. D. H. Kaplan, Joel Dirlam and Robert Lanzilotti has lent substantial credence to the idea that oligopolists stabilize margins by employing a target rate of return. This concept, inherent to target return pricing, is designed to achieve a desired rate of return on capital over the business cycle.[7] A grafting of the target rate of return onto the structure of the full cost price essentially means that the ex ante margin consists of average expected profits equal to the target return in addition to overhead costs. Accordingly, the level of the full cost price is the sum of unit direct costs and ex ante margins

(1) $P_{FC} = UDC + \bar{M}$

Recalling the two previously stated assumptions, the full cost price will change in the short run only because of a change in the prices of variable inputs, and the absolute change in price and in unit direct costs should be approximately the same.

(2) $d(P_{FC}) \simeq d(UDC); d\bar{M} \simeq 0$

Therefore, the proportionate changes between price and its components will be

(3) $\dfrac{d\bar{M}}{M} < \dfrac{d\,P_{FC}}{P_{FC}} < \dfrac{d\,UDC}{UDC}$

What is implied by this argument is not the type of absolute price rigidity conveyed by Sweezy's kinked demand curve or by Rothschild's vision of oligopolistic war strategy, but the rigidity of margins in the maintenance of which prices can be expected to change only in accordance with the movement of direct costs. The degree of that response and the lack of any response to pure swings in demand depend on the inflexibility of ex ante margins. To gauge the relativity of the price rigidity in this model, I use as a basis of comparison price-margin behavior implicit in the theory of perfect competition, the ideal standard of price flexibility.

COMPETITIVE MARGINS AND PRICES

Consider the ex post identity:

(4) $P \equiv UDC + M$

in perfectly competitive equilibrium, price equals marginal cost, therefore

(5) $P = MC = UDC + M$

By a familiar transformation, marginal cost can be expressed as a product of UDC and the elasticity of the total direct cost function or

$$\frac{d(TDC)}{d\,Q} \cdot \frac{Q}{TDC} \quad \text{or} \quad k$$

(6) $MC \equiv UDC \cdot k$

then rewriting (5) as

(7) $P = UDC \cdot k = UDC + M$

From (7), the elasticity of the total direct cost function can then be defined as the fraction of margins in unit direct costs

(8) $k = 1 + \dfrac{M}{UDC}$

If k is stable for short periods, the expectation is that in competition, prices and unit direct costs and margins will change about proportionally

(9) $\dfrac{dP}{p} \simeq \dfrac{d\,UDC}{UDC} \simeq \dfrac{dM}{M}$

In a related study, I looked at a sample of unconcentrated industries with concentration ratios less than 50% (1935) during the Great Depression to find that the average percentage of M/UDC is 40.9, 41.8, and 43.2 in 1929, 1931, and 1933 respectively. Therefore, the assumption of a stable k seems reasonable, especially in view of the precipitous decreases in prices and costs during that period.

Equations (3) and (9) generate a number of testable propositions concerning the relationships of prices and their determinants in a dual market world. Here, stress is laid on margin behavior as a key to an explanation of price change. The theoretical conclusions pertain to the Marshallian short run and, for that reason, might have the greatest validity in brief periods (say a year). The competitive margin in equation (9) is an ex post residual between price and costs and is anticipated to vary in recessions and booms significantly more than the full cost margin in equation (3), an ex ante decision variable. In recessions, the full cost margin should fall less than the competitive margin and in booms, the full cost margin should rise relatively less.

A CAVEAT

Price-cost margins measured from census data have entered the literature of industrial organization as a proxy for profits,[8] but the composition of margins has remained something of secret until T. Hultgren.[9] Hultgren examined the components of margins with information drawn from the Federal Trade Commission and the Securities and Exchange Commission's *Quarterly Financial Report for*

Manufacturing Corporations, blown up to provide estimates for the population of manufacturing corporations. According to Hultgren, depreciation and depletion constitute most of the overhead costs (net of salaries), and although profits before taxes are considerably larger than overhead costs, the ratio exhibits a steady declining trend through the postwar cycles. At the peak of the cycle in the third quarter of 1948, profits before taxes were about five times greater than overhead, while at the peak in 1960, they were something less than three times as large.[10] Moreover, the peak to trough changes in the relationship are striking; in the severest postwar recession between the first quarter of 1957 and the second quarter of 1958, the ratio of profits before taxes to overhead costs declined by about 43%, depreciation and depletion per unit of output rose 23% and profits before taxes per unit of output declined 27.5%.[11] As the stock of capital expanded and the ratio of profits to overhead declined secularly, even the mild recession of 1960-1961 provoked sizable shifts in the magnitude of overhead and profits in unit output: depreciation and depletion increased 14.3%, while profits before taxes declined 21.4%. Unfortunately, Hultgren does not tell us how these ratios varied over a cross section of corporations, but the results warn us that the census margin is not an unambiguous proxy for profits or anything else unless adjusted for cycle and trend.

The findings give added weight to the argument by John Blair [12] and others that during several postwar recessions, the rise in unit overhead costs and the decrease in unit profits were sharp enough to encourage oligopolists to raise prices in order to recover part of the disappearing profits. As I interpret the thesis of the unlagged inflationary recession, prices in strategic concentrated industries rise with labor and raw materials costs and rise a quantum further to restore profits. In unconcentrated industries, price rises are a partial or a complete adjustment to increases in direct costs, the extent of the adjustment depending on the degree of competition and conditions of demand. In the language of the full cost model, when the composition of the ex post margin diverges from that of the ex ante margin, and the increase in unit overhead cost threatens the target return, the ex ante full cost margin will be deliberately increased. W. J. Yordan, Jr. observed the unique expansion of margins in a small sample of concentrated industries during the 1957-1958 recession, while margins among his unconcentrated industries were stable.[13]

I would want to amend the forecasts of the dual market model to account for the upward revaluation of full cost margins, especially in the deep recessions of the 1950's; in the shallower recessions of 1960-1961 and 1969-1970, this factor would presumably be less powerful. Other real world intrusions also modify the theoretical conclusions as applied to the postwar years: the continuous rise in wages, salaries, and raw materials would certainly have an impact on margins, if the adjustments in prices fail to get reflected in our annual observations; longer run forces, such as the inflation in the cost capital, in the prices of capital goods, and in the values of depletable resources would increase the size of margins in year-to-year comparisons, the time period employed in this short-run analysis. The short-run dictates of the model are fulfilled by the relatively brief postwar recessions which averaged in duration between nine and twelve months, but decidedly unfulfilled by the much longer expansions which, in the periods studied, varied from twenty-one months to over eight years. Qualified by these considerations, the hypotheses concerning margin behavior in the postwar cycles are: during recessions, full cost margins will rise by more than competitive margins; during periods when demand is increasing to capacity, full cost margins will rise by less than competitive margins; during periods of recovery and noninflationary growth, there is no presumption about the differential behavior of full cost and competitive margins.

MARGIN BEHAVIOR 1952-1970

The *Annual Survey of Manufactures* furnishes reliable data for a large sample of four-digit industries, making possible a fairly continuous series of margins. Margins are computed by deducting from value of shipments the sum of wages, salaries, raw material costs, and the cost of electricity. Changes in unit margins are the most appropriate data for testing the hypotheses; however, output indexes are unavailable for intercensal years. Instead, changes in the proportion of margins in value of shipments is the dependent variable which, of course, is equivalent to changes in the proportion of unit margins in census price. In recognition of a relationship between concentration to price change that may well be discontinuous, the results are presented here in tabular form. In three concentration groups, average annual changes in the ratio of unit margins to price and their statistical significance is recorded in Table I. The subsample of industries in each concentration group differs in size between some periods because of the widespread redefinition of industries in the 1958 census and the sometime vagaries of the survey data.

Recession Periods

The time series span four reference cycle recessions of contrasting severity and of durations that do not, in each case, accommodate the calendar year.

| | Percent Change | |
Peak — Trough	Current GNP	Constant GNP
(2Q) 1953 — (1Q) 1954	−1.9%	−3.4%
(1Q) 1957 — (2Q) 1958	−2.6	−3.9
(1Q) 1960 — (1Q) 1961	−0.3	−1.6
(4Q) 1969 — (4Q) 1970	+4.5	−0.8

When the trough occurs in the first two quarters of the year, the subsequent recovery within the year may obscure the impact of the recession, so an additional pairing is made between the year of the trough and two years previous. Also, when the peak occurs early in the year, an additional pairing is made between that year and the previous year.

The increase in the ratio of unit margins to price in the highest concentration group is larger than in the lowest concentration group — the most relevant comparison — in the recession years of the 1950's. The medium concentration group is ambiguous both in market structure and price policy. That the average increase in margins for the group is sometimes lower than in the least concentrated group may be a fault of the classification scheme or a hint of non-linearity in the functional relationship of margin change and concentration. The method of classification underestimates the significance of concentration: in linear regressions designed to remove some static and unreported here, concentration is significant at the 5% level of probability and better. The pervasive inflation ignited by the Vietnam War apparently continued into the downswing of 1969-1970 when income fell by three billion constant dollars. So far as the data go, there is no evidence that the relatively small decrease in aggregate demand encouraged concentrated industries to raise prices in defense of profits.

Table IX—I

CHANGES IN
MARGINS AS A PROPORTION OF VALUE OF SHIPMENTS, 1952-1970,
AVERAGED BY CONCENTRATION GROUPS,
EIGHT LARGEST PRODUCERS

Years	I 1-40	N	II 41-70	N	III 71-100	N	Significant Differences Between X's of Groups I, II and III
			RECESSION PERIODS				
1954/1952	0.996	25	1.024	33	1.083	30	I, III between 5-10%
1954/1953	1.014	30	1.031	38	1.086	30	I, III between 5-10%
1957/1956	1.041	39	1.012	42	1.074	37	II, III at 5%
1958/1956	1.059	39	1.025	42	1.145	37	I, III between 5-10%
1958/1957	1.016	39	1.018	42	1.034	37	— — — — — — — — —
1960/1959	0.990	31	1.020	42	0.968	39	I, III at 5%
1961/1960	1.024	31	0.997	42	1.043	39	II, III at 2.5%; I, II at 5%
1970/1969	1.034	31	1.018	34	.973	33	— — — — — — — — —
			POST 1965 INFLATION				
1967/1966	1.085	35	1.005	41	1.027	37	I, II at 0.5%; I, III at 2.5%
1967/1965	1.078	35	0.993	41	1.002	37	I, II at 0.5%; I, III at 0.5%
1968/1967	.974	31	1.005	34	1.061	33	— — — — — — — — —
1969/1968	.984	31	.989	34	.989	33	— — — — — — — — —
			RECOVERY AND GROWTH PERIODS				
1955/1954	1.028	38	1.014	35	1.071	36	— — — — — — — — —
1956/1955	1.002	38	1.019	35	0.972	36	— — — — — — — — —
1959/1958	1.011	31	1.032	43	1.030	39	— — — — — — — — —
1962/1961	1.015	31	1.011	43	0.997	39	— — — — — — — — —
1963/1962	1.080	31	1.052	43	1.053	39	— — — — — — — — —
1964/1963	0.997	31	1.000	43	1.033	39	— — — — — — — — —
1965/1964	1.008	31	1.023	43	1.010	39	— — — — — — — — —
1966/1965	0.985	35	1.002	41	0.988	37	— — — — — — — — —

*The concentration ratios varied with the years compared:

Comparisons	Concentration Ratio
1952-1956	1954
1957-1960	1958
1961-1965	1963
1966-1970	1967

Post 1965 Inflation

In the initial years of the current inflation, the growth of margins in the highest concentration group was distinctly slower than in the least concentrated group. As the inflation progressed from 1967 to 1969, becoming a long-run phenomenon, institutionalized into high interest rates and morbid expectations of future price rises, the distinction dissipates. Indeed, between 1968 and 1969, there is an apparent squeeze on margins across all industries. I am not surprised that the proposed short-run model does not provide answers to long run inflation — merely disappointed.

Recovery and Growth Periods

In those years when demand and capacity grew together, when neither recessions nor excess demand provoked inflation, the short run effects of concentration on margins and, consequently, on prices are negligible. I interpret this evidence as favorable to the thesis that concentration exerts an influence on margins and prices at specific times and for specific reasons.

Table II presents a different measure of margins, inclusive of salaries. Treating salaries as overhead, which probably are more important in concentrated industries, does not disturb the configuration or the meaning of the findings in Table I.

CONCLUSIONS

The influence of concentration on price movements is viewed as a corollary of the primary influence of concentration on the behavior of margins. A dual market model, comprised of perfect competitors and oligopolists adopting the logic of the full cost price, generates several hypotheses about price-margin behavior in the short run. The empirical results indicate that concentrated industries exercised their market power to increase margins and therefore prices in the recessions of 1953-1954 and 1957-1958 significantly more than unconcentrated industries. The findings are somewhat weaker, although in the right direction for the recession of 1960-1961; in the downswing of 1969-1970, the effects of the excess demand inflation of prior years inhibit an increase in margins across all industries. In the open inflation beginning in 1966, unconcentrated industries increased their margins and prices significantly more than concentrated indus-

Table IX—II

CHANGES IN
MARGINS (INCLUSIVE OF SALARIES) AS A PROPORTION
OF VALUE OF SHIPMENTS, 1952-1970, AVERAGED BY
CONCENTRATION GROUPS, EIGHT LARGEST PRODUCERS

Years	I 1-40	N	II 41-70	N	III 71-100	N	Significant Differences Between X's of Groups I, II and III
RECESSION PERIODS							
1954/1952	1.025	25	1.038	33	1.078	30	I, III approx. 10%
1954/1953	1.021	30	1.027	38	1.075	30	— — — — — — — — —
1957/1956	1.032	39	1.018	42	1.063	37	I, III at 5%; II, III at 2.5%
1960/1959	1.002	31	1.052	42	0.981	39	II, III at 2.5%
1958/1956	1.055	39	1.028	42	1.101	37	I, III bet.5-10%;II,III at1%
1958/1957	1.028	39	1.007	42	1.045	37	II, III between 5-10%
1961/1960	1.023	31	1.004	42	1.033	39	II, III at 5%
1970/1969	1.045	31	1.027	34	.984	33	— — — — — — — — —
POST 1965 INFLATION							
1967/1966	1.077	35	1.014	41	1.017	37	I, II at 0.5%; I, III at 0.5%
1967/1965	1.054	35	0.999	41	0.999	37	I, II at 1%; I, III at 0.5%
1968/1967	1.008	31	1.011	34	1.023	33	— — — — — — — — —
1969/1968	.990	31	.998	34	.995	33	— — — — — — — — —
RECOVERY AND GROWTH PERIODS							
1955/1954	1.004	38	1.007	35	1.062	36	I, III at 5%; II, III at 5%
1956/1955	1.026	38	1.022	35	0.953	36	I, III at 5%; II, III at 5%
1959/1958	0.998	31	1.014	43	1.023	39	— — — — — — — — —
1962/1961	0.996	31	1.001	43	0.992	39	— — — — — — — — —
1963/1962	1.059	31	1.015	43	1.027	39	I, II between 5-10%
1964/1963	0.993	31	1.000	43	1.022	39	— — — — — — — — —
1965/1964	0.999	31	1.009	43	1.002	39	— — — — — — — — —
1966/1965	0.992	35	1.002	41	0.990	37	— — — — — — — — —

*The concentration ratios varied with the years compared:

Comparisons	Concentration Ratio
1952-1956	1954
1957-1960	1958
1961-1965	1963
1966-1970	1967

tries between 1966 and 1967. The reverse was true for 1967-1968: in the highest concentrated group, unit margins in price rose 6% and decreased nearly 3% in the least concentrated group. In Table I, these differences are not significant, although the regression coefficient for concentration is. From 1968 on, the impact of concentration on margins and of margins on prices deteriorates. We do not know enough about how firms adapt their price policies to the disequilibrium of inflation. What the findings do show is that the brake applied to price increases by concentrated industries during booms is short lived. Nothing more could be expected either from a belief in the full cost rule or a consideration of the profit incentives of oligopolists.

This essay began by asking "why" and "when" relative prices of concentrated industries would differ in behavior from unconcentrated industries. The answers seem interesting enough to stimulate further inquiry toward perhaps a more definitive resolution of an old problem.

NOTES

NOTES

INTRODUCTION

1. John M. Blair, *Economic Concentration, Harcourt Brace Jovanovich,* 1972, p. 544.
2. *Forbes,* January 1, 1975, CXIV, 1, p. 136.
3. Except for the latest recession, the source for the table is: Julius Shiskin, Commissioner of Labor Statistics, "The Changing Business Cycle," *New York Times,* December 1, 1974, p. F12.
4. This behavior was first observed in the United States during the 1954 and 1958 recessions; cf., 86th. Cong., 1st Sess., Senate Subcommittee on Antitrust and Monopoly, *Hearings on Administered Prices,* Pt. 10, 1959, pp. 4997-5013. "Price Behavior of Administered versus Market Price Products in the Current Inflation" by John M. Blair; 91st Cong., 2nd Sess., Joint Economic Committee, *Hearings on the 1970 Midyear Review of the State of the Economy,* Pt. 2, 1970 (testimony of Gardiner C. Means and John M. Blair, pp. 226-277, 285-289).
5. Computed from United Nations, *Monthly Bulletins of Statistics.* Neither for France, the United Kingdom, nor the Federal Republic of Germany is a general index of wholesale prices published. For the purposes of isolating the effect on their general price structure of imported raw materials, which in these countries are more important than in the United States, the index of "domestic" goods is used for France and "finished" goods for the United Kingdom and the Federal Republic of Germany. In the United Kingdom, production declined 6%, while wholesale prices rose 13%; in France production fell 4%, while prices increased 28%; and in West Germany, output decreased 6%, while prices rose 5%.

CHAPTER ONE

1. Gardiner C. Means, *The Structure of the American Economy,* National Resources Committee, 1939, pp. 200-201.
2. *The Behavior of Industrial Prices,* National Bureau of Economic Research, 1971, Table 5-5, p. 65. Other data on frequency of price change is presented but in such a confused fashion that it sheds little light on the frequency of price changes paid by individual buyers. For an analysis of the price data and a critique of this report by the present writer see "The Administered-Price Thesis Reconfirmed." *American Economic Review,* Vol. LXII, No. 3, June 1972, pp. 292-306.
3. See "The Administered Price Thesis Reconfirmed," *Op cit.*
4. *Steel and the Post-War Inflation,* Joint Economic Committee, 86th Congress, 1st Session, Nov. 6, 1959.
5. See John M. Blair, *Economic Concentration,* New York, 1972, pp. 640-642.
6. The total of demand deposits and currency (M_1) was not significantly greater at the end of 1957 than at the end of 1955, $135.9 billion as against $135.2 billion.
7. The corn blight of 1970 contributed some "crop-failure" effect.
8. After paying taxes and allowing for the plant and equipment used up in production (depreciation etc.) the remaining income of nonfinancial corporations in the last half of 1972 amounted to $941 billion. Of this $824 billion went as compensation to employees covering wages, salaries and supplements while $117 billion went as compensation to capital covering interest and profits after taxes whether or not distributed as dividends.
9. The government's power to interfere with the pricing process might be further limited

by relating it to the rate of administrative inflation. If there were little administrative inflation as indicated by an appropriate index, the government power might be limited to the issuance of guidelines and the calling on the few corporations subject to its control to report and justify price increases. If the rate of administrative inflation were higher, the government could require pre-reporting of planned price changes which would provide an opportunity to persuade those which appeared to exceed the guidelines. Finally, the power to control prices or force rollbacks might accrue to government only if the rate of administrative inflation were high.

CHAPTER TWO

1. cf. Milton Friedman in *Guidelines, Informal Controls and the Market Place*, edited by G. Schultz and R. Aliber, Chicago 1966.

2. 74th Cong., 1st Sess., S. Doc. 13, *Industrial Prices and Their Relative Inflexibility* by Gardiner C. Means, 1935.

3. John M. Blair, *Economic Concentration*, Harcourt, Brace, Jovanovich, New York, 1972, Chapter 17, pp. 438-466.

4. For a fuller discussion of these "industry-sector" data, see, John M. Blair, "Market Power and Inflation," *Journal of Economic Issues*, March, 1974.

5. Willard L. Thorp and Walter Crowder, *The Structure of Industry*, Monograph No. 27, Temporary National Economic Committee (TNEC), 1941.

6. National Resources Committee, *The Structure of the American Economy*, 1939, Pt. 1 (prepared under the direction of Gardner C. Means).

7. For a delineation of the deleted product classes, see Blair, "Market Power and Inflation," *op. cit.*

8. Both the concentration ratios and the value of shipments "weights" are for 1967 (Bureau of the Census, 1967 Census of Manufacturers, *Concentration Ratios in Manufacturing*, Pt. 2, "Product Class Concentration Ratios," 1971).

9. The principal difference between the aggregate and the selective basis for the sample as a whole was a lesser decline in the former, for the unconcentrated products, reflecting (a), (b), and (c) above. The difference for the concentrated group was only half of a percentage point. The showings on the aggregate basis are as follows:

Concentration Ratio	No. of Products	Change (12/69 - 12/70)
50% and Over	155	5.4%
25-49%	144	0.6
Under 25%	70	−1.4
Total	369	2.0

10. *Ibid.*, pp. 364-366.

11. *Annual Report of the Council on Economic Advisors*, January, 1973, p. 61.

12. *Ibid.*

13. *Ibid.*

14. Economic Report of the President, February 1974, p. 91.

15. Paul H. Earl, "A Disaggregate Analysis of the Economic Stabalization Program," *Western Economic Journal* (forthcoming).

16. R.F. Lanzalotti, Mary F. Hamilton, and Blaine Roberts, *Phase II in Review: The Price Commission*, Brookings Institution (forthcoming).

17. Thomas S. Kuhn, *The Structure of Scientific Revolutions*, Chicago 1962, pp. 52, 95; 77.

18. *Ibid.*, pp. x, 96.

19. *Ibid.*, pp. 52-3.

20. The principal contributors to the body of concepts on which this model is based are as follows:

Donaldson Brown, "Pricing Policy in Relation to Financial Control," *Management and Administration*, Feb., March, April, 1924, pp. 195-98, 283-86, 417-22; R.L. Hall and C.J.

Hitch, "Price Theory and Business Behavior," *Oxford Economic Papers,* May, 1939;   C.C. Saxton, *The Economics of Price Determination,* London, 1942; Richard A. Lester, "Shortcomings of Marginal Analysis for Wage-Employment Problems," *American Economic Review,* March 1946. For an opposing point of view, see Fritz Machlup, "Marginal Analysis and Empirical Research," *American Economic Review,* Sept., 1946; Joel Dean, *Managerial Economics,* Englewood Cliffs, N.J., 1951; Alfred R. Oxenfeldt, *Industrial Pricing and Market Practices,* Englewood Cliffs, N.J. 1951;Richard B. Heflebower, "Full Costs, Cost Changes and Prices," in *Business Concentration and Price Policy,* National Bureau of Economic Research, 1955, p. 361; Robert F. Lanzilotti, "Pricing Objectives in Large Companies," *American Economic Review,* December 1958; Walter Adams and Robert P. Lanzilotti, "The Reality of Administered Prices," in: *Administered Prices: A Compendum as Public Policy,* 1963; Gardiner C. Means, *Pricing Power and the Public Interest,* New York, 1962; and *The Corporate Revolution in America,* New York 1962; John M. Blair, *Economic Concentration, op. cit.,* 1972, Chapter 18 and "Administered Prices: A Phenomenon in Search of a Theory," *American Economic Review,* May 1959.

21. Thomas S. Kuhn, *op. cit.,* p. 24.

22. *Ibid.,* p. 78.

23. *Ibid.,* p. 96.

24. See Blair, *Economic Concentration, op. cit.,* pp. 640-643.

25. *Ibid.,* p. 673.

CHAPTER THREE

1. P. Sargant Florence, *Atlas of Economic Structure and Policies,* Oxford, 1970 (hereafter, *Atlas*), figure 54 and text, p. 117. The Annual British Abstracts of Statistics do not calculate the annual rates of unemployment.

2. Chart I is based on statistics up until the year 1973, when the base year, expressed as 100, was changed from 1963 to 1970.

3. National Institute, *Economic Review,* May 1974, appendix, tables 7 and 18.

4. *Ibid.,* table 18; and May 1973 issue.

5. E.g., Introduction, in D. H. Robertson, *Money,* Cambridge, 1922.

6. M. H. Dobb, *Wages,* Cambridge Economic Handbook, Cambridge, 1946, pp. 29ff. The differences in the trend of wage rates and weekly earnings, and, for that matter, from that of retail prices are so wide that they should be confirmed from other sources. Quoting the index numbers in the appendix (Tables 8 and 9) of the National Institute's *Economic Review,* the trend as from 100 in the year 1963 up to the fourth quarter of 1972 was for retail prices to 163.5, for wage rates to 200.1, and for weekly earnings to 218.9. A different method of calculation for price changes is the Consumer Price Index (appendix, Table 18) which, in the last quarter of 1972, stood at 164.2, differing only by 0.7 from the alternative calculation given above of 163.5.

From 1972 to the last quarter of 1973, the outpacing of the retail and Consumer Prices indexes by the weekly wage rates and earnings indexes continued unabated.

7. I quote part of my review of Wesley Mitchell's *Types of Economic Theory* (*Political Science Quarterly,* 1968, pp. 164-5): "Mitchell relates each of the main theorists to the particular historical conditions and problems of the time, for instance, Adam Smith to mercantilism, or Jeremy Bentham to the still subsisting feudal traditions of England. In our own day, Keynes could similarly be related to the urgent problem of the inter-war unemployment. His solution then . . . , still urged by the trade unions, is not necessarily applicable today."

8. Exactly how much of each policy, sacking or pricing-up, will depend largely on the supply of money. In 1972, money was more available under the government's growth strategy, and up-pricing prevailed over unemployment as shown in Table I, i.e., straight inflation over stagflation. High wage claims in the climate of growth, not money, must be considered the *prime* cause at work, however.

9. Index numbers are provided (National Institute, *Economic Review,* November 1973, table 6) for demand as well as supply (e.g., population, total insured). Unfilled vacancies

averaged 1.05% of the labor force in 1964-66, but in the subsequent six years, the jobs demanding labor in vain fell considerably, and in no single year rose above 0.87%. Demand does not seem to have increased, but in using the vacancy rate as a proxy of demand, it should be said that only changes in the rate are signficant since a certain proportion of vacancies are normally not reported to the Employment Exchanges from which the statistics are gathered.

10. D. Jackson and H. A. Turner, *Do Trade Unions Cause Inflation?* Cambridge, 1972, p. 13.

11. In my *Statistical Methods in Economics and Political Science,* London, 1929, pp. 25-6, I asked "who is it that actually changes the price of any article when it is changed? ... The person or persons who have the initiative in adjusting retail prices in shops are probably very different when the article is monopolized or is a proprietary article, than when it is a 'staple' article produced competitively. But this important and interesting type of information is not usually vouchsafed in text books. The usual wording is that "prices are fixed" or "are determined," etc., not that so and so decides or would probably decide to change prices."

12. R. H. Tawney, *Equality,* London, 1929, pp. 71-2, 75.

13. I have repeatedly drawn attention to the effect of the English public schools on the English attitude toward management; cf., my *Logic of Industrial Organization,* London, 1933, pp. 252-5. (Hereafter referred to as *Logic* 1933. A later work titled *Logic of British and American Industry* ran into three London editions. These are referred to as *Logic,* 1953, 1961, 1972.)

14. J. L. and Barbara Hammond, *The Town Labourer 1760-1832,* London, 1918, and *The Rise of Modern History,* London, 1925.

15. G.D.H. Cole, *The World of Labour,* London, 1913.

16. A. Carr-Saunders, P. S. Florence, and R. Peers, *Consumers Cooperation in Great Britain,* London, 1938, expecially part IV.

17. *Ibid.*

18. *Ibid.,* pp. 453-58; also, Independent Commission (Gaitskell) *Report,* p. 145.

19. Allan Flanders, *Trade Unions,* London, 1952, gives the whole list, p. 31.

20. Royal Commission on Trade Unions and Employers' Associations 1965-1968, Chairman Lord Donovan, *Report,* p. 188.

21. *Times,* (London), April 17, 1972.

22. W. Dibelius, *England,* English trans., London, 1929, pp. 136-7.

23. In industrial policy, labor in fact adopts a conservative line. As I wrote in 1933 (*Logic,* p. 161) "the trade practices which the Unions establish and defend, if necessary by striking, are conservative and difficult to adjust to any new requirements of technical efficiency."

24. Ferdynand Zweig, *The British Worker,* London, 1952, pp. 189-90.

25. *Report, op. cit.,* p. 95. For a comparison for the years 1955-1964, see Richard Caves, ed., *Britain's Economic Prospects,* Washington, D.C. 1968, p. 333.

26. In a recent Fabian pamphlet (tract 402, p. 9), Mr. Wedgwood Benn, then a minister in the Labour government of 1966-70, seemed to rejoice in the economic vulnerability to strikes of this interdependence. The new citizen's bargaining power, he writes, "is immensely greater than it was, and is the greatest in those advanced industries where interdependence has gone furthest, and the cost of dislocation is greatest."

27. Economist Brief Booklets, no. 10, p. 6.

28. Birmingham (England) *Post,* February 8, 1972.

29. For a detailed table of industries in Britain's mixed economy governed respectively by state enterprise and private-capitalist enterprise, see my *Logic,* 1972, pp. 268-271.

30. The similarity of Britain and America has recently been again demonstrated by F. L. Pryor, "An International Comparison of Concentration Ratios," *Review of Economics and Statistics,* May 1972.

31. Adolph Berle and Gardiner C. Means, *The Modern Corporation and Private Property,* New York, 1934; P. Sargant Florence, *Ownership, Control and Success of Large Companies,* London, 1961, chapters three and five.

32. Florence, *op. cit.,* pp. 196-217.

33. In view of the growing take-overs and mergers in Britain since 1951, this sort of analysis should be repeated.

34. See the introduction to my *Logic,* 1972.

35. P. W. S. Andrews, *Manufacturing Business,* London, 1949; see also, R. H. Barback, *The Pricing of Manufactures,* London, 1964, and R. C. Skinner, "The Determination of Selling Price," *Journal of Industrial Economics,* July 1970; as well as A. M. Alfred, "Company Pricing Policy I" *Ibid.,* November 1972.

36. K. D. George, "The Changing Structure of Competitive Industry," *Economic Journal,* supplement, March, 1972, p. 361. George indicates that in the five-year span, 1958-63, concentration increased in the manufacturing sector in a total of 141 industries (of which 101 were large increases), and that concentration decreases occurred in a total of 67 industries (of which only 36 were large decreases). Thus, industries with large increases (3% or more) outnumbered large decreases (-3% or more) by 2.75 to l.

37. P. Sargant Florence, *Ownership, Control and Success of Large Companies,* London, 1961, p. 191.

38. As early as 1933, in *Logic,* and later, in *Logic,* 1953. The English situation is illustrated and discussed in greater detail in my *Atlas,* pp. 118-124, figure 56.

39. Caves, ed., *op. cit.,* p. 285.

40. Florence, *Logic,* 1972, pp. 30-1, 39-40.

41. *Ibid.,* table VI gives a full list of nationalized industries.

42. The prices of which certainly rose rapidly in Britain after 1965, but the rise was partly due to that of imported materials after the devaluation of 1967.

43. Florence, *Atlas,* figure 21.

44. Indeed, a further possibility of testing empirically whether increasing wage costs are at present a predominant factor for inflation is to differentiate labor intensive and capital intensive industries. In the former, wage costs will predominate among the total of costs; in the latter, capital costs may well be of equal or greater importance. Price index numbers are published in Britain separately for service industries and for building, both labor intensive. From 1963 to 1971, the price of services rose 52.4%, capital goods building 40.1%, and housing 63.6%, including local taxation. On the other hand, the prices of all manufactured goods, requiring the use generally of less labor and of more capital equipment, rose only 37.7%. National Institute, *Economic Review,* November 1971, p. 83.

45. And recommended, instead, the Indian civil service. Where now are the men who fell for that advice?

46. See Florence, *Logic,* 1972, pp. 374-6, and P. Sargant Florence, *Economics and Sociology of Industry,* 2ed., London, 1969, pp. 53.

47. From 1972 onwards, however, the money stock started to rise heavily. But it still remains to ask how far this rise was not due to the credit money which banks had to extend to managements to avoid bankruptcy in face of the increased wage bill when prices were restricted and full employment was more or less guarenteed.

48. Alfred Marshall, *Principles of Economics,* var. eds., Book V, chapter five, §8.

49. The general history of British incomes policy has been admirably described and assessed by David C. Smith in a contribution to *Britain's Economic Prospects,* edited by Caves, *op. cit.,* and also in Lloyd Ulman and Robert Flanagan, *Wage Restraint: A Study of Incomes Policy in Western Europe,* Berkeley, Calif., 1971, pp. 11-47.

50. Siege is the only word to apply to the stopping, by sheer number of the crowd, of trucks trying to carry coke out of the Saltley Gas Works in the center of Birmingham. The police, present in large numbers, had to retreat back to quarters. This action settled the issue of the strike, and the Labour party (Birmingham) planned, when they regained control of the City Council, to erect some kind of monument at the spot. (Birmingham *Post,* March 1972.)

51. Florence, *Logic,* 1972, VI, §1.

52. Adam Smith, *Wealth of Nations,* var. eds., Book I, chapter X.

53. Florence, *Economics and Sociology of Industry,* 2ed., London, 1969.

54. I well remember, at a broadcast forum in Birmingham, declaring from the chair that

wages must not be completely fair, otherwise every worker being precisely compensated for the real cost of his work would be satisfied where he was, mobility and shifts in manpower would cease except by sacking and deaths, and the economy would become frozen. My remarks were greeted with howls of denunciation from both employers as well as workers in the audience. Both were moved, perhaps, by the idea of a "just price," which ruled in the static, undynamic medieval economy.

55. Ulman and Flanagan, *op. cit.*, pp. 18ff.

56. As of December 31, 1970, see Report of Registrar of Friendly Societies, February 1972.

57. *Economist,* October 19, 1973.

58. Florence, *Logic,* 1972, p. 262; i.e., the state unsocialistically leaving wage-planning to collective bargaining between workers and employers — without representation of the consumer or the public interest. Though accused of failure and abandoned by both parties, the special adjudicating organs, boards, or commissions set up by both parties did introduce *some* stability. Failure is here a matter of degree.

CHAPTER FOUR

1. Alain Chenincourt, *L'Inflation ou l'Anti-Croissance* (Paris, 1971), p. 19.

2. Maurice Parodi, *L'Economie et la Société Française de 1945 à 1970* (Paris, 1971), p. 66.

3. OECD, *France* (Paris, 1972), p. 11. Professor A. Cotta, it should be noted, sees the rate of inflation in France, 1967-1972, as not differing substantially from that experienced by England, Germany, and the United States. See *Inflation et Croissance en France depuis 1962* (Paris, 1974) pp. 41-42.

4. *Ibid.*; Stillman, Bellini, Pfaff, Schloesing and Story, *L'Envoi de la France dans les Années 80* (Paris, 1973), *passim.*

5. "Le Nouvel Indice Mensuel des Prix de l'I.N.S.E.E.," *Actualités-Service,* No. 122, May, 1971.

6. C. Gruson, *Origine et Espoirs de la Planification* (Paris, 1968), pp. 121-218; J.P. Courthoux, *La Politique des Revenus* (Paris, 1968), pp. 70-71.

7. *Le Monde,* Oct. 21, 1970.

8. Differences in weighting and sampling are discussed in "L'Indice des Prix à la Consommation," Conseil Economique et Social, *Journal Officiel,* March 27, 1973, pp. 223-241.

9. OECD, *France* (Paris, 1972), p. 12; Institut National de la Statistique et des Etudes Economiques, *Bulletin Mensuel de la Statistique,* June, 1972; OECD, *Inflation: The Present Problem* (Paris, 1970), p. 61. (Henceforth cited, *Inflation.*)

10. I.N.S.E.E., *Tendances de la Conjoncture, Perspectives,* June, 1974, p. 23.

11. Claude Malhomme, "Les prix agricoles dans l'inflation," *Economie et Statistic,* December, 1972, p. 22.

12. I.N.S.E.E., *Tendances de la Conjoncture,* June, 1974, p. 25.

13. OECD, *The Problem of Rising Prices* (Paris, 1961), p. 46.

14. *Inflation,* p. 10.

15. OECD, *Les Politiques Actuelles de la Lutte Contre l'Inflation* (Paris, 1971), p. 29.

16. OECD, *France* (Paris, 1972), p. 47; Ministère de l'Economie et des Finances, *Notes Bleus,* November 3, 1973, p. 3.

17. I.N.S.E.E., *Tendances de la Conjoncture, Perspectives,* August, 1971, p. 35; *Perspectives,* June, 1974, pp. 15-21.

18. J. H. David, "Un Modèle de l'Economie Française inspiré par des Thèses Monetaristes," Banque de France, *Bulletin Trimestriel,* No. 5, 1972, pp. 23-56. David's short-run model shows maximum impact of changes in the money supply when there is little excess capacity. Going somewhat further in adopting the monetarist position, another economist attributes increases in the money supply, and hence inflation, to the banks unbridled cupidity, which has led to unhealthy expansion of loans and deposits: S.C. Kolm, "Qui sont les instigateurs de l'inflation? " *Le Monde,* Feb. 22, 1972. Critics point out that Kolm failed to take into account that banks must pay interest to attract savings. *Le Monde,*

Feb. 29, 1972, p. 18.

19. Donald Hodgman, "The French System of Monetary and Credit Controls," Banca Nazionale del Lavoro, *Quarterly Review*, November 1971, p. 348.

20. A. Piettre, "Faux Dogmes Economiques," *Le Monde*, Feb. 27, Feb. 28, 1971; I.N.S.E.E., *Tendances de la Conjoncture*, December 1971, pp. 100-101, June, 1974, p. 124; I.N.S.E.E., *Comptes de la Nation, 1971, Part 1*, 1972, p. 78.

21. I.N.S.E.E., *Comptes de la Nation 1972*, 2 (Paris, 1973), p. 9; and see, generally, on growth rates in France, data summarized in Stillman, *et. al., op. cit.*, esp. p. 50.

22. Parodi, *op. cit.*, p. 92.

23. Chenincourt, *op. cit.*, p. 71.

24. Pierre Uri, *Rapport sur la Capacité concurrentielle de la Communauté Européenne*, European Communities (Bruxelles, 1971), pp. 48 and I/1/14.

25. Parodi, *op. cit.*, pp. 96 and 99.

26. *Ibid.*, p. 107.

27. I.N.S.E.E., *Comptes de la Nation 1972*, 2 (Paris, 1973), p. 53.

28. Chenincourt, *op. cit.*, p. 106.

29. Ministère de l'Economie et des Finances, "Comptes du Commerce, 1969-1971," as cited in J. P. Mockers, *Etude sur le rôle essentiel de certains revenus non-salariaux dans le développement de l'inflation en France* (manuscript, 1973), p. 159.

30. "Les Industries Alimentaires," *Les Echos*, Nov. 2, 1972, p. 81. See also, "Les grandes surfaces d'évraient effectuer le quart des ventes d'alimentation cette année," *Les Echos*, Jan. 15, 1973, and "Le commerce vend deja à peu près 43.6 percent de l'alimentation en France," *Les Echos*, Jan. 31, 1973.

31. Chenincourt, *op. cit.*, p. 168.

32. "L'Activité et les Comptes du Commerce de 1969 à 1970," Ministère de l'Economie et des Finances, *Service de l'Information* (1972), p. 5.

33. Lionel Stoleru, *L'Imperatif Industriel* (Paris, 1969), p. 107.

34. Ministère de l'Economie et des Finances, *Le Budget de 1971*, p. 50.

35. Uri, *op. cit.*, p. 52.

36. John Shean, *Promotion and Control of Industry in Postwar France* (Cambridge, 1963), p. 201. According to reliable sources, foreign competition has never managed to corral more than 5% of the government-dominated market for electrical machinery and equipment.

37. *L'Expansion*, February, 1971, pp. 37-38.

38. Commission des Communautés Européenes, *La Politique Industrielle de la Communauté*, March, 1970, pp. 96-97.

39. Parodi, *op. cit.*, p. 144.

40. Testimony of Jacques Houssiaux, in *Economic Concentration, Part 7A*, Senate Committee on Antitrust and Monopoly, pp. 3967-3969 (1963).

41. Alexis de Tocqueville, *L'Ancien Régime et la Révolution* (Paris, 1967), pp. 133-145.

42. C. W. Cole, *French Mercantilism, 1683-1700* (New York, 1943), p. 272.

43. Chenincourt, *op. cit.*, p. 123.

44. John J. McArthur and Bruce Scott, *Industrial Planning in France* (Cambridge, 1969), p. 229.

45. See Michel Crozier, *La Société Bloquée, passim*, and Jean-Jacques Servan-Schreiber and Michel Albert, *The Radical Alternative* (New York, 1971), pp. 99-100.

46. Stoleru, *op. cit.*, p. 202.

47. McArthur and Scott, *op. cit.*, p. 202.

48. Chenincourt, *op. cit.*, p. 97. In some areas, such as the marketing of fresh fruits and vegetables, lumber, and dresses, sales without invoices permit the seller to avoid the T.V.A. tax.

49. *Journal Officiel*, December 30, 1973, p. 14139. For a survey of the background of anti-competitive policies, see W.J. Adams, "Malthusianism, Protectionism and Stagnation: A Case Study in French Commercial Policy," U.S. House Committee on Ways and Means, 90th. Cong. 2nd Sess., *Hearings on Foreign Trade and Tariff Proposals*, Part 4, 1968, pp. 1434-1446.

50. H. W. de Jong, *Ondernemingsconcentratie* (Leyden, 1971), p. 121.

51. Parodi, *op. cit.*, pp. 154-165, and Yves Morvan, *La Concentration de l'Industrie Française* (Paris, 1972), p. 106.

52. Jean-François Ruges, *Le téléphone pour tous* (Paris, 1970), pp. 86-89.

53. On French antitrust law, see Jean Guyénot, *Le Droit des Ententes Industrielles* (Paris, 1972). For the work of the Commission, see André and Danielle Schilte, *La Politique Française à l'Egard des Ententes et des Positions Dominantes,* Mémoire No. 419, Université de Paris I, Oct., 1971.

54. Schilte, *op. cit.*, pp. 88-89.

55. Schilte, *op. cit.*, p. 31.

56. *Le Monde*, April 17, 1971, and *Bulletin Officiel des Services des Prix,* April 17, 1971. The oil cartel is described in *Le Monde*, Feb. 12, 1973, and March 7, 1973. Somewhat embarrassed by the disclosures, and by a report of the Commission on Ententes, the Ministry of Economics and Finances issued a document that attempted to define, in advance, those crisis situations that would justify market sharing and similar practices by petroleum refiners. *Bulletin Officiel des Services des Prix,* Feb. 20, 1974, pp. 38-40.

57. Commissariat Général du Plan, Préparation du VIe Plan, *Rapport du Comité, Concurrence* (Paris, 1971), p. 18.

58. M. Aglietta and R. Courbis, "Un Outil du Plan: le Modèle Fifi," *Economie et Statistique,* No. 1, May 1969, pp. 45-66.

59. The published wholesale price statistics aside from food products, which are largely non-processed, cover only 218 items, with a disproportionate emphasis on coal (48 prices) and chemical products (33 prices). Using 40 price series, including 5 textile products and 11 foods, plus certain other products or groups of products chosen because it was possible to compute concentration ratios for the sector based on employment, Phlips attempted to measure the relation between concentration and price change from 1959 to 1965. *Effects of Industrial Concentration* (Amsterdam, 1971), pp. 23-24, 33-34. Apart from the bizarre character of the sample (which included steel tubes—but no other steel products), Phlips' conclusion that concentration had no influence on price behavior has been subjected to criticism on other grounds. See H. Ross, "Illusions in Testing for Administered Prices," and L. Phlips, "Illusions in Testing for Administered Prices: A Reply," *Journal of Industrial Economics,* Vol. XXI, No. 2, April, 1973, pp. 187-199. See also, Morvan, *op. cit.*, pp. 430-431.

60. Commissariat Général du Plan, Préparation du VIe Plan, Rapport de la Commission, *Economie Générale et Financement* (Paris, 1971), pp. 66-67.

61. Commissariat Général du Plan, Préparation du VIe Plan, *Rapport du Comité, Concurrence* (Paris, 1971), p. 63.

62. Chenincourt, *op. cit.*, p. 108.

63. Philippe-Jean Terasse, "L'Evolution de la Réglementation des Prix depuis 1945," *Concurrence,* 1971, reprinted in *La Documentation Française, Problemes Economiques,* February 2, 1972, pp. 9-13.

64. OECD, *Pour un Politique des Prix, des Profits et des Autres Revenus Non-Salariaux* (Paris, 1964), pp. 65-68.

65. Louis Frank, *Les Prix* (Paris, 1968), pp. 58-59; "Huit années de valse-hésitation entre la liberté et le control," *Le Monde,* March 15, 1972, p. 26.

66. P. Aranda, "Les Contrats de Programme," *Entreprise,* June 22, 1967; *Le Monde,* March 2, 1972, p. 27.

67. "Huit années de valse-hésitation entre la liberté et le control," *Le Monde,* March 15, 1972, p. 26.

68. J. F. Bourg, "La Gendarme peut-il être bon enfant? " *L'Expansion,* Feb., 1971, p. 60.

69. Ministère de l'Economie et des Finances, Service de l'Information, "L'Application du Contrat Anti-Hausse, au 1er Novembre 1971" (1971).

70. Ministère de l'Economie et des Finances, Service de l'Information, "La Programmation Annuelle des Prix, 1er Avril 1972—1er Avril 1973" (1972).

71. *Entreprise,* June 16, 1972, p. 47.

72. *Entreprise,* June 2, 1972, pp. 16-34.

73. *Le Figaro,* December 8, 1972; *Le Monde,* December 7 and December 8, 1972; Ministère de l'Economie et des Finances. *Notes Bleus,* December 23, 1971, p. 8.

74. Commission of the European Communities, Studies, Competition: Approximation of Legislation Series, *The Effects of National Price Controls in the European Economic Community,* No. 9 (1970); and see the authoritative study of Jean Charpy, *La Politique Des Prix* (Paris, 1973), especially pp. 221-270.

75. H. Lepage, "Control des Prix: Comment en Sortir," *Enterprise,* Feb. 25, 1972, p. 84.

76. Chenincourt, *op. cit.,* pp. 117-121.

77. Bourg, *op. cit.,* p. 62.

78. Communication from Professor Max Peyrard.

79. cf. Cotta, *op. cit.,* pp. 93-94.

80. Cotta, *op. cit.,* Table 31, pp. 107-108.

81. For summaries of OECD's econometric studies see, *Inflation,* pp. 69-75; *cf:* Mockers, *op. cit.,* pp. 31-36.

82. Lloyd Ulman and Robert Flanagan, *Wage Restraints: A Study of Income Policies in Western Europe* (Berkeley, 1971), p. 150.

83. See Ministère du Travail de l'Emploi et de la Population, *Statistiques Sociales,* Supplement C15, Nov., 1971, p. 127, and Gilbert Mathieu, "Peut-on justifier une forte inégalité des salaires? " *Le Monde, Selection Hebdomadaire,* May 4-10, 1972, p. 9.

84. I.N.S.E.E., *Comptes de la Nation,* 1971, Part 2, pp. 91 and 96. All social assistance and similar transfers accounted for 18.0 percent of total household income in 1959 and 22.7 percent of total household income in 1959 and 22.7 percent in 1971. Medical and old-age payments accounted for the increase.

85. Parodi, *op. cit.,* p. 317.

86. J. P. Mockers, *op. cit.,* pp. 13-47, and *passim.*

87. Journal Officiel, *Conjoncture Economique au premier semèstre 1972,* p. 525.

88. I.N.S.E.E., *Tendances de la Conjoncture, Perspectives,* June 1974, p. 13.

89. Because of the clandestine methods by which foreign workers have been introduced into France, it is difficult to know what their exact number may be. M. Fontanet, Minister of Labor, stated that there were 2 million foreign workers in France in the spring of 1971. (*Le Monde,* June 27-28, 1971.) According to estimates of Maurice Parodi, there were between 1.5 and 1.7 million foreign workers in France in 1973.

90. I.N.S.E.E., *Tendances de la Conjoncture,* Supplement, August, 1971, Note de Synthèse, p. 21.

91. *Entreprise,* June 2, 1972.

CHAPTER FIVE

1. In May 1971 the inflation rate was 6%, the unemployed number only 142,900 or 7%, and the job vacancies amounted to 720,000. The unemployment figures of the United States and the Federal Republic of Germany are only conditionally comparable. The American figures are based on interviews of households, the German statistics are based on the official figures of the Federal Labor Office which gets its information from the local labor offices. In the Federal Republic, furthermore, the number of vacancies is registered and published.

2. For the concept of competition, cf. Helmut Arndt, *Mardt und Macht* (Competition and Economic Power), 2ed., Tuebingen, 1973, pp. 92-98 and: *idem., Mikroökonomische Theorie,* vol. 2, *Marktprozesse* (The Market Process), Tuebingen, 1966.

3. The concept of target pricing is used in different ways. "Target pricing" as defined, for instance, by Gardiner C. Means, applies to the setting of a long-run target rate of return such that the target would be achieved on the average of the business cycle, not each year. The term "target pricing" is used on the other hand (for instance by John M. Blair) to characterize a policy of achieving at least a constant annual profit regardless of the volume sold. In this paper target pricing implies that prices tend to rise when sales diminish, not, however, that prices do not increase when sales rise.

4. In 1974, the German car producers increased their prices in spite of a decrease of demand. This price increase, however, was not caused by "target pricing," but by a cost explosion. Volkswagen suffered losses — for the first time in its history.

5. Herbert Giersch, in: Helmut Arndt (ed.), *Lohnpolitik und Einkommensverteilung,* (Wage Policy and Income Distribution) Berlin, 1969, pp. 786-87.

6. The index excluding rents rose from 100 (1962) to 132.8 (1972) in West Germany; the inflation rate in the USA in the same time from 100 to 138.3.

7. This was pointed out long ago by David Hume, in "On the Balance of Trade," in *Political Discourses,* Edinburgh, 1752.

8. With regard to recent economic consequences of the oil crisis, the German government and the German Bundesbank have begun to change this policy.

9. Report for 1968-69 of the Board of Advisors (Sachverstäendigenrat), p. 38. This Board advises the Federal government on economic questions.

10. See, for instance, the high production of Opel (GM) and Ford in West Germany in Table III.

11. John Maynard Keynes, *The General Theory of Employment, Interest, and Money,* London and New York, 1936.

12. These are nominal figures, i.e., including the price increases.

13. Wiebke Jensen, *Welthandel und Rohstoffmärkte* (World Trade and the Raw Material Markets), Weltkonjunkturdienst (HWWA), 1974, no. 3.

CHAPTER SIX

1. This is the contention in a book by C.P. Kindleberger, which contains an important contribution to the explanation of European economic growth during the 1950's. But Kindleberger's deduction from his Lewis-like model of classical output growth with "unlimited supplies of labour," *viz.* that continental European growth would subside with the drying up of this abundant supply, has not yet come true. During the 1960's another factor — increased international competition — rose to a position of prime importance. cf. C.P. Kindleberger, *Europe's Postwar Growth, The Role of Labor Supply,* Cambridge, Mass., 1967.

2. OECD, *Economic Outloook,* July 1973 (pp. 14-15) and December 1973 (pp. 24-25)

3. *Ibid.,* pp. 13-14. See also: "The Role of Commodity Prices in the Current Inflation," in: *Economic Outlook,* December 1973, pp. 99 *ff.*

4. See W. Adams, *The Structure of American Industry,* 4th ed., New York, 1971. Automobile and beer production in the U.S. would seem to exemplify our main pattern.

5. The process has been worked out more fully in my book, *Dynamische Concentratietheorie,* Leiden, 1972.

6. See H. Arndt (ed.), *Die Konzentration in der Wirtschaft,* (On Economic Concentration) 2 ed., Berlin, 1971. The factual information in the text was taken from the contributions by V. G. Venturini (on Italy, P. 121-61), A. P. Weber (France, pp. 107-21), W. Kilger and O. Karl (West Germany, pp. 401-35) and H. W. de Jong (Benelux, pp. 37-65). See also, The E.E.C. memorandum on Industrial policy (1970).

7. Gross domestic product of extractive and manufacturing industries. The fact that the level of the share has a bias in the upward direction because the G.D.P. equals added value does not invalidate the trend.

8. OECD, *Inflation, The Present Problem,* December, 1970, pp. 66-68.

9. V. Terpstra, *American Marketing in the Common Market,* Praeger, International Studies in Economics, New York 1967.

10. See E.E.C., Annual Reports, recent years. Also first and second Report on Competition Policy 1972 and 1973.

11. Terpstra, *op. cit.* p. 118, a theme also heard in other contexts.

12. See M.R. Mok, "The Cartel policy of the E.E.C. Commission, 1962-67," *Common Market Law Review,* November 1968.

13. See Official Journals of the European Communities No. C 12 of January 30, 1970.

14. Cheese prices on the Dutch market have been kept high by the branch organization

in order to recoup the losses from selling at "dumping prices" to the French market. The main Dutch coffee roaster — having a 50% market share — was forced, in the fall of 1972, to lower its prices by the Ministry of Economic Affairs.

15. There were about 500 national price cartels in the Netherlands on January 1, 1970. As cartels are not *per se* forbidden, but have to be registered in a secret cartel register, it is not known to what extent they inflicted damage on the economy. In the German economy the number of cartels has been reduced — by means of vigorous action — to about 250. No one should be any more optimistic about the number of cases in other E.E.C. countries.

16. L. Bussmann, *Der Einfluss der Konzentration auf Preise und Gewinne,* Koln 1965, pp. 118-124.

17. OECD, *Inflation, op. cit.,* p. 60.

18. See F.J.A. Huygen, "Some prospects for the education of physicians in the Netherlands." Boerhaave Conference on Medical Education and Methods, Dec. 1967, in: *Universiteit en Hogeschool,* vol. 14, no. 5.

19. Early in 1974, there was a waiting list of 112,000 for new telephone connections. The average waiting time was 3.8 months and the "introduction fee," about $100 per connection. Yet, the responsible Minister refused to allow new investments to be financed in order to cope with the backlog.

CHAPTER SEVEN

1. P. J. D. Wiles, "Soviet-Type Inflation" (mimeographed manuscript), p. 66. Excess demand is his sole criterion for the existence of inflation. See also, P. J. D. Wiles, *The Political Economy of Communism,* Cambridge, 1962, pp. 135-36 and pp. 261-62, and *Communist International Economics,* New York 1968, Chapter 3 and pp. 43-55.

2. P. J. D. Wiles, "Soviet-Type Inflation," *op cit.* For a discussion of Statistical problems, see Morris Bornstein, "Soviet Price Statistics," in *Soviet Economic Statistics,* edited by Vladimir G. Treml and John P. Hardt, Durham, N.C., 1972, pp. 355-96.

3. Keith Bush, "Soviet Inflation," in *Banking, Money and Credit in Eastern Europe: Colloquium,* M. Yves Laulan, ed., Brussels, 1973, pp. 97. The statement dates from 1960.

4. *Ibid.*

5. With respect to demand-pull inflation in a socialist command type economy, the government directly influences most investment expenditures and all government expenditures. Although savings are not directly controlled, they are relatively small and subject to influence. More important is the fact that the government has a free rein in setting tax policy. Changes in tax rates can, in theory at least, be employed to mop up any serious excess in aggregated demand. Similarly, in socialist command type economies, the government controls all the variables which might cause cost-push inflation. Wage rates are set by a government committee, except in Yugoslavia, as are the prices of raw materials and finished products. Therefore, the essential ingredients of cost-push inflation are under direct government control in almost all socialist economies.

6. Albert Boiter, "When the Kettle Boils Over," *Problems of Communism,* XIII, No. 1, Jan.-Feb., 1964, pp. 33-43.

7. Franklyn D. Holzman, "Soviet Inflationary Pressures, 1928-1957: Causes and Cures," *The Quarterly Journal of Economics,* LXXIV, No. 2, May 1960, pp. 175-81.

8. *Ibid,* pp. 182-86.

9. S. Partigul, *Voprosy ekonomiki,* No. 12, December, 1969, pp. 47-58. Translated under the title "Tailoring Demand to Fit Production," in, *Current Digest of the Soviet Press,* XXII, No. 13, 1970, p. 2.

10. *Trud,* November 3, 1971.

11. *Radio Liberty Dispatch,* December 21, 1972. Citations are to *Trud,* September 14, 1971 (footnotes 11 and 12) and to *Trud,* November 3, 1971 (footnote 15).

12. Yurii Vladimirovich Yakovets, *Tseny v planovom khoziaistve,* Moscow, 1974, p. 72.

13. *Ibid,* p. 61.

14. *Radio Liberty Dispatch,* December 21, 1972 and January 5, 1973, p. 6.

15. Michael Kaser, *Soviet Economics,* New York, 1970, p. 143; Norton T. Dodge, "Fifty

Years of Soviet Labor," in *The Development of the Soviet Economy,* Vladimir Treml, ed., New York, 1968, pp. 160-62; David W. Bronson and Constance B. Krueger, "The Revolution in Soviet Farm Household Income, 1953-1967," in *The Soviet Rural Community,* James R. Millar, ed., Urbana, 1971, p. 227; and David W. Bronson and Barbara S. Severin, "Soviet Consumer Welfare: The Brezhnev Era," in *Soviet Economic Prospect for the Seventies,* Joint Economic Committee, Washington, D.C., 1973, pp. 378 and 380.

16. Although there is no proof of this, it is difficult to believe that the productivity of the lowest paid workers, many of whom are unskilled and poorly educated, could have increased more than modestly over the past two decades.

17. David W. Bronson and Barbara S. Severin, "Soviet Consumer Welfare: The Brezhev Era," in *Soviet Economic Prospects for the Seventies,* Joint Economic Committee, Washington, D.C., 1973, p. 378.

18. *Ibid,* p. 379.

19. See Holzman, *op. cit.,* for a full discussion.

20. Robert M. Fearn, "Controls over Wage Funds and Inflationary Pressures in the USSR," *Industrial and Labor Relations Review,* XVIII, No. 2, January, 1965, pp. 186-95.

21. *Ibid,* p. 187.

22. *Ibid,* p. 186.

23. *Narodnoe Khoziaistvo SSSR v 1970 g.,* Moscow, 1971, p. 601.

24. These are usually defined as average branch costs. Costs as calculated by the Soviets omitted until recently large elements of interest and rent, and depreciation was generally low. Marginal cost pricing is not accepted by the Price Committee.

25. Keith Bush, "Soviet Inflation" in *Banking, Money and Credit in Eastern Europe: Colloquium,* M. Yves Laulan, ed., Brussels, 1973, p. 99.

26. *Ibid.*

27. *Ibid.*

28. The State Price Committee was formed in 1965 by the merger of the Price Bureau of USSR Gosplan with the Commission of the Presidium of the USSR Council of Ministers. See Morris Bornstein, "Soviet Price Theory and Policy" in *The Soviet Economy: A Book of Readings,* Morris Bornstein and Daniel Fusfeld, eds., 4th ed., Homewood 1974, pp. 85-116.

29. *Izvestiia,* Nov. 30, 1968. Translated in *Current Digest of the Soviet Press,* XX, no. 48, 196, p. 25. For further evidence, see Norton T. Dodge, Statement in Hearings Before the Subcommittee on Antitrust and Monopoly, U.S. Senate, *Economic Concentration: Part 7 — Concentration Outside the United States,* Washington, D.C., 1968, pp. 3739-57.

30. V. Sitnin, *Pravda,* July 10, 1970. Translated in *Current Digest of the Soviet Press,* XXII, No. 30, p. 13.

31. P. Maizenberg, "Improvements in the Wholesale Price System," *Voprosy ekonomiki,* No. 6, 1970, pp. 63-64. See also, Abraham S. Bedier's recent article, "The Price Level of Soviet Machinery in the 1960s," *Soviet Studies,* XXVI, July, 1974, no. 3, especially p. 376.

32. P. Kuligin, "Improvement of Price Formation under the Economic Reform," *Nauchnye doklady vyssei shkoly — ekonomicheskie nauki,* No. 4, 1969 (in *Problems of Economics,* October, 1969, pp. 33.)

33. A. Eremin, "The Enterprise and the System of Production Management," *Voprosy ekonomiki,* No. 9, 1967. pp. 46-47.

34. G. Popov and N. Petrov, *Pravda,* September 12, 1973, Translated in *Current Digest of the Soviet Press,* XXV, No. 37, 1973, pp. 6-7.

35. "Resolution on Industrial Associations," *Current Digest of the Soviet Press,* XXV, No. 14, 1973, pp. 1-2.

36. For a further description of functions see Alice C. Gorlin, "Socialist Corporations: The Wave of the Future in the USSR," in Morris Bornstein and Daniel R. Fusfeld, eds., *op. cit.,* pp. 522-35. For possible dangers, see Dodge, statement in hearings.

37. John M. Montias, statement in hearings before the Subcommittee on Antitrust and Monopoly, U.S. Senate, *Economic Concentration: Part 7 — Concentration Outside the United States,* Washington, D. C., 1968, pp. 3785-92.

38. *Ibid.* p. 3792.

39. Jeno Wilcsek, *Figyelo,* No. 4, January 26, 1972, p. 3.

40. *Ibid.*

41. George R. Feiwel, *New Economic Patterns in Czechoslovakia: Impact of Growth, Planning, and the Market,* New York, 1968.

42. Joel Dirlam, "Problems of Market Power and Public Policy in Yugoslavia," in *Comparative Economic Systems: Models and Cases,* Morris Bornstein, ed., 3ed., Homewood 1974, pp. 201-17.

43. Joel Dirlam, statement in hearings before the Subcommittee on Antitrust and Monopoly, U.S. Senate, *Economic Concentration: Part 7 — Concentration Outside the United States,* Washington, D.C., 1968, pp. 3758-84.

44. *Ibid.* pp. 3766-67.

45. Joel Dirlam, "Problems of Market Power and Public Policy in Yugoslavia," in *Comparative Economic Systems: Models and Cases,* Morris Bornstein, ed., 3ed. Homewood 1974, p. 211.

46. John M. Blair, *Economic Concentration: Structure, Behavior and Public Policy,* New York, 1972, p. 703.

47. Joel Dirlam, "Problems of Market Power and Public Policy in Yugoslavia," *op. cit.,* p. 212.

48. *Ibid,* p. 217.

CHAPTER EIGHT

1. The yields on Aaa corporate bonds dropped from 1929 and 1933 peaks of 4.73 and 5.01 to 2.53 in 1946, then rose, though of course not evenly, to 4.38 in 1960, and an annual peak of 8.04 in 1970. They were at 7.65 in mid-December 1973.

2. See Otto Eckstein and Roger Brinner, *The Inflation Process in the United States, A Study for U.S. Congress,* Joint Economic Committee, 92d Cong., 2d Sess., February 22, 1972, for a specific finding that an average annual inflation rate of as little as 2.5% over a two-year period greatly increases the sensitivity of wages to prices and a demonstration that this increased sensitivity explained the perverse behavior of wages in the United States during the 1969-70 recession. It is questionable that this model could have predicted the restrained wage settlements during the accelerated inflation of 1973, but it would presumably, and presumably correctly, predict much more inflationary settlements in 1974, or greatly intensified labor unrest.

3. It is entirely likely, thus, that the essentially noninflationary character of the 1961-65 recovery reflected the application of those brakes in the preceding five years or so; that another dose of the same medicine became necessary in the late 1960's only because of the irresponsible monetary and fiscal policies of 1966-68; and that it too could have worked had we but persevered.

4. John M. Blair, "Administered Prices: A Phenomenon in Search of a Theory," *American Economic Review, Papers and Proceedings,* XLIX, May, 1959, pp. 431-50; Martin J. Bailey, "Discussion," *ibid.,* p. 460.

5. We should emphasize the arbitrariness of labelling some inflations as attributable to the pull of demand, others to the exercise of market power. All inflations typically contain mixtures of both elements, with some price or wage increases occurring (or price or wage decreases failing to occur) in periods of general demand-pull that would not have occurred but for the presence of market power; and with some price and wage increases occurring in "market power" inflations that are fully explicable in terms of changes in demand and supply conditions in those particular markets without any substantial influence of market power. But this observation is not wholly symmetrical. As we will see, the role of market power in periods of demand-pull is clearly less crucial than the role of demand factors in "market-power" inflation — which is another way of saying that the identification of "market power inflation" is typically the more difficult and arbitrary. When, therefore, we classify the price increases of 1939-48, 1950-53, 1965-69, and 1972-73 as preponderantly of the former type, and those of 1954-58 and 1969-71 as exhibiting characteristics of the latter, we are, if anything, underestimating the relative influence of demand forces — especially those influences that operate only with a lag.

6. It is particularly easy to confuse the cost-push variety, as we use the term here, with demand-pull because the pressure of excessive demand in classic inflation gets transmitted via product markets into the markets for labor and for other production inputs, and thus presents sellers of goods and services with both the opportunity (because of rising demand) and the pressure (from the cost side) to raise prices. So "cost-push" occurs under "demand-pull" as well. But the necessary and sufficient impelling force in such cases is the pull of demand. Instead, in true cost-push inflations, as we refer to them here, costs move up in spite of the fact that labor markets (and other inputs) are *not* for the most part characterized by demand outrunning supply.

7. I presume it would be possible to construct a scenario according to which market power might be unnecessary. If, for example, demand was increasing sufficiently for products supplied under conditions of increasing cost to offset the price effects of a decrease in demand for products supplied under constant or decreasing costs, the general price level might increase while aggregate demand was declining, entirely apart from the influence of monopoly. But any such sequence of events would bear so little resemblance to the events we are attempting here to describe that the exercise seems pointless.

8. Leonard W. Weiss, "Concentration and Labor Earnings," *American Economic Review,* LVI, March, 1966, pp. 96-117. And whether this seems merely to represent the higher price that they are required to pay for the generally higher apparent "qualifications" of their workers (Weiss finds that when he introduces such indicia of labor "quality" as race, education, and geographic origin, the statistically measured influence of concentration falls to insignificance), or reflects also their superior *ability* to attract such workers, or, at the extreme, to indulge their managers' preferences for discrimination in employment on grounds of race, religion, or sex (Armen A. Alchian and Reuben A. Kessel, "Competition and the Pursuit of Pecuniary Gain," in Universities-National Bureau Committee for Economic Research, *Aspects of Labor Economics,* Princeton, 1962, p. 163), it clearly suggests that monopoly power in *product* markets does have an influence at least on wage levels. We will consider later whether it may also influence their behavior over time.

9. But, the economist will interject, if that is so why would wages not already have been raised so as fully to exploit that inelasticity? If unions are wage-increase maximizers, why would they not have gotten the maximum increase the previous time around? No profit-maximizing monopolist prices on the inelastic portion of his demand curve (that puts it imprecisely, but with sufficient clarity to raise the question here). That would mean that he was failing fully to exploit his monopoly power, the measure of which is, precisely, the extent to which demand for his services is inelastic. What we have here is a simplified statement of the proposition, which the proponent of the market power inflation thesis must confront, that monopoly can account for prices *being higher* than they would otherwise be, but cannot explain why they would *keep rising faster or further* over time than they otherwise would.

Two possible parts of an answer in the present context are that labor unions are almost certainly not profit maximizers, or even wage maximizers in any static sense; and, second, that the determinants of the wage increases they can get each time around are subject to so many influences, economic and noneconomic, and *change* so drastically over time as to make any static, once-and-for-all determination of the optimal wage — analogous to the profit maximizing price — completely meaningless as a basis for either explaining or predicting actual wage behavior.

10. See, for example, P. Sargant Florence's essay in this volume.

Along similar lines, see the very persuasive essay of Peter Wiles, laying heavy emphasis on such noneconomic forces making for chronic cost inflation as the communications revolution, the New Left, rivalry and jealousies among trade unions and between their leaders, and "national character":

> "In a nation where the national character is plainly changing — rising crime, sex-and-drug permissiveness, less self-discipline in dress, speech and deportment, less respect for hard work, less religion, loosening of the nuclear family, breakdown of a deferential class structure . . . we must also expect less restraint at the bargaining table, less concern for consequences. I do not disapprove *per se* of most of the changes listed, quite the contrary. I only assert that, good or bad, they raise prices." ("Cost Inflation and the

State of Economic Theory," *Economic Journal,* June, 1973, pp. 392-3 and *passim.*)

Wiles makes a telling counterargument to the economist who would respond that "national character" is unnecessary and irrelevant to the explanation of inflation:

"National character would be a parameter also in any purely monetarist model that seriously came to grips with the factual world. Such models too have to explain Latin America and Britain. *Because* they — quite falsely — deny a role to trade unions they raise the question of the national character of central bankers and senior ministers." (*Ibid.*)

How else could they *explain* the divergent monetary policies that go so far in turn to explain the presence and varying degrees of inflation in different countries? We return to this kind of consideration in our concluding remarks.

11. The result of a situation where, as Tobin puts it, "one man's reference wages are another man's wages" is that "there is something arbitrary and conventional, indeterminate and unstable, in the process of wage-setting. In the same market circumstances, the reference pattern might be 8% per year or 3% per year or zero, depending on the historical prelude." "Inflation and Unemployment," *American Economic Review,* LXII, March, 1972, p. 13.

12. In an efficiently functioning market system, prices in industries experiencing above-average increases in productivity would decline relative to the prices in less progressive industries, reflecting their declining real costs and encouraging their purchase. If wage increases vary from industry to industry in accordance with the behavior of their respective man-hour productivities, this would cause their money costs and prices instead to move uniformly, thus concealing the divergent trends of their real costs.

13. Another factor inflating some service prices in recent years has been the increasing unionization of their employees, notably hospital workers, teachers, municipal and state employees generally — police, firemen, sanitation workers and so on.

14. Changes in product prices are likely to show greater dispersion than in wages because, among other things, of differences in rates of productivity improvement; but this fact itself suggests that wages do tend to move together, regardless of inter-industry differences in output, employment, and ability to pay.

15. I find that Peter Wiles has said most of these things in not much different terms:

"What, in particular, if trade-union jealousy — a new and pernicious form of the demonstration effect — is the motive force, and social services and tax rebates will cushion those laid off well enough for the period extending to the trade-union leader's time horizon? What, in other words, if strikers and wage-bargainers are insensitive to unemployment, and only the long-term unemployed and the nation suffer? . . .

"This rivalry leads to leap-frogging. . . . It is not that other unions directly *expect higher prices* . . . They *expect similar surrenders,* and know that by enforcing such surrenders they will *create higher prices.* Moreover, they tolerate a little more unemployment, since they expect a passive or even inflationary monetary policy, from a government more humane than themselves, to float it off in time." (*Op. cit.,* pp. 382. 388.)

16. Sen. Doc. 13, 74th Cong., 1st Sess.

17. Vol. I, Washington, 1939, Chapter 8.

18. Willard Thorp and Walter Crowder, "Concentration and Product Characteristics as Factors in Price-Quantity Behavior," *American Economic Review, Papers and Proceedings,* XXX, Feb., 1941, pp. 390-408.

19. Richard Ruggles, "The Nature of Price Flexibility and the Determinants of Relative Price Changes in the Economy," in: Universities — National Bureau Committee for Economic Research, *Business Concentration and Price Policy,* Princeton, 1955, pp. 441-95.

20. Alfred C. Neal, *Industrial Concentration and Price Inflexibility,* Washington, American Council on Public Affairs, 1942. See also John M. Blair, "Means, Thorp and Neal on Price Inflexibility," *Review of Economics and Statistics,* XXXVIII, Nov., 1956, pp. 427-35; Jules Bachman, "Economic Concentration and Price Inflexibility," and Blair, "Rejoinder," *ibid.,* XL, Nov., 1958, pp. 399-406.

21. Ruggles, *op. cit.;* F. M. Scherer, *Industrial Market Structure and Economic Per-*

formance, Chicago, 1970, Chapters 12 and 13; John M. Blair, *Economic Concentration,* New York, 1972, Chapters 16, 17.

22. The necessary conditions would be that (a) the seller's average variable costs (and hence his marginal cost function) be linear, and (b) as demand increases and decreases it does not change in its elasticity, and (c) as variable costs go up and down, the demand that they encounter remains of unchanged elasticity. On this demonstration and the exposition immediately following, see John B. Moore and Lester S. Levy, "Price Flexibility and Industrial Concentration," *Southern Economic Journal,* XXI, April, 1955, pp. 435-40.

23. I set aside for the time being the intriguing argument by John Blair in this volume that in order to achieve target returns on an annual basis, firms are departing even further from the competitive norm and pricing counter-cyclically.

24. Ruggles defines "inflexibility" in principle as prices fluctuating less than *marginal* costs. This means a percentage markup above marginal costs varying inversely with the cycle. But in his statistical tests he is forced to compare prices with average direct cost since marginal cost data are, of course, unavailable. This would be a correct test of inflexibility, as he defines it, only if direct costs per unit of output are constant (hence, the same as marginal costs) over the relevant range of output, an unlikely situation even in manufacturing. If, instead, as there seems reason to believe, the average variable cost function is even mildly U-shaped, the marginal cost curve, which a purely competitive price would follow, will be even more so. In that event, administered prices embodying a fixed percentage markup over (average) *direct* costs (which is roughly what Ruggles found in manufacturing) will in fact be exhibiting more rigidity than would purely competitive prices, and would actually mean that the degree to which the seller was exploiting his monopoly power (which is measured by the relation of price to *marginal* cost) *was* varying inversely with the cycle. The criterion of rigidity that Ruggles applies in his statistical tests — that percentage markups above *average direct* cost vary inversely with the cycle — is therefore excessively demanding. Even constant percentage markups of this kind would probably involve inversely fluctuating markups over *marginal* cost, would require monopoly power, and therefore be a sign of rigidity.

25. They will fluctuate even more at those levels of output at which increases tend to involve declining average variable costs, as seems to be typical.

26. Armen A. Alchian, "Uncertainty, Evolution, and Economic Theory," *Journal of Political Economy,* LVIII (1950), reprinted in American Economic Association, *Readings in Industrial Organization and Public Policy,* Homewood, 1958.

27. Neal, *op. cit.*, and Howard N. Ross, *The Theory and Evidence of Price Flexibility,* unpublished dissertation, Columbia University, 1964. Neal finds no such relationship for the 1931-33 period, but Ross convincingly demonstrates that this was because of the hitherto overlooked sharp demand inflation during the course of the latter year. "Full Cost-Administered Prices," ms., 1973.

28. Wiles makes this point in an even more radical way. As he sees it (and, indeed, as some of Means' early writings suggest), identification of administered prices, and of the kind of behavior they exhibit, with monopoly power is a mistake: "they are and were far more widespread, since they characterize imperfect competition as a whole and have no particular connection with monopoly." In effect, he comes close to saying there are simply two categories of prices — those set by and in an open market, closely approximating the model of perfect competition; and (a much greater number of) those that are administered, determined in imperfectly competitive markets, where short-term profit maximization is simply impossible, and prices are essentially set on the basis of direct costs plus a conventional mark-up. *Ibid.,* pp. 382 and ff.

29. What of the criticisms of Means that the B.L.S. price indexes he uses are fatally flawed on this account? Without attempting to do justice to these criticisms, I merely record my opinion that they qualify but do not destroy the validity of his observations — that those markets in which quoted prices change frequently are typically more nearly purely competitive than those in which they change infrequently, and that the actual transactions prices in the former category tend also to fluctuate with greater amplitude over the business cycle than the latter. Both the Neal and the Ross studies, which found a significant impact

of concentration on the resistance of margins to the 1929-31 decline, did in fact use unit product realizations, as computed from the Census, rather than BLS indexes, precisely in order to take this qualification into account. And see also Means' demonstration that the transactions price data compiled by Stigler and Kendahl continue to show relative cyclical rigidity in the administered group. "The Administered Price Thesis Re-confirmed," *American Economic Review*, LXII, June, 1972, pp. 292-306.

30. Daniel S. Hamermesh, "Market Power and Wage Inflation," *Southern Economic Journal*, XXXIX, Oct., 1972, pp. 204-12.

31. As we will see, if one asks the question how do prices in concentrated industries typically behave, one is likely to get relatively weak statistical results. If instead one asks, what was the nature of *those* markets in which prices or margins in fact behaved in a particular way, one is likely to get much more clear-cut results. See p. 262, and especially note 35, below.

32. See the references to Bachman, Blair, and Ruggles, above.

33. Charles L. Schultze, *Recent Inflation in the United States*, Joint Economic Committee, Study Paper No. 1, 86th Cong., 1st Sess., 1959; and Richard T. Selden, "Cost-Push versus Demand-Pull Inflation," *Journal of Political Economy*, LXVII, Feb., 1959, pp. 1-20.

34. Horace J. DePodwin and Richard T. Selden, "Business Pricing Policies and Inflation," *Journal of Political Economy*, LXXI, April, 1963, pp. 116-27; Leonard W. Weiss, "Business Pricing Policies and Inflation Reconsidered," *ibid.*, LXXIV, April, 1966, pp. 177-87.

35. Note therefore that the charts Means presents in his contribution to this volume, as in his original testimony setting forth this hypothesis, reflect the relative weights of the industries concerned in the general price level.

A striking illustration of the difference in the answers one gets when one asks (a) how consistently was concentration associated with price increases during the 1950's, and (b) how consistently were *those (perverse)* price increases *that actually occurred* in the 1950's associated *with concentration* is provided by the following brief summary of findings by John A. Henning.

Henning computed estimates of expected price changes for 214 U.S. manufacturing industries over the period 1954-61 on the basis of the estimated changes in their average direct costs and, on the basis of these, related the "residual price variation" (RPV) — i.e., the differences between actual and expected price changes — to market concentration. In one test, he divides his sample into two groups — 31 prices that rose most relative to direct costs, and 218 that rose less — and then divides each of these into two groups, of high and low concentration, with the following results:

	Low CR (under 45%)	High CR (over 45%)	Total	"Predictive accuracy" of	
				High RPV as predictor of high CR	High CR as predictor of high RPV
High RPV	1	30	31		
Low RPV	109	109	218	93%	10%
	Low CR (under 65%)	High CR (over 65%)	Total		
High RPV	5	26	31		
Low RPV	156	62	218	75%	20%

John A. Henning, *Relative Price Behavior and Market Concentration: Problems of Theory, Measurement, and Testing*, unpublished dissertation, Cornell University, 1965, p. 77. Obviously the answer to question (a) is "not at all," and to question (b) "very consistently."

36. Weiss, *op. cit.* Also, Bruce T. Allen, "Market Concentration and Wage Increases: U.S. Manufacturing, 1947-1964," *Industrial and Labor Relations Review,* XXI, April, 1968, pp. 353-66.

37. "The Administered-Price Thesis Denied: Comment," *American Economic Review,* LXIV, March, 1974, pp. 232-34.

38. See Weiss, *op. cit.,* and Allen, *op. cit.*

39. John Kenneth Galbraith "Market Structure and Stabilization Policy," *Review of Economics and Statistics,* XXXIX, May, 1957, pp. 124-33. See also M. A. Adelman, "Steel, Administered Prices and Inflation," *Quarterly Journal of Economics,* Feb., 1961, pp. 16-40.

40. *Op. cit.*

41. Harvey J. Leibenstein, "Allocative Efficiency vs. 'X-Efficiency,' " *American Economic Review,* LVI, June, 1966, pp. 392-415.

42. Gardner Ackley, *Macroeconomic Theory,* New York, 1961, pp. 425-57.

APPENDIX

1. George J. Stigler and James K. Kindahl, *The Behavior of Industrial Prices,* New York, 1970.

2. Howard N. Ross, "Illusions in Testing for Administered Prices," *Journal of Industrial Economics,* April, 1973, XXI, 187-95.

3. R.R. Neild, *Pricing and Employment in the Trade Cycle* Cambridge, 1963; Wesley J. Yordan Jr., "Industrial Concentration and Price Flexibility," *Review of Economics and Statistics,* August 1961, XLIII, 287-94.

4. R.H. Day, D.J. Aigner and K.R. Smith, "Safety Margins and Profit Maximization in the Theory of the Firm," *Journal of Political Economy,* November/December 1971, LXXIX, 1293-301.

5. A clear and accurate summary of the full-cost literature appears in John M. Blair, *Economic Concentration,* New York, 1972, 469-76.

6. P.W.S. Andrews, *Manufacturing Business,* London, 1955.

7. A.D.H. Kaplan, J. Dirlam and R. Lanzilotti, *Pricing in Big Business,* Washington, 1958.

8. Norman R. Collins and Lee E. Preston, *Concentration and Price-Cost Margins in Manufacturing Industries,* Berkeley, 1968; Howard J. Sherman, *Profits in the United States,* Ithaca, 1968.

9. Thor Hultgren, *Cost, Prices and Profits: Their Cyclical Relations,* New York, 1965.

10. *Ibid.,* Table 33, p. 58 and Table B-1, pp. 189-91.

11. *Ibid.,* derived by the author from the above tables.

12. John M. Blair, "Market Power and Inflation: A Short-Run Target Return Model," *Journal of Economic Issues,* June 1974, VIII, 453-78.

13. Wesley J. Yordan Jr., "A Model of Price Flexibility: Comment," *American Economic Review,* June 1961, LI, 390-92.

INDEX

INDEX

Numbers in parenthesis indicate Chapter, Introduction (I), or Appendix (A).

Ackley, Gardner: 271, 304n42(8)
Adams, Walter J.: 288n20(2), 293n49(4), 296n4(6)
Adelman, M.A.: 304n39(8)
Administered prices: 4, 85, 244; cause of inflation, 251-268; inflexibility of, 5-7, 252, 254-255; market price compared, 4-5, 252; rising costs and, 267
Administrative inflation: 11-22; control efforts, 12-22; endemic character, 12, 239, 240-243; labor role, 11; limiting, 28-30; planned stagnation and, 18-19; profit levels and, 11, 12
Aglietta, M.: 294n58(4)
Agricultural sector: E.E.C., 165-166, 190; France, 111, 136; prices, 14, 15, 17, 21, 36, 42, 43-44, 49, 190; socialist countries, 214, 220-223, 227-228
Aigner, D.J.: 304n4(A)
Albert, Michel: 293n45(4)
Alchian, Armen A.: 302n26(8)
Alfred, A.M.: 291n35(3)
Allen, Bruce T.: 304n36(8)
Aluminum industry: 60; foreign competition, 38
Amalgamated Engineers and Foundrymen (Great Britain): 98
Ammonia industry, infrequency of price changes: 5-6
Amplitude, price changes, concentrated industries: 35-36, 38
Andrews, P.W.S.: 87, 277
Annual Survey of Manufactures: 281
Anti-hausse contracts (France): 124-126
Antitrust: E.E.C. policy, 192-197; limitations of existing legislation, 30; and pricing behavior, 65; Yugoslavia, 235-236, 238
Anti-Trust and Monopoly Committee (U.S. Senate): 11

Apparel industry, prices: 42-43, 49, 50
Aranda, P.: 294n66(4)
Armand-Rueff report: 117
Arndt, Helmut: 128, 171
Arrow, Kenneth J.: 137n
Associations, Soviet industrial: 231-232
Aujac, Henri: 77
Automation: 90; and featherbedding, 81
Automobile industry: sensitivity to price changes, vi-vii; West European, 141-142, 143, 144, 147, 186, 196-197

Bachman, Jules: 302n20(8)
Bailey, Martin J.: 299n4(8)
Bain, Joe S.: 89
Balance of payments: Great Britain, 90; U.S. deficit, 28, 109, 158
Banque de France: 109
Banque de Paris et des Pays-Bas: 118
Banque d'Indo-Chine: 118
Barback, R.H.: 291n35(3)
Bedier, Abraham S.: 298n31(7)
Beer market, West Germany: 200-202
Belgium (*see also* Benelux countries): employment, 166; stagnation in, 175
Benelux countries: 183; trade with West Germany and Italy, 171-175, 188
Benn, Wedgwood: 290n26(3)
Bentham, Jeremy: 289n7(3)
Berle, Adolph: 290n31(3)
Blackstone, Erwin A.: 239n
Blair, John M.: vi, 143, 235-236, 260, 263, 264, 280, 287n5(I), 288n3(2), 288n20(2), 289n24(2), 295n3(5), 299n4(8), 302n20(8), 302n21(8), 304n5(A)
Board of Advisors (West Germany): 157
Boiter, Albert: 297n6(7)
Bornstein, Morris: 297n2(7), 298n28(7)

305